FIELD GUIDE TO
COVERING
LOCAL NEWS

How to Report on Cops, Courts, Schools, Emergencies and Government

Fred Bayles

Boston University

Los Angeles | London | New Delhi
Singapore | Washington DC

To all the past and future ink-stained wretches (real and virtual)

Los Angeles | London | New Delhi
Singapore | Washington DC

For information:

CQ Press
An Imprint of SAGE Publications, Inc.
2455 Teller Road
Thousand Oaks, California 91320
E-mail: order@sagepub.com

SAGE Publications Ltd.
1 Oliver's Yard
55 City Road
London, EC1Y 1SP
United Kingdom

SAGE Publications India Pvt. Ltd.
B 1/I 1 Mohan Cooperative Industrial Area
Mathura Road, New Delhi 110 044
India

SAGE Publications Asia-Pacific Pte. Ltd.
33 Pekin Street #02-01
Far East Square
Singapore 048763

Copyright © 2012 by CQ Press, an Imprint of SAGE Publications, Inc. CQ Press is a registered trademark of Congressional Quarterly Inc.

All rights reserved. No part of this book may be reproduced or utilized in any form or by any means, electronic or mechanical, including photocopying, recording, or by any information storage and retrieval system, without permission in writing from the publisher.

Printed in the United States of America

Library of Congress Cataloging-in-Publication Data

Bayles, Fred.

Field guide to covering local news: how to report on cops, courts, schools, emergencies and government/Fred Bayles.

p. cm.
Includes index.

ISBN 978-1-60871-001-0

1. Journalism, Regional—Vocational guidance. 2. Local mass media—Vocational guidance. 3. Reporters and reporting—Vocational guidance. I. Title.

PN4784.L6B39 2012
070.4'33—dc23   2011033667

Acquisitions Editor: Christina Mueller
Production Editor: Laura Stewart
Copy Editor: Janine Stanley-Dunham
Typesetter: C&M Digitals, Ltd.
Proofreader: Emily Bakely
Indexer: Maria Sosnowski
Cover Designer: Myself Included Design
Marketing Manager: Chris O'Brien

This book is printed on acid-free paper.
12 13 14 15 16 10 9 8 7 6 5 4 3 2

BRIEF CONTENTS

CONTENTS

INTRODUCTION

Over the past decade daily journalism has been battered by immense change. As people turned to the Internet for their news, sports — even classified ads — daily print circulation (and local television news ratings) plummeted, forcing many once-proud news organizations to cut back or close. The survivors have eliminated staff, reduced the depth of their coverage and even downsized the dimensions of the paper. A parade of new Web-based models has been tried. Words such as *blogs*, *tweets* and *crowd sourcing* have become part of the newsroom vocabulary as media organizations, both new and traditional, seek formulas for survival and success.

More recently there have been signs that the publishers, editors and reporters are figuring out ways to attract and hold an audience. Ironically, one of the most successful "trends" is definitely old school.

Known by various names — community news, public affairs and, now, hyperlocal — local news is flourishing on websites around the nation produced by newspapers, new media organizations and citizen journalists. These sites provide fast, comprehensive and interactive coverage of towns and neighborhoods, producing the kinds of stories often ignored in the past by the traditional media.

Unlike the old model of metro dailies, these news sites focus on specific communities, developing strong relationships with their audience. Residents can add comments to stories. They serve as tipsters to what's happening in their community, leading to important stories that wouldn't have found room in the finite space of a newspaper. Some sites are experimenting with interactive features, asking audiences for ideas about governance or inviting their input for a map detailing the worst road conditions in the area.

This trend has created hundreds of reporting jobs around the country, providing an important training ground for new reporters. It's a wonderful opportunity. If you can learn to cover the offices and officials that make a community function, you'll have the basics to cover almost anything.

But community reporting can be a challenge, even for the pros. In the past, reporters were assigned to specific beats. Someone covered the schools; someone handled the police and fire departments. Another reporter had the City Hall beat. Now, with general cutbacks among newspapers and media outlets, young reporters are expected to cover a combination of these beats on a daily basis.

This type of reporting can include days in court and nights at public meetings. It can mean poring over daily police reports at the precinct house and monitoring the radio for fire calls. Sitting in meetings, listening to citizens complain about traffic lights, sewer bills and school curriculum, may not be what you dream of doing as a reporter. Most writers aspire to document the bugles of history, not the hum of everyday life. But, working a local beat, especially for the first time, can be both an exhilarating and a challenging experience. This is where you can develop a lifetime of skills and smarts. The confidence you build talking with the cops and prosecutors, the councilwomen and road commissioners will inform all your later work.

During my two decades as a national correspondent, I came to understand that the successes of colleagues and competitors were grounded in our earlier days of covering the town halls, district courts, police and the other mainstays of local news. The time spent chatting up assistant district attorneys in bars and courthouse hallways taught us that prosecutors like to gossip as much as anyone. So, when sent across the country to cover a murder case of national interest, we knew that instead of waiting around for the daily press conference where the district attorney would offer only scraps of news, it was better to reach out to people behind the scenes, perhaps someone who had worked in the DA's office and had been speaking with former colleagues. These early lessons could mean the difference between a story that breaks news and a story that is little more than a glorified news release.

In the movie *Karate Kid*, Mr. Miyagi, the karate sensei, has his student, Daniel, do menial tasks of repetition: painting a long fence *(brush up, brush down)* or waxing a fleet of cars *(wax on, wax off)*. After watching Daniel grumble his way through these jobs, we learn that the repeated physical motion has developed the autonomic skills and reflexes Daniel needs to become a karate master. Covering the beats outlined in this book will help develop the reflexes you need to become a consummate reporter — a confident, skilled pro.

But don't get the impression that community reporting is the equivalent of waxing Mr. Miyagi's Cadillacs. Covering local news can be both fun and rewarding. Stories about a town council vote on a parking ordinance, the house fire that spread to an entire city block, the police chase that ended with a car smashing into the local donut shop are often followed more closely by the residents of your community than a bill making its way through Congress.

How does one prepare for community beats? I run a program that takes mostly inexperienced students and throws them into the deep end of the pool — covering deadline stories for newspapers around Massachusetts. The students' questions and anxieties are grounded in their daily experience: How do you talk to the cops? How do you approach politicians? What can you do when a key figure in your story won't call you back? How do you find sources to inform and balance your reporting?

Students aren't the only ones asking such questions. The growing numbers of citizen journalists have similar issues: How do you find the right information or the right person to talk to? How do you wade through the increasingly complex stream of data and warring facts? How do you prepare for an interview? How do you ask that tough question?

My time as a reporter and educator has reinforced my conviction that these skills don't come from textbooks. Classroom drills alone can't prepare you for reporting the details of a three-car fatal, including interviews with authorities and victims' families, with a deadline ticking away in your head.

The intent of this little book is to smooth the path to community reporting through concise, practical answers to the questions young reporters ask as they head off to their assignments. The chapters are intended to help young professionals and citizen journalists navigate the unfamiliar shoals of government, the courts, public safety and education and provide insights to refresh and reinforce their growing journalistic skills.

A final note. As the news business works through its changes, the theorists and consultants continue to prophesize a future where traditional journalism — and journalists — will be obsolete. Blogging, social networks and news aggregation will replace the beat reporter, they say. But despite the drama of uncertainty that accompanies any big change, I am confident the community reporter will be more relevant than ever.

Soon after I started my first reporting job, the newspaper automated its back shop, going from mechanical typesetting to a computerized system. Although the changes affected only the production staff, Human Resources sent a memo to all employees, including the reporters, promising to retrain us on new technologies.

The old journeyman reporter who sat at the desk in front of me — a salty guy who spent his years in newsrooms around the Northeast — considered the memo for a minute, then whirled around on his chair.

"I want to learn how to run the reporting machine," he said.

The craft of reporting will remain an important skill no matter what form the news media takes in the future. It doesn't matter how the news is delivered, be it the traditional newspaper on the doorstep or a Twitter feed on your smartphone. The ability to get the facts right and communicate them well will always be the basis of the news we read or watch. No matter what the future holds, there will always be a need for someone to run the reporting machine.

Think of this book as an instruction manual on how to do so.

Acknowledgements

Although only one name appears under its title, this book would not exist without the help of a long list of people.

Family first. Nothing much gets done around here without Paula. I get dizzy just thinking about her kind patience, wise counsel and support through the years. When I began this project, I envisioned it as a tutorial for Cara. As it turned out, she tutored me, making this book much more complete.

CQ Press is next. Thanks to Aron Keesbury, who came up with the original idea; to Charisse Kiino for taking it up; to Christina Mueller for shepherding it through the shoals; to Jane Harrigan and her endless torrent of ideas; to Janine Stanley-Dunham for her sharp eye and deft hand and to Laura Stewart for turning it all into the book you are reading.

Finally the big list. Thanks to Matt Goisman, Rob Mitchell, Ruben Rosario, Stephanie Slater, Mark Puente, Stan Finger, Steve Johnson, Steve Ruda, Anne Stuart, Richard Dyer, Bob Khan, John Pepitone, Linda Deutsch, Annette McGregor, Harland Braun, Henry Lee, Trish Mehaffey, Audrey Marks, DeWayne Lehman, Ruben Vives, Jeff Gottlieb, Jon Celock, Jaime Sarrio, Molly A.K. Connors, Jesse Register, Emily Alpert, Holly Hacker, Joshua Benton, Linda Perlstein and V.D. Donovan.

Fred Bayles
Boston University

OPERATING INSTRUCTIONS
FOR YOUR
FIELD GUIDE

There are many fine textbooks on the subject of news writing and reporting. Library and bookstore shelves groan under the weight of tomes that offer in-depth analysis, contextual history, deconstructed examples and theoretical insight.

This is not one of those books.

As the name implies, this field guide is meant to educate and guide students and new reporters as they take on the beats of government, public safety, schools and the courts. It is not a compendium of all aspects of community reporting. It doesn't offer expansive reviews of the broader issues of journalism and society. If it did, you wouldn't be able to stick it in your pocket as you go out on assignment.

The approach is straightforward. Part I provides an overview of new and tried-and-true tools and techniques you will use to report and produce the news. You will read how to find and evaluate sources of information, interview subjects, work with editors and file stories in the various mediums demanded by today's news organizations.

Part II looks at five major community beats. Each chapter identifies the players you will need to know and the places you will have to go to get your stories. Other sections detail what records and data you'll need for each beat — how to find them and how to use them. Each chapter includes a section on the Web — how to use it in reporting and in delivering your work. Lists are provided to help you develop a daily routine of making the rounds. There are exercises to build your confidence and knowledge of how to report complex issues and present them in lively, engaging ways.

Each chapter comes with a glossary of terms to help the newcomer understand the language of the beat. "Beat Backgrounders" throughout the book offer concise explanations on the issues and the structures of each beat. What is the difference between civil and criminal courts? What is the division of powers between the legislative, executive and judicial? How are police departments organized? What is a three-alarm fire? Another recurring feature, "Judgment Call," discusses the moral and legal issues facing reporters.

Each chapter also provides a step-by-step instruction on how to cover the significant story within each beat. You will learn how to cover a trial, how to report on a government hearing, how to gather information from the chaos of a fire scene and how to work with, and sometimes around, police officials to cover a criminal investigation.

You will hear the voices of experienced reporters who have excelled at their work. You will also hear the perspectives that the politicians, bureaucrats, lawyers, and fire and police officials have about reporters. We include examples of excellence in reporting along with tips on how to take the beat beyond the daily routine.

Each chapter also takes you through the types of stories each beat involves, explaining what information you need to know and the ways of presenting it across the range of media platforms (print, video, audio, interactive media). Finally, each chapter includes an example of typical beat stories, with notes explaining how the reporter/writer put together the story.

The hope is that this book gets dog eared and scuffed from regular use and becomes a valued possession — a set of training wheels for new reporters and a reassuring friend to more experienced journalists.

As you'll find, reporting is a particularly idiosyncratic craft; there is no one right way to cover a story. The information and tips within the covers of this guide are tools that have worked for me and for fellow journalists over the years. As a reporter you'll develop your own methods that work for you. To that end, we'd love to hear about your approach to reporting and examples of your (and others') spectacular successes and tragic failures. We are collecting them at our website, www.reportersfieldguide.com.

Feel free to stop by anytime.

DEVELOPING
BEAT SKILLS

PART I

CHAPTER 1

BEAT REPORTING IN THE DIGITAL AGE: SHOE LEATHER AND SOCIAL MEDIA

BEAT BACKGROUNDER

Privacy Issues ▶ p. 21

G ood beat reporting has always been, and will always be, about people.

Reporters succeed by developing contacts with the officials, activists, patrol officers, firefighters, teachers and citizens in their communities. These are the people who provide the tips, ideas and information you need to stay on top of what's happening.

Reporters' stories succeed when they are populated with people who illustrate and explain the larger issues. How are students and their parents affected by new testing standards? What's the personal toll of the fire that destroyed several stores on Oak Street? Why are homeowners angry about a change in parking regulations in their neighborhood? Stories without these human elements are flat and ineffective. The piece may be accurate, but it won't be complete. Worse still, it will be boring.

Finding the people and the background information crucial to your beat has become easier with today's tools. A few keystrokes on your computer or smartphone can hunt up background information on anyone or anything. The Web provides instant access to facts and data that once took a half day of phone calls and reference work to find.

The Internet also helps reporters cast a wide net to gather the personal stories, public reaction and commentary buzzing through social networking sites. Google, Facebook, Twitter and other tools show you and your audience what matters to the community. Crowd sourcing not only allows you to find the people affected by breaking news but also points you toward new issues and angles. You can tap into individuals' knowledge and gather their stories at the speed demanded by the 24/7 news cycle.

But, as handy as these tools are, you can't rely on them to do a complete job. That's where shoe leather comes in. You need to get out from behind your computer, haunt the public offices and walk the streets to talk with officials and residents. Personal, face-to-face contact almost always gives you something more substantial and more authentic than a phone call or e-mail dialogue.

Many new reporters fret about getting out and meeting people. They may be shy or lack the confidence it takes to approach strangers and ask them questions. Most of that uncertainty fades as you discover just how much fun reporting can be. It is exhilarating when that stranger gives you the quote or bit of information that brings your story alive. It's exciting when a source provides you with a tip that leads to an exclusive. Your confidence will grow with each interview, each story, each success. This chapter offers advice on how to quicken the path to that confidence.

Assembling Your Tools

The best tools any reporter can have are curiosity and the ability to see potential stories everywhere. Every person you talk to, every tweet or bulletin board poster you read, every change you notice in your community should raise the question, What is *that* about? Why is it happening? Whom will it affect?

You will need other tools. A notebook and a couple of pens and pencils are still essential, but today's reporters carry a heavier load than a ballpoint pen and spiral steno pad; they need skills that go beyond shorthand and typing. Media organizations want sound and video for their websites; they may rely on reporters to be photographers as well. Most require reporters to file blog posts and news updates directly to the Web from the field.

Traditional Tools

A well-organized notebook remains the reporter's most important asset. It provides an immutable record of your days, weeks and months of reporting. It is portable and unobtrusive. It doesn't need charging or batteries. It won't crash or lose important data (unless you lose the whole pad — a tragedy for any reporter).

Notebooks are not just for interview notes. Think of it as your professional diary — a daily record of what you've seen, what you've heard and what you've thought. Jot down the lede that occurs to you as you leave an interview; make note of the story idea that flits through your mind as you sit in traffic. Collect threads of conversations you may be able to use in the future. If a community relations police officer mentions a new set of gang graffiti in her neighborhood, write it down. It might be relevant if violence breaks out between gangs. When a neighborhood activist complains about an abandoned building on Aspen Street, put that in the notebook with a note to ask the building inspector about it. If a town council member talks about a new initiative he's considering for noise restrictions, write down his comments for use if he does file the proposed regulation. Make an entry about that interesting poster for a community meeting of a group you've never heard of, and check it out when you get back to your computer.

Remember to refer back to all those things you've written down. Disciplined reporters review their notes every day or so and transcribe them into computer files that are categorized by subject.

A collection of good notebooks will serve you through the years if you catalog their contents. Write the date you started the new book on the cover along with the date when you fill the last page. Date the first entry you make each day. Note the different stories you covered with this notebook on a list inside the cover. All this will help when you're trying to find that important quote or observation.

It may seem archaic to discuss writing implements in the digital age, but you'll need something with which to write all those things down. Carry at least two different color pens, one for notes and the other to highlight important sections you'll want to find quickly. Have a pencil with you for the times you're taking notes outdoors. Pencils work in colder weather, which may gum up pens. Pencils can also write on rain-wet paper; pens can't.

21st-Century Tools

At this writing, Patch.com and some other Web-only publications welcome new reporters with a box of equipment that can include a laptop with a full suite of editing programs, a video camera, a digital sound recorder and a wireless network card. Reporters working for other companies get by with less. Your smartphone alone probably has many of the features you'll need, but if your organization doesn't provide equipment, look into buying a good video camera that can record broadcast quality sound.

This book doesn't presume to suggest what makes and models of equipment you should use; technology changes too rapidly for that. It won't offer tutorials on Final Cut

Pro or Audacity or whatever the state-of-the-art editing programs will be by the time you read this. Your organization will have its own standards for the types of video and audio files it wants and the platforms it uses to edit them. Look into classes on shooting and producing sound and video if you haven't had the training. The same advice applies to basic Web design. Many community colleges and adult education centers offer quick tutorials on the essentials. Don't expect your organization to train you. You will be expected to know these skills.

Digital Notes You will likely take a lot of notes on your computer, interviewing people on the phone and researching details and facts from documents and online sites. It's a good idea to keep these raw files to refer to in the future. Clean up your notes as soon as you can after an interview; they'll be easier to understand later when your memory isn't as fresh. Just as you do with your notebook, categorize and date the notes. Computer files can be searched by name, topic or date. Keep notes in related files (city council, fire, crimes). Collect any phone numbers or e-mail addresses and put them in those subject-specific files. Be sure to regularly back up all files on a portable hard drive or other type of storage medium, and keep important material in an online drop box you can access from anywhere. Most people fail to make backup a routine and suffer for it when the hard drive fails.

Use the calendar in your computer or phone to remind you about future meetings or the next steps in a continuing story. When you cover an arrest, note the arraignment date in your calendar. If a committee begins a study on health care benefits for city workers, make a note in the calendar to check in with committee members a week or two before the report is due.

The Web A 2011 study, "The Social Side of the Internet," by the Pew Internet and American Life Project, found that online activity is an essential tool for civic, social, religious and advocacy groups. According to the survey, 82 percent of social media users belong to such groups; the Internet is key to the way these groups communicate, organize and plan.

You can tap into this information by signing up with the civic and professional association sites that are subjects for your beat. Establish a routine for checking their websites. Read the relevant local blogs and other online sites. Search for groups centered on local issues: the environment, schools, and neighborhood watch groups. The institutions you cover, such as the police department, municipal court or school district, may have their own websites or blogs.

Use online tools such as Google Alerts to keep track of what's happening. For example, you can set up an alert to let you know any time there is a reference on the Internet to your town's "Shady Manor" neighborhood. You can refine your searches ("Shady Manor and Springfield"). Set up the results as an RSS feed on Google Reader and on your smartphone. This reduces the risk that they'll be buried in the e-mail pile. Much of what will show up isn't useful (apartment ads, stories that have been over-covered), but occasionally you'll find a nugget of a story.

The Web can also be used to build on what reporters have always done: gauging what your sources and audience care about. Face-to-face reporting will always have huge advantages. But when you're getting started on a story, crowd sourcing can give you a sense of what's out there. Establish a blog on your news organization's site. Write posts asking for people's thoughts on your next story — say, the impact of school district budget cuts on students. You might try crowd sourcing "assignments," for example, asking audience members what parts of the school budget *they* would cut and posting their suggestions as a sidebar to your main story.

Social media sites can be another tremendous resource for tapping into people and their experiences. They can help build relationships that will boost your reporting. Check http://search.twitter.com to see if Twitter has established a hash tag or keyword for an event or an issue. Establish a personal Twitter feed to let your audience know what you're working on and to hear what's on their minds. Monitor Facebook for people and groups relevant to your beat. YouTube and other video sites may provide you-are-there visuals of fires or car accidents you can link to (once you get permission). Professional sites such as Poynter.org can give you great tips on using blogs, Twitter and Facebook.

Bear in mind, however, that the people who respond to you through the Web are a self-selected group. They have the means, the time and the passion to weigh in on a subject, but they may not represent a majority of opinion. Don't be lulled into thinking that what you're hearing from your audience represents something larger. You'll need to gauge the thinking of others out there who don't use the Web as a sounding board

Also, remain skeptical about what you read. There is a lot of mischief on the Web. Consider anything you find there as a tip that needs to be checked. That professional-looking website of the Citizens for/Against *(fill in the blank)* may represent nothing more than one angry individual sitting in front of a basement computer, nursing a beer and a grudge. That fantastic series of tweets about how a family survived a paralyzing blizzard might be just that: fantastic. The story may not be true; the person who wrote it may not be who he or she claims to be. Thorough, careful reporters take the extra steps to verify who and what they are sourcing and citing. They use real shoe leather to confirm and expand what they've found in their virtual reporting. So follow up whatever you read on the Web. Contact the people directly. Don't cut and paste rumor and gossip.

Preparing for the Beat

Before you start working any beat, you'll need to research the people and institutions you'll be covering. Join the LISTSERVs your sources are likely to use. Subscribe to RSS feeds from groups related to your beat so you don't have to constantly troll websites. An example: *Education Week*, a publication for educators, sends out RSS feeds on 75 topics, from testing to finances to charter schools. Join professional groups that are specific to your beat, such as Criminal Justice Journalists or the Education Writers Association, to see what other reporters are doing.

History Lessons

Immerse yourself in the archives to see what's been written about your beat. Read the past stories done by your news organization and its competitors. If you're lucky, your news organization will have a good archive and access to a national database such as Lexis-Nexis. If not, your local library may provide access.

Understanding the past puts the present in perspective. Has the size of your police force changed over the years? Are there more or fewer students in the public schools? How has the employment picture changed? Does Main Street have more or fewer shops than a few years ago? What disasters, fires or accidents are engrained in the city's culture? What scandals or folklore is part of the city's self-image? Make notes on the background data you find. What are the past budget numbers? What have court caseloads been over the past decade? Read the police and fire logs to see where the trouble spots are in your community.

Make a list of the players you will encounter on the beat. Learn the names of the judges, clerks, lawyers and officers who work in the courthouse. Chart the chain of command at the police stations and firehouses. Look up organizational structure for the school department and municipal agencies.

Learn about the personal histories of the major figures on your beat. Were the police chief and other high-ranking officers involved in any significant cases in the past? Did the fire chief come up through the ranks? What's the political history of the mayor? How has the composition of the town council changed through the years? What important cases did the judge handle before presiding over the murder case you are currently covering? The more you know about your sources' history, the better you will understand how to approach and speak with them.

You shouldn't expect to know everything. You certainly don't want to act as if you do. Nobody likes know-it-alls, especially when they *don't* know it all. So ask lots of questions. Consider all this research as preparation for a job interview. Instead of meeting with a potential employer, you'll be meeting with a variety of potential contacts. You want to show them you are smart enough and care enough to know the value of preparation.

Develop Contacts

If you're taking over the beat from another reporter, have him or her take you around to meet the people you'll be covering. It will give your sources a sense of continuity. Interview your predecessor. Ask which sources are helpful and which are likely to make your life difficult. Find out the best time and method for contacting the mayor or police chief.

Meet the public information officers and department spokespeople. Seek out the community groups, civic associations, professional organizations and bloggers who can bring you up to speed on the beat. All will be valuable contacts in your daily work. Go everywhere. Attend everything. Hand out business cards and collect names, phone numbers and e-mail addresses.

Start a beat blog so the audience can see what you're working on and chime in with ideas. Post links to your stories to show the community you're on the job. Your contacts will share your stories with their friends, raising the number of clicks to your site. That will help enhance your reputation and hopefully generate online comments you can learn from. If people see you as a reliable contact who follows up on their tips, you'll be the first person they call with news.

Find Good Starter Stories

Establish yourself by writing introductory stories about the personalities and issues you'll be covering. Reporters call these "handshake stories" because they introduce you to your sources and audience. Find something to write about the police chief; profile Officer Friendly. Spend a shift with a dispatcher and write about the job. Write about what it's like to be a councilwoman serving her first term. Profile a retiring firefighter and use his memories as an insight into the history of the department. These stories don't have to be puff pieces; they can be informative and compelling for your audience, help sources grow comfortable with you and provide you with a good overview of your beat.

Look through the clips and online archives for stories that need updating. Did the police ever find the armed robber who escaped from the jail? Did the new sewer system fix the chronic flooding problem on the east side of town? How is the sex-education class that was so controversial two years ago working out? Asking questions about old stories can point you to a ready supply of new ones.

DAILY REPORTING

You have your bag of real and virtual tools. You've studied the history, issues and people on your beat. You've met your contacts and written some introductory stories. Now comes what may be the hardest part of the beat — maintaining a daily flow of stories that will inform and entertain your audience.

The chapters in Part II of this book explain the routines for specific beats: the rounds to make, the types of stories to pursue and the ways to report and write them. This section highlights some tips and techniques for whatever beat you're assigned. Each journalist develops his or her own style of reporting through experience, trial and error. That education continues through your whole career. Here is a framework on which you can start building your own system.

Reaching the People You Need

As a reporter, you'll face no greater frustration than waiting for callbacks from the people you need for a story. Talking with reporters is low on the list of most people's priorities. They have busy lives; they may not have the time to speak with you when you need them. They may not want to talk at all, or they may take their time crafting a statement that comes too late and says too little. A reporter needs the skills to get people to talk. This is crucial to getting the information you need, especially the different perspectives to an important issue. Here are some hard-learned lessons in getting what you need.

Reach out early and often. The longer you wait to contact a person, the longer it will take to get a response. If you know what story you'll be working on tomorrow, send out e-mails — and perhaps text messages — to sources tonight, telling them you need to speak with them about a specific issue. E-mail extends your ability to contact people past business hours. People check their e-mail and texts regularly and respond quickly, even through the night. Most find it easier to hit the reply button than to pick up the phone. Contacts may set a time when you can call in the morning, or at least put you on their calendar. This technique helps set up your day with a schedule of interviews that can ease your morning jitters.

If you don't get a response, follow up your e-mail with a call as early as is polite. Having a list of your contacts' cell phone numbers is invaluable; a call during the morning commute can catch them in their cars with nothing better to do than speak with you.

If you don't reach them, leave a voice mail explaining quickly and concisely why you need to speak with them. Don't be passive about waiting for a call back. Call again in an hour or two. Leave another message explaining why it is important you speak with them right away. Be polite and don't exaggerate; you'll lose the credibility if you portray every contact as a crisis.

Stop leaving messages once you've dropped a couple of voice mails, but keep calling until you get a real voice. You may feel a bit pushy, but that's your job. Producing a complete, accurate story is much more important than worrying about being perceived as too aggressive.

Get Past the Gatekeepers

Sometimes you'll find your access to the person you need barred by a secretary, public relations person or some other intermediary. These people are protective of their bosses. They see their job as shielding superiors from interruptions and distractions. In their view, reporters aren't crucial to the day's business, especially if the subject is less than pleasant. Some of these gatekeepers will be helpful; others will be so hostile that you may wonder if your request is being passed on.

Yelling and threats won't help; that approach only gives them a reason to shut you off. You don't want that, especially if this is someone you will be dealing with regularly. Remain calm. Make it clear why you need to speak with the boss; frame your explanation to show that it would be to everyone's advantage. Appeal to their loyalty. Explain that you just want their boss' side of the story or that you need to check a critical fact that would be embarrassing to you and them if it were wrong. Try playing on their fears. Point out that the boss might not be happy if your story doesn't include his or her input. As a final incentive, ask for the intermediary's name and explain that you'll need to name someone in the story to explain why you weren't able to talk with the person in question. This is not a ploy, as we'll show later.

Knock on Doors

Don't rely just on the phone or e-mail. If you have the time, go to the person's office or home. People are generally polite; they find it much harder to slam the door in your face than to hang up the phone on you. Be respectful. Explain why it is important to get their side of the story. They may not answer your question directly, but you can usually tease some comment out of them. If the person says, "I have no comment," you might try commiserating. Say, "I guess this whole episode must be hard for you"; then wait for a response. Every veteran reporter has a story of how he or she got a terrific quote or important information by simply showing up at door of someone who didn't want to talk.

When All Else Fails . . .

Sometimes you just can't get the people you need for a story. They won't respond to your calls or e-mails, or they will decline to speak with you. In the latter case, simply explain in your story that the person would not comment. If you didn't speak with her directly, quote who gave you that information.

In cases where you haven't heard back from the person by deadline, detail your efforts to reach the person. Say he didn't respond to phone calls or e-mails. Provide specifics: *Joe Smith did not respond to multiple attempts to reach him by phone and e-mail.* This is important. You need to show you made a good-faith effort to produce a balanced story.

Keep trying even after you're published. If your story appears online first, send a link to the person in a email explaining that you'd still like to include him in the piece. Seeing the story on the Web may change his mind and you can add his voice to the story with a few quick tweaks.

Interviewing Etiquette

Interviewing a person on the street or the mayor in her office carries some rules of etiquette and some ethical questions.

You should never misrepresent yourself; always tell people you are a reporter. (Reporters, on rare occasion, do go undercover, but that is a subject well beyond the scope of beat reporting.) Wearing your media identification can add to your credibility and assuage the hesitation a person might have when approached by an inquiring stranger. Identify whom you work for and explain why you are asking the question. Make it clear this conversation could wind up in a story. This is an important step for people not experienced with reporters; they may not understand their name will be published along with their words.

You'll want the person's name, town, profession and, if relevant, age. Reporters have differing opinions on when to ask those questions. Some people find it off-putting to be asked private details at the beginning of a conversation; they may stop talking. Asking about the issue you're reporting may be a gentler way to lead them into a discussion that can end with questions about their personal information. The risk, however, is that they could decline to give their name after you've interviewed them, making your efforts a waste of time.

judgment call

Unnamed Sources

Named sources are an essential element of good journalism. Attributing quotes or information to someone by name, place and profession adds credibility. As the Society of Professional Journalists code of ethics puts it, "The public is entitled to as much information as possible on sources' reliability." Attribution shows your audience where the information is coming from and reassures them you're not making it up. In an ideal world, every person in every story would be named.

In the real world, however, you'll face situations when sources will give you important information only on the condition that you don't identify them. They

judgment call

may be fearful of losing their jobs or being ostracized by friends and co-workers. Or they may have an agenda — they hate their boss or they're feuding with a neighbor and may be telling you something about that person that is not entirely true. You have to balance a request for anonymity against the importance of the information.

Ask the person's reasons for remaining anonymous and what she fears will happen if she speaks for attribution. The answer can help you decide. A mother who tells you about the problems of getting special education services might have a good reason not to have her son identified as a special needs student. A woman who says she has dirt on an ex-husband she clearly hates should raise warning flags.

Then there are the times when people may not understand they *need* anonymity. They may come to you because they are troubled by something they think is immoral or illegal but not realize they are putting themselves in jeopardy. An employee may be fired for talking; someone who has signed a confidentiality agreement may be sued. As a reporter, you have the responsibility to make sure a source won't be harmed by a story. Make sure you both understand the consequences. Confer with your editors; they may take the decision out of your hands. If they say no and you can't use the information from the source, try to confirm it elsewhere. Sometimes you can leverage what you know to get someone else to speak to the issue.

Think in Multiple Media

Words aren't the only way to convey ideas. Stories also can be told with photos, video or sound. Charts and maps can often describe concepts better than words. News websites are hungry for all these images and sound. You'll need to think in multiple media.

Few organizations have the staff to send a photographer/videographer/sound engineer along with a reporter on assignment, so it may be up to you to shoot pictures and record audio and video in addition to your print duties. Tackling all these jobs at once can be tricky, but with help and experience you'll find each medium benefits the others.

The first step is to think about which medium would be best for the story. Audio, video and still photos help you to convey setting, emotion and personality in ways that words alone can't. The convergence of all these tools is true multimedia storytelling. If you are covering a scene where action is taking place — a fire, protest rally, water main break — capture images of the flames, the street action, the gush of water, while the action is still occurring, and post it before you start interviewing people. Alert your editors to watch for additional visuals your audience may be posting on YouTube or to your website.

Follow some of basic rules of photography. Move in close, fill the frame, focus carefully, avoid extraneous detail and capture the highlights of the action. Shoot from different angles. You will learn some skills by trial and error, but if your organization has a photo staff, ask them for tips and spend some time with them to see how they work.

You should be thinking about sound as well. You might grab an official on the scene for a quickly recorded interview about what's going on. Getting these snippets of breaking news onto your website is time-critical. The sooner you do it, the more clicks your site will get, building an audience for the stories that follow. If you're covering a meeting, it's wise to collect audio and video of what you think will be illustrative moments of the session.

If your story is less urgent — a leisurely interview or a color piece involving just a few people — do your notebook work first. Cameras can get between you and your subject. Many people become self-conscious knowing they're being recorded; they start speaking more to the camera than to you. Once you finish the conversation, you can bring out the camera and ask your subject if she could repeat a statement about a certain issue. The person will feel more comfortable knowing her video exposure is limited.

Gathering audio alone is less obtrusive than shooting pictures and video. After you turn on the recorder, you and your subject will soon forget it's there, and you'll be able to capture some subtleties of the person's tone and speech patterns. For extensive audio recording, use an external microphone rather than the one inside your recorder. If you're covering a meeting or other public forum, you may be able to connect to a feed from the podium microphones. You can also use your video camera to do double duty, capturing sound on the audio channel that you can use to create MP3s or other audio files. Whichever way you decide to go, keep good notes to track where these sound bites can be found.

Think about capturing ambient sound and images related to the story: the chants of protesters for a demonstration story, the sounds of road construction for a piece on a public works project. A story about a city councilor might include video of him walking down the corridors of City Hall. These "B rolls" of sight and sound can help pull your audience into the scene and into your story.

Study the multimedia stories that win journalism awards. Get inspired about what's possible. Journalists who do a lot of multimedia work are more than willing to share tips. Training courses and websites are great sources of advice. All these steps will help you convey important stories through various mediums. New technological developments do not change the elements of good storytelling. They simply provide you with more paths toward the same goal.

PRIVACY ISSUES

Your multimedia duties will require knowledge of privacy laws.

Generally, the rule is that anything happening in public places is fair game. The same is true for government meetings. Private organizations, such as fraternal and religious groups, advocacy coalitions, and business groups, such as the local chamber of commerce, have the right to bar you and/or your recording devices from their meetings. You should always ask first before you start recording in these situations.

Be aware of privacy concerns. Parents should be asked for permission to publish images of their children. Medical patients are protected under privacy rules. So are victims of sexual crimes. Again, if you have doubts, check your state's privacy laws and regulations.

New technology and concerns over terrorism have raised questions about the use of cameras, particularly those in cell phones. In a number of cases, people taking pictures of police making arrests have themselves been taken into custody and charged with illegal surveillance. Citizens have a right to observe and photograph police activities as long as they don't interfere with officers. But the officers have claimed that since the cell phone can transmit the picture, its use violates state wiretapping laws. Most of these cases have been thrown out of court, but you should be aware this is an unsettled issue of law in some jurisdictions.

The right to shoot pictures in public places has also been challenged under homeland security laws. Photographers have been stopped and their cameras or phones confiscated because they were filming public places that, according to officials, could be targets for terrorists. Again, these cases are usually dropped (in one case the photographer collected damages from the police). But you should be aware of the gray areas of enforcement. Check with your local bar association or civil liberties organization to understand your rights.

INTERVIEWING

Checklists

No matter what the beat, the art of the interview can offer some of the toughest challenges and biggest rewards for a reporter. It requires a set of competing skills. You must be a knowledgeable, coherent questioner and a careful listener at the same time. You need to take careful notes while analyzing what your subject is saying. (Using a recording device doesn't count. More on that later. . . .) You have to ask follow-up questions on minor details while staying focused on the big picture. You need to establish a rapport with your subject while remaining a dispassionate observer. You have to think in different media, including video and audio. And as this all goes on, you'll be hearing a play-by-play commentary bouncing around your brain: *Should I challenge him on that point? What does that vague term mean? What's her body language communicating? How can I describe this person's speech patterns and gestures to give the audience insight about who he or she is?*

An interview can be an exhausting experience. Done well, it can also be exhilarating, educational and even life changing. Interviews give you a peek into another person's life, skills and knowledge. The firefighter shares what he was thinking as he escaped a collapsing building. The politician provides tips on the art of persuasion by explaining how she got her colleagues to compromise on a controversial bill. The cop describing how he handled a domestic violence call reveals his childhood experiences dealing with an alcoholic father. No other profession, short of psychiatry, offers such an intimate glimpse into a stranger's mind.

To be a good interviewer, you must learn when to speak and when to listen. You have to swallow your pride and keep asking for a translation of the language in a legal brief, admitting you don't understand until you do. You need to analyze your own performance after each interview, asking yourself what worked and what didn't.

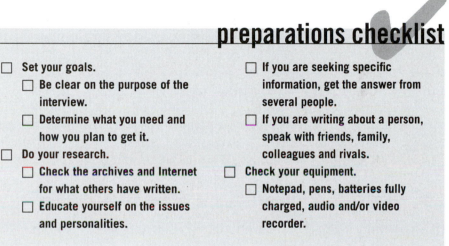

preparations checklist

- ☐ Set your goals.
  - ☐ Be clear on the purpose of the interview.
  - ☐ Determine what you need and how you plan to get it.
- ☐ Do your research.
  - ☐ Check the archives and Internet for what others have written.
  - ☐ Educate yourself on the issues and personalities.
- ☐ If you are seeking specific information, get the answer from several people.
- ☐ If you are writing about a person, speak with friends, family, colleagues and rivals.
- ☐ Check your equipment.
  - ☐ Notepad, pens, batteries fully charged, audio and/or video recorder.

PREPARATION

The most important part of interviewing is the groundwork necessary before you ask your first question. Blundering into an interview with a few half-formed questions and no clear goal will not serve you well. Your subject will consider you a shallow ignoramus and choose his or her words with excruciating care — ultimately providing you with nothing but meaningless clichés. You will lose your chance to gain good information and possibly deny yourself a valuable source in the future.

Many interviews are little more than a few hurried questions to a police spokeswoman at a crime scene or a councilman rushing to a vote. Even so, you need to give some thought to how you phrase your question to get the answer you need. That can make the difference between a mediocre outcome and a potential revelation.

Set Your Goals

Determine what you hope to accomplish in the interview. Are you looking for a specific fact, detail or opinion? Do you need confirmation of what someone else has said? Are you starting out on a longer project and simply gathering as much information about the subject as you can? Or are you planning a profile that needs personal details about the person you are interviewing? Your level of success rises dramatically if you have a clear idea before the interview of what you want in your notebook when you walk out of the interview. The goal can be as simple as getting that one quote that confirms the name of the person under investigation or as complex as getting someone to give you a timeline of events that led to the mayor's resignation.

Some reporters set their goals by drawing up a detailed list of questions they can refer to during the interview. Other reporters don't like this sort of scripted question-and-answer format; they prefer to keep the interview more conversational and spontaneous. The nature of the interview will often decide which approach to take. You won't need a list of questions for a lighter story about a firehouse's master chef. An interview with a politician answering charges of corruption will require a detailed checklist of the accusations your subject needs to address. It is always good to have a few questions written in your notebook to remind you of your goals, but the best questions can come in reaction to what your subject just said. Your experiences will teach you which approach works best in different scenarios.

Research Your Subject

If you're preparing for a longer interview, learn all you can about your subject and the larger issues you plan to feature in your story. Search engines and online databases such as LexisNexis and Google will show you what others have written and suggest new angles for your story. A check of Facebook, LinkedIn and other social networking sites will provide more personal information about the subject's family, friends and colleagues.

Conversations with your subject's co-workers, underlings and rivals can provide anecdotes that add to your understanding of your subject, as will conversations with the subject's friends and family. This homework will provide more material for your interview. The wife of a politician might tell you how he tries out speeches at the family breakfast table. A mention of that to the politician may lead him to explain his deep fear of public speaking. It may be a small revelation, but it could offer a terrific insight for the story.

Assume anything you say to friends and family will go straight back to the source. Frame the conversation by explaining your desire to understand the person you will be interviewing. In most cases, your subject will be understanding and even a bit flattered that you've taken the time to ask around.

Once you've gathered all this preliminary information, you'll need to stifle the tendency we all have to show off what we know. You walk a thin line when you go into an interview armed with research. Nobody likes a know-it-all, yet demonstrating your knowledge is important in letting the subject know you can't be misled. Make a casual reference to some detail that shows you've done your homework. Ask the fire chief why the department is choosing a Ferrara pumper rather than one built by American LaFrance. But don't show off too much. The interview is not about you.

Come Equipped

In just a few years reporters have gone from using reel-to-reel tape recorders the size of a small toaster oven to a digital stick smaller than a pen. The technology may have changed, but one inexorable fact has not: Machines and their operators fail with regularity. Batteries give out. You forget to turn on the microphone or turn off the pause button. Circumstances conspire to defeat you even when the machine works. Background noise drowns out your subject, or some quirk in the room's acoustics make voices fade in and out. So always take notes. It will keep you focused, and your scribbles are guaranteed to be there when you start putting the story together.

That's not to say you shouldn't use a recorder. Reviewing an interview, if you have the time, offers subtle cues and insights you're too busy to notice during the actual event. You can catch pauses, shifts in tone, words that are emphasized and answers that are rushed. Recording also protects you if someone questions a quote. And your organization is probably eager to post audio or video on its website.

So record interviews, but take copious notes, too. Try to ignore the recorder once you start. Some devices allow you to mark a passage by pushing a button; some have a counter you can discretely note for later playback. But take the attitude that something will go wrong. If you never expect your recording to come out and you keep good notes, you won't be disappointed.

Avoid doing interviews by e-mail. An exchange of written questions and answers can never match the spontaneity of a conversation. E-mailed answers sound like what they are: written statements. It is much harder to follow up on nuances within the answers. Much is lost and little is gained.

The Interview

☐ **Establish a relationship.**
  ☐ Start with small talk; let the subject know who you are.
  ☐ Explain why you're there.
☐ **Set ground rules.**
  ☐ Get permission to record.
  ☐ Determine what's on and off the record.

☐ **Consider your questions.**
  ☐ Frame them to avoid limited yes/no answers.
  ☐ Start with easy questions and work toward the tough ones.
☐ **Follow up.**
  ☐ Pursue what is unclear; don't accept an incomplete answer.
☐ Reserve the right to call again.

You've done your research. You've set your goals. You've double-checked the recorder. Now it's time for the interview.

Social Niceties

Shake hands and make eye contact. These little social niceties have their reasons. The handshake developed as a way to show you weren't armed. Many people feel reassured when you look them in the eye. Be polite. Show you're not a threat.

Repeat why you are there and what the story will be about. You probably mentioned this when setting up the interview, but it's always good to make sure your subject understands. It should dispel some of the anxiety he might be feeling.

Look around. Note the décor, the family pictures, the award plaques. Admire the dried lizard's head on the desk. Ask where it came from. This allows for some nonthreatening conversation to set your subject at ease. It also can provide you with some good details for your story. That lizard's head may have a terrific story behind it that offers insight into your subject.

This chitchat also helps the subject get to know you. Slip in a mention of your family, your pets, your interests. Find some commonality that shows you're just another person doing his or her job and not some bloodthirsty inquisitioner.

But don't get carried away with the small talk. Your subject may not have the patience; the police chief may be a brusque character in a rush to get back to business. Take your cues from them as to the level and speed of conversation.

Set Ground Rules Ask for permission to record the interview. Usually there are no objections; it's to everyone's advantage to have a clear record of what is said. Subjects may want to make their own recordings. That's fine. Follow the same etiquette when doing a phone interview. The laws about recording phone conversations vary from state to state, so the best policy is to be up-front about what you're doing. So there is no question later, record the subject giving you permission to record.

If you're interviewing someone who objects to being recorded, make it clear your goal is to protect him or her against inaccuracies. If the objections continue, drop the request, put the recorder away and resolve to take better notes.

You may face questions about what will be on or off the record. Many times subjects will stop in the middle of an interview and ask that the next answer be off the record.

Sometimes someone will ask that the entire interview be off the record. The prosecuting attorney may agree to give you background on the case but doesn't want to be quoted. A school superintendent, who wants to float an idea about a curriculum change, will ask you not to attribute the information to him. You should always try to dissuade someone from going off the record. If the person persists, agree to keep that specific answer off the record but push to go back on the record once you move to the next question. Tell your subjects you'll honor the off-the-record request but reserve the right to get back to them later to explain how you would use the information. Once time passes and your subject better understands your goals, he or she will be more likely to agree to attribution. Be very, very clear as to what is on and what is off record. Carefully mark each off-record answer in your notes.

Employ Different Types of Questions Ask open-ended questions instead of a series of fact checks. Don't start with "You joined the police force in 1984?" Ask what changes have taken place in policing since the subject started back in 1984. Ask what event or incident stands out in his or her mind. Dig deeper whenever possible.

The way you frame questions can bring out anecdotes, details and explanations:

▶ *Why* is a word you can never wear out. It requires the subject to respond with something more than a one-syllable answer.

▶ *What was that like?* This draws out personal recollections. Such answers give readers a much better sense of a time, an event and the person.

▶ *Give me an example* also draws out your subject and can lead to other specifics that will broaden your readers' understanding.

No matter how many good questions you come prepared with, better ones may reveal themselves during the conversation. When the defense lawyer says she worked just for a year as an assistant prosecutor, asking why reveals that she felt the deck is stacked against defendants — leading to an insight into why she defends accused murderers. When a fire chief speaks generally about the burdens of command, asking for an example brings out an anecdote of how he felt the first time he saw one of his firefighters injured.

Repeat Questions Until They Are Answered Don't accept a partial or evasive answer. Some people, particularly politicians, are skilled at turning your question into a talking point that has nothing to do with what you asked. Don't be shy about calling them out: "I know, Alderman Johnson, that you say you've supported the sludge plant proposal because it will bring jobs, but I'm asking, again, how do you explain the big campaign contribution from the plant's owner?" If he doesn't answer, rephrase the question. Don't give him wiggle room. Did he or didn't he? Yes or no? Tell the subjects you want to present their side but their answer doesn't do that. Tell them you don't want to misrepresent them, but if they don't answer the question, you'll have to note that in your story.

Listen Play a recording of your last interview. If you hear your voice as often as your subject's, you aren't listening enough. You're there to hear what the person you're interviewing has to say. Keep your comments to a minimum. New reporters often talk too much when they're nervous. Learn to stifle yourself.

Use Silence Most people abhor silence and will rush to fill it with the sound of their own voice. If your subject gives a pat answer or is not forthcoming, stop talking and simply look at the person. Think about what you'd like for dinner. Make a laundry list. Pick a lottery number. Just don't say anything. Most times the interviewee will start talking just to break the tension.

Asking the Tough Questions Too many new journalists think the way to get information is to confront their subject like the reporters they've seen on television. Mike Wallace, a hard-nosed interviewer of *60 Minutes* fame, and his imitators set such behavior for a generation of reporters. That is unfortunate. Those theatrics are primarily a show for the camera. It is unnecessary and unproductive in a regular interview.

You can ask a tough question without acting tough. Be conversational. Make it clear you want to get their side of the story. For example, "The Jonesville Neighborhood Association says they hardly ever see a patrol car in their area despite a rise in purse snatchings. What would you say to them?" If there are no specific critics to cite, say you're playing devil's advocate. Or put it on your boss. Say: "My editor wants me to ask you about the rumors of your cross-dressing." Whatever the tactic, you shouldn't worry about offending your subject. He or she is probably expecting the question and may have agreed to the interview to rebut the accusations.

Sometimes a tough question will be unexpected. It may be the whole reason you're talking with the subject; the rest of the conversation was mostly pretense. You're really not interested in their work for charity. You've come to confront them with accusations that they have been lying, stealing, cheating or breaking one of the other Ten Commandments. Save that question for the end of the interview. Spring it after you get all the ancillary material you may need. This tactic might not be polite, but getting the necessary information is your duty to your story and your audience.

Finishing Up

You may hear something interesting during the course of an interview that you want to pursue, but you don't want to interrupt the flow of conversation. Mark it in your notebook with a question mark and come back to it. Never be afraid to go over something you don't understand. Many of the people you report on specialize in a certain field. That usually means they speak in a specialized language. If you don't know what some terms your source is using mean, there's a very good chance some of your audience won't know either. Ask for definitions. Although most of the people you interview want you to get the facts right, you'll probably run into a few who treat you like an idiot. That may be a ploy to throw you off balance. Pay it no mind. It's more important what your readers, viewers and editors think of your story than what some assistant deputy secretary for transportation thinks of you.

Ask Follow-On Questions

Here are two questions you should never hesitate to ask at the end of an interview:

▶ Is there anything I didn't ask that you think I should?

▶ Who else would be good to speak to for this story?

The first question may get your subject to search his or her mind for something neither of you thought about. It may also be disarming enough to get them to talk about something they've been waiting for you to address. The second question is more straightforward. Your subject might be eager for you to speak with someone who can offer better details.

Reserve the Right to Call Back

You will probably have follow-up questions and facts to check after you've gone over your notes. Don't hesitate to call to clarify these questions. In most cases, your subjects will be eager to make sure that you get the facts right and present their position accurately. It's in their best interest. A follow-up call is also a way to continue your relationship, and it may lead to additional information.

Saying Good-Bye

Ending an interview can be remarkably hard, especially if it has gone well. There's something unique about the interviewer/interviewee dynamic. You are strangers, yet within an hour you have asked and they have answered questions of a fairly intimate nature. Maybe you've talked about their successes, their failures, their families and their life's passions. You've raised issues that may have required some soul searching. They've told you stories they might not have thought about for some time or never shared with anyone before. As cautious as they may be about being interviewed, many people relax and feel freed by talking to a nonjudgmental stranger who hangs on their every word. This intimacy, which comes on so quickly, ends just as abruptly. It's important to honor that moment, to be thankful and respectful of your subject. After all they've just given you a bit of themselves.

THE AFTERMATH

post-interview checklist

- ☐ Review notes.
- ☐ Transcribe recordings.
- ☐ Write yourself a memo to remember details.
- ☐ Debrief yourself.

If you're not on deadline, the temptation is to go home and kick back. Watch television. Open a bottle of something. Give yourself a well-deserved break. Well, not yet. If you put your notes aside and let them grow cold, you risk losing a lot. Impressions fade. Context withers. You need to get it all down in a memo to yourself while the experience is fresh and you can still make out what you've scribbled on your pad.

If you've recorded the interview, now is the time to start transcribing. It isn't fun; it certainly isn't glamorous to spend an evening with your notes, your recorder and your computer. You don't have to transcribe every word — conversations often wander away from the point of the interview. Concentrate on the parts that are critical to the story you want to tell. Even so, transcription is boring and time consuming. The alternative — incomplete notes and foggy memories — is much more painful.

Debrief Yourself

Finally, it's always good to spend a few minutes analyzing the interview. Did you get what you wanted? Were you able to read your subject? Did you come off too hard? Too soft? What could you have done better? After 30 years I still go through this exercise to see what I can learn about my technique and myself. I highly recommend it. A conversation with the runner-up in a local pie-baking contest might not seem like much, but the experience may give you some insight to make you that much better an interviewer when, years in the future, you get some face time with the queen of England.

CHAPTER 3

WORKING WITH
EDITORS

Newsrooms come in all sorts of configurations; with the advent of the Internet some have become virtual. Many reporters now work out of their homes or coffee shops, using cell phone, text and e-mail. But whether or not you have a desk at your organization's headquarters, you will have an editor or editors. Understanding their care and feeding is essential to your success.

Learning how to work with editors is a basic job skill, right up there with reporting, writing and production. A large part of your day-to-day work — and longer-term career — is in the hands of editors. They decide what beat you'll cover, approve your story ideas, set deadlines and mold how your final story will look and where and when it will appear. You might have supernatural talents for finding news and producing fascinating, evocative stories, but unless you understand the editors' worldview and each one's specific idiosyncrasies, your job will be a lot more frustrating and a lot less fun. Working well with a good editor can make your stories better and earn you an important mentor.

Editors come with various titles and duties. Depending on how your organization is structured, you may work with an assignment editor, city editor, news editor, feature editor or managing editor. You will deal with copy editors and desk editors. Web editor/producers, photo editors and graphics editors will help tell your stories.

Whatever their title, most editors are overworked, with short attention spans and, on occasion, even shorter fuses. Editors are constantly multitasking. Reporters clamor for their attention; higher-level editors second-guess their decisions. Deadlines are always looming; the nature of news can create a constant state of near crisis. News meetings eat into their editing time; readers and viewers question their judgments with a constant stream of e-mails and calls. One of the better editors I worked for described his job as being nibbled to death by ducks.

So how does a reporter deal with these beleaguered souls? The best word of advice: *communication*. Editors need to know what ideas you plan to pursue, where you are throughout the day, when you plan to file and what you will do for them next. It isn't always easy to provide this information and get the feedback you need. Editors can be hard to reach; they may not have the time or patience to listen to all the details about your run-in with the mayor. And they often have limited memories: What you told them this morning may be forgotten by lunch.

The overriding principle is to keep communication brief and use multiple media. Speak face-to-face when you can; call when you can't. But also send brief e-mails and texts. Having a written record is an important backup for both of you to refer to if questions arise in the future about what was agreed on in the past.

Introductions

Get to know your editors the same way you'd develop relationships with important sources. Go out for lunch, coffee or a beer. Before you do, research their careers, just as you would an interview subject. Find out the big projects they have worked on; track their careers from their early days. Talk to other reporters who've worked with them. All this will give you a better understanding of the editors you will be working with.

Use your chat with the editor to find out more about their past successes and lessons learned from failure. Discuss their journalistic philosophies; ask for examples of what they look for in their reporters and the stories they produce. Ask about their families and outside interests. Then provide them with the same information about yourself.

Establish guidelines. What will your duties be? What kind of stories are they looking for and what kind of production do they expect — how many daily stories, how many longer news features or weekend pieces? What multimedia duties will you have? Ask for specific examples. Find out the criteria that will be used to judge your work: The number and size of the pieces you produce? The number of clicks on your online stories? Find out whether the newsroom has a formal evaluation process and when it should take place.

Establish the day-to-day procedures. Should you check in each morning? What time would be best? What form of communication do the editors prefer: Phone? E-mail? How often do they want to hear from you during the day? What is the deadline structure? What are the filing procedures? Take notes during your conversation; then follow up with a memo outlining your understanding of the details you've discussed. This is an important step. This written record of the conversation will become your script of expectations. Most editors will appreciate the effort.

from the source

Rob Mitchell,
Vermont state editor, the Rutland Herald

Rob Mitchell learned about reporters while growing up in a family of editors.

His grandfather was editor of the Rutland Herald for 45 years; his father was an editor at the paper before becoming publisher in 1978. Mitchell, now state editor for the Herald and Barre-Montpelier Times-Argus, remembers each had his own way of working with reporters.

"My grandfather was okay with having different personalities in the newsroom, taking a bunch of egos and getting them working in the same general direction," he recalls. "My father has drilled into me that an editor has to be both demanding and nurturing to reporters. You have to push them and tell them when they do a good job."

Mitchell is adding his own pages to the family's reporter playbook as his newspapers transition to all-day deadlines on their websites. The challenge, he says, is marrying traditional reporting skills with the new requirements of updates, summaries and blogs, on the virtual newspapers as well as Facebook and Twitter.

All this, he says, changes the rhythm of the newsroom. "Reporters are tracking three or four things throughout the day. It's a continuous flow rather than a gradual buildup to a crescendo of pressure at the end of the day."

Mitchell says these new duties can make it tempting for reporters to stay at their desks, poring over news releases and working the phones rather than going down to City Hall or the police station to find out what's happening.

"Reporters don't get out of the newsroom as much as they used to. They don't rely on the face-to-face schmoozing," Mitchell says. "A good editor will pry a reporter out of the seat. Usually the reporter will come back and grudgingly say, 'Yeah, I got more out there.'"

Mitchell appreciates the different styles of reporting he sees in his newsroom. Editors, he says, have to recognize that reporters can have various ways of getting to the same place.

"One reporter may get a tip, then go back and do a lot of research before making calls. Another reporter will say, 'Okay,' call 10 people and start asking dumb questions until he has what he needs," he says. "It's really fun to see those different personalities work side by side and turn in incredible stories."

Here are some of Mitchell's tips for reporters:

▶ *Be brave.* "As a reporter you have to be fearless about looking like an idiot or calling someone back four or five times to make sure you are absolutely clear about what they said."

▶ *Own up to mistakes.* "It gets me angry if a reporter makes a mistake and refuses to admit it. If you get a call that you've got something wrong, fix it. Once you start taking it personally, it becomes about you and not the mistake."

from the source

- ▶ *Deliver on your promises.* "It really ticks me off when reporters give me a budget line [a summary of the story they are working on] and then don't come through because they didn't get off their butts. As an editor I want my reporters to push away all the obstacles and get the story."
- ▶ *Find the joy.* "I really appreciate reporters who can look at an old subject with fresh eyes and come up with something unique," he says. "I want someone who goes out in the street and finds an interesting story by talking to an ordinary person."
- ▶ *Remember the rewards.* "To survive in this industry, you have to keep sight of what is great about it. The pay is crappy, the hours are long and no one appreciates us. But this job allows you to learn something new every day."

PITCHING STORIES

Editors rely on reporters to come up with stories ideas — lots and lots of story ideas. It's logical that stories should flow up from reporters. They're the ones familiar with their subject; they encounter the issues and personalities on their beats every day.

Pitching your story ideas to an editor is an important skill. A successful pitch allows you to do the stories *you* think are important. It also shows that you are enthusiastic and engaged. Editors don't want reporters to sit around waiting for direction. If you do that, prepare to be saddled with story ideas that you won't like, that waste your time and that disappoint your editor's expectations.

But don't expect editors to accept vague ideas. Telling your editor, "I want to do a story about fire calls," isn't going to satisfy him or her. Editors need to know more, but they don't always have time to hear every detail. Therein lies the art of the pitch.

Some busy editors may bark, "Just give me the headline." Others may ask for the elevator pitch, a reference to the business world where a worker has to get his or her message across to the boss in the time it takes them to ride the elevator to the 22nd floor. What they are looking for is the focus of the story.

Think your pitch through before you start talking. What makes your story timely? What's the impact — the reason your audience will want to read it? Cite some details to make your point. Say you want to look into the time it takes various firehouses to respond to calls. Explain that you've heard complaints that some neighborhoods get a quicker response than others. List the people and resources you plan to tap. Draw up an outline you can refer to when you make the pitch; it will help focus your thoughts. If you're not entirely sure where the story is headed, explain that you're researching the idea to see if it will pan out. Don't make promises you can't keep. If you oversell too many stories, the editors will begin to doubt your ability to deliver.

Your editors will have their own story ideas. Some will be drawn from their knowledge and experience; presumably they've been in the business longer than you and know something about the background and personalities of your beat. A majority of their ideas will lead to great stories. A skilled editor can see the big picture that reporters may miss in the day-to-day scramble for news.

But sometimes the editors' story ideas may be vague or even misguided, based on a snippet of conversation they overheard or a line or two they read on the Web. They may even do what you have been warned against: suggesting a story about a subject without offering details or specifics to show you what they have in mind.

When such a situation comes up, don't be dismissive. Be enthusiastic; dig deeper to see if you can turn the idea into something better. No one, particularly editors, appreciates seeing her grand idea dismissed out of hand. Ask where the idea came from. She may have misread something in an article that you can track down and refer her to (*the story actually was about martins in the forest, not Martians*). Try to engage your editor and grow that seed of a suggestion into a fully realized story plan. Go off and do the research. If the idea is sound, proceed from there. If the idea is flawed, try to move the editor's suggestion into the realm of the possible. Explain that although there are no Martians, the spread of martins in the forest is a terrific story — then detail how you would proceed. Thank her for the tip. Keep her invested in the story. If you do, it can lead to better placement in the paper or on the website.

Communicating Through the Day

Editors want to know what you are doing for them — both today and in the longer term. Their motivation is simple. They begin each morning faced with an empty space for both the website and the print edition. They need to be reassured they can count on you to feed the hungry beast. But you need to be realistic about keeping your daily promises.

Check in each morning. Send an e-mail detailing your plan for the day: what you will produce today and what you are working on for later in the week. Follow up your message with a call to the editor to see if he or she has suggestions about the stories you are working on. Get answers to the two most important questions every writer faces: When is your piece due, and how long can it be?

Offer regular updates on how your stories are progressing. Let your editors know when a source confirms your story; warn them when a story isn't going well. If that is the case, your editor may have good ideas on other places to look or other sources to seek. You can discuss whether you should reshape the idea or go on to another project. Either way, your editor doesn't like to be surprised with a finished story that looks nothing like what he or she was expecting.

If you're working on a story you think could top the website or make it onto the front page, make your pitch early. Explain the significance of the piece and why you think it will be of great interest to your audience. If your story will contain information that no one else has, make that clear. That fact may be the most important selling point for good placement of your story. Also mention the great photos the photographer took, the chart you're working on with the graphics people, the audio or video that will attract the Web audience.

But don't oversell. If you tout everything as a top story and then fail to deliver, your credibility will shrink and even your best stories will face skepticism. There's no shame in having your story run inside the newspaper or further down on the website. Plenty of people read those stories too. Nobody makes the front page every day. At the end of the day, your editors will appreciate your help in filling some of that empty space.

Even if your editor is the type who doesn't like frequent updates, be sure to tell him immediately if something changes: a new, important story pops up, an expected story changes significantly, or a story isn't going to be ready for deadline. Editors may not seem happy to get these calls, but that annoyance won't compare to their frustration if you neglect to tell them something they need to know.

EDITING WITH YOUR EDITOR

Some reporters have issues with being edited. They think every change makes their story worse, or they feel challenged when an editor makes it better. But don't let your insecurities get in the way of an important collaborative process. Everyone needs an editor. A second set of eyes can spot gaps in your reporting, typos in your writing and places where you could improve your organization. A good editor spares you embarrassment and teaches you to be a better journalist. Even a not-so-good editor keeps you on your toes. You may think your story is crystal clear, but if the editor doesn't understand some section, chances are your audience won't either.

Here are some tips to make the editing process easier for both of you:

Give Your Editors Enough Time

Filing your story right on deadline will put more pressure on the editors to do a quick-and-dirty job. A rushed process often allows errors to slip through. Try to get your work to the editor as early as possible. If the story is waiting for a final callback from the police spokesperson, send the draft to your editor with a note explaining where you'll put the additional information. This will provide time for feedback before the editor is overwhelmed by the rush of copy later in the day.

Be Clear on What Changes They Want

Editors have different styles. Some are surgical with very specific changes and questions. Others are more philosophical. They may shower you with general observations, tales of past stories and a range of ideas about your story that may be more of a suggestion than a request.

Just as a reporter should never be afraid to ask "dumb" questions of a source, you shouldn't be shy about asking your editor exactly what he or she wants. If you don't understand an editing change or a question, persist until you do. But watch your tone. Make it clear that you're asking for clarification and not challenging the editor.

Don't Repeat Mistakes

Few things annoy editors more than seeing the same errors repeated in your copy. Misspellings of names, repeated misspellings of the same words and constantly misplaced commas will hurt your reputation and raise questions about your credibility. You should be familiar with your organization's style rules. Whether it's *The Associated Press Stylebook*, another manual or your organization's own style guide, use the book even if you think you know the proper style. Again, if you don't understand some editing change in your story, ask questions until you do.

Don't Argue Over Words

The newsroom is not a democratic institution. The editor is the final gatekeeper for what appears in the paper or on the website. Little time can be spent in debate over a phrase or word. So don't waste time quibbling about where a quote should go or whether you really needed that adverb the editor removed. Reserve your objections for the times when you feel the editor has introduced an error, made your work awkward or given the audience the wrong idea. It is then that you should explain clearly why the original was more accurate.

judgment call

Balancing Your Loyalties

You may face a time when you have to stand up to your editors. You may feel they've done something to your story that gives a false impression or is just flat wrong. They may leave out some essential section they consider too controversial. They may want to present something as simple fact when it requires explanation and qualification. In extreme cases, your editor might want you to do a story that you feel is unfair to the subject, or he may call you off a story involving a prominent person or institution.

judgment call

Thankfully, such issues come up rarely. Few editors or news organizations have personal vendettas or agendas. Nearly everyone wants to get it right. Still, you may be faced with occasions that raise some tough questions. To whom do you owe your loyalty: the editor who wants to name the source of your information or the person you promised to keep anonymous? Do you remain silent when a part of your story you consider essential is removed because the editors fear it will create too much controversy in the community? Or when your story is softened to reduce the risk of a lawsuit even though you know your facts are right? Do you agree to an edit that includes changes you consider misleading? Or do you take a principled stand at the risk of your job?

You can often prevail through solid reporting. Use the details and records to show why your story should stand. If you must do a story you don't feel right about, take the extra steps to balance the editor's preconceptions with detailed research and extensive interviews. It's hard for editors to ignore facts. They'll change their minds when presented the evidence.

If these approaches don't work, you face harder choices. You can refuse an assignment on moral grounds. You can ask that your name be removed from an edited story that you feel is wrong or unfair. You can make your case to the managing editor or editor in chief.

Ultimately, however, if you regularly find yourself in situations where your standards clash with those of your superiors, it may be time to find another job. In a perfect world truth prevails as long as you remain loyal to the story and your audience. But the world isn't perfect.

Make a Thorough Final Review

Editors may send your story back several times with questions and changes. Carefully review the final version for anything that would embarrass you or your organization. Remember, your name is on the story; your audience will hold you responsible for any typo or factual error.

Admit to Errors and Fix Them Quickly

Mistakes can creep into your work despite the best efforts of you and your editors. When you discover a mistake — usually courtesy of an online comment or a call from an observant reader — let your editor know immediately. Correct the error on the webpage and prepare a correction or clarification for the print edition. Don't hide the error. You only make the situation worse by letting a mistake go.

Other Editors, Other Issues

Although you're likely to work regularly with one or two editors, you will deal with editors and supervisors from other departments. Your organization may have web producers, a photo and video department and perhaps a graphics department that produces charts, graphs and designs that help tell your story. The same rule applies to all of them: *Communicate early and often.*

If you have a photo/video department, learn the procedure for letting the editors know you will be interviewing the new school superintendent so they can assign someone to provide the visuals for your story. Don't just tell them the time and place. Share what you've learned from your reporting. Knowing the superintendent is a black belt in karate who does community gardening on the weekend may get the photo/video people thinking about visuals that are more interesting and revealing than a standard headshot. Tell the graphics department supervisor you're working on a detailed story about fire response times that would be enhanced by charts illustrating your findings. Give them plenty of advance warning on your deadline.

Your story's final stop will be the copy desk. Copy editors are often the most undervalued people in a newsroom. They are paid and promoted for finding mistakes in grammar, punctuation, math and logic. What may seem like nitpicking to you is deadly serious business to them. Copy editors may disagree on certain grammar and punctuation rules. They have strong personal opinions about certain words and usage. You should respect them by studying their likes and dislikes. You make their job and your life a little easier if you make the effort to avoid making the same mistakes.

CHAPTER 4

FILING IN THE
DIGITAL AGE

Some of the loneliest moments in a reporter's life come when he or she sits down to write.

The calls have been made; the research is done. Now comes the time to turn that legwork into a compelling story. The blank screen awaits you, but you still face questions — lots of questions.

What is this story about? What kind of lede would best draw people in? What do you leave in? What do you take out? How can you incorporate audio, video and HTML links? These questions become more urgent with the Web's persistent deadline hanging over your head. No wonder some writers sit paralyzed, hoping that inspiration — or fear — will get them past the awful inertia.

You can get over these mental speed bumps if you start by laying out the story in your mind before you sit down to write. Before you even begin the interviews and research, think about the points you want to make, whom you will talk to and what information you will need. You won't have a clear idea of how the story will look — you're still finding out about it. But with each conversation and every bit of information you gather, the framework of the story should begin to emerge. The interview with the angry parent will need a response from the school superintendent. A statement by the plaintiff in a lawsuit requires research on the case and a balancing comment from the defendant. As you collect the parts, you'll start to see where they go and what else you need to complete the story.

Write an Outline

As you gather information for your story, especially a longer, in-depth piece, sketch out an outline of the basic narrative or storyline. Where will you put the background on the robbery arrest? Does the sharp quote from the police spokesman go before or after that

on the web

Tweeting and Live Blogging

As you put together your story, you'll probably write shorter, less formal versions for your website, Facebook account and Twitter feeds. By tweeting, "Councilwoman Flanders and housing head getting into heated debate at Fawlty Towers forum" — and other tweets that follow — you can beat the competition, ease some of the deadline pressure and build an audience for the story that may be a few hours away. The immediacy can be compelling and fun. Tips for this practice, called "live tweeting," can be found on the website: www.twitterjournalism.com/2009/06/28/tips-for-live-tweeting-an-event.

You should build a Twitter following. Make yourself easy to find (use your name without spaces, for example), and identify yourself as a reporter in your profile. This allows followers to weigh in with useful tips. When a gunman took hostages at the Discovery Channel headquarters in Silver Spring, Md., the website TBD enhanced its coverage with tweets and texts from people at the scene, giving its readers a comprehensive, up-to-the-minute view of what was happening. Re-tweeting information like this can help your story. People may have tips on snow day school cancellations or news from a crime scene. But do additional reporting to be sure you are passing on fact, not gossip.

Tweet links to your final story, but remember not everyone is on Twitter. So go old school and e-mail the story link to those in the community who might be interested. They will appreciate the notice and think of you when they have an issue they want covered.

section? Will you need a transition to the statement from the suspect's lawyer? Keep thinking how the focus and flow of the story have changed with each new bit of reporting. Framing the points, ideas and transitions as you go will show what you still need to report. The technique will also help you to think about what audio or video package should accompany your work.

Find Your Lede

Even after you've decided on the main points of your story, you still have dozens of options for the first paragraph or opening sequence. Writers can get stuck trying to come up with those one or two perfect sentences that summarize their reporting in an economical, engaging way that will catch and hold their audience's interest. If they spend too much time on the lede, deadline pressures may make the rest of the story feel rushed and incomplete.

Various techniques can help you get around the "*What's my lede?*" roadblock.

This Story Is About . . .

Come up with a headline you would write to grab readers and convey the point of your story. If you can't come up with a headline, you probably have more thinking to do about the focus of the story.

Or consider how you would answer a friend who asks what you're working on? Start out by saying, "This story is about"; then finish the thought out loud while you type it. Example: This story is about . . . *a plan by the traffic department to eliminate congestion on the East Side by making several streets one way.*

Not exactly riveting prose, but it's a start. Now think about other things you'd tell your friend. You might add: *The people who live in the area are so upset that they're putting signs on their lawns to protest the plan.*

That's more interesting; you've told your friend something about the impact this plan is having on people. Then think about the details you would mention to hold your friend's interest: *A lot of the signs say, "I Don't Want to Be One Way."* (Mentioning this should remind you to get a picture of the sign to accompany your story.)

This imaginary conversation has conjured up elements of a good lede. With a little rearranging, you might write: *Some East Side residents, angered by a Traffic Department plan to limit travel on their streets, are placing lawn signs declaring: I Don't Want to Be One Way.*

Now leave the lede and get on with the rest of the story. As you write, other facts may come up that could go in the lede. Maybe you'll add a word or two as to why the plan has been put forward or when it is scheduled to take effect. Your notes may have details about how many streets and homes would be affected.

Try Different Approaches

Think beyond a lede that relies on the five Ws (who, what, when, where and why). The *what (as in what is this story about?)* is the most important element. The other Ws can get in the way of a lede's flow. Consider the best way to communicate the central element of the story. Sometimes complicated issues can be better explained by an anecdote or through a real person's eyes. Here are two sample ledes for a story:

Seventy people, some in wheelchairs and walkers, crowded into the city's Elder Affairs Office on Thursday to protest a plan that would reduce subsidies to neighborhood adult day care centers by 30 percent, limiting the number of clients who can be served at the facilities.

This lede has the basic elements, plus some details and color to show you were there. But does it communicate what this means to those affected by the proposal? Using someone's personal experience might better explain the impact of the issue:

As the only child of an aging father with dementia, Karen Jones relies on the Sunnyside Adult Day Care Center to provide therapy and other services to her father while she works as a clerk in an insurance office.

"At home he was at risk for a fall, but now he has professionals to help with the dementia," she told a group of demonstrators outside the city's Elder Affairs office on Thursday. "I don't know what I'd do if this program is closed."

Jones was one of 75 people, some in wheelchairs and walkers, protesting a proposed 30 percent funding cut to neighborhood adult day care centers. If the reduction goes through, Jones' father could be among an estimated 10 seniors who would lose their spots at Sunnyside.

This anecdotal lede shows the personal toll the budget cuts would take. The *nut graf* — so called because it explains the crux of the story (in this case the details of the cuts) — comes in the third paragraph (or "graf"), moving the individual perspective of Ms. Jones' lament into the context of the larger issue.

Both these examples work, as could dozens of other kinds of ledes. You could start with short snippets from other people's experiences. You could visit the adult day care center and start the story with a description of the scene there and then explain those services may end soon for some people. You'll experiment with hundreds of ledes in your career, and make your choices based on what you know about your audience's interests and what's unique about each story.

Show Impact and Context

As you write, ask yourself: *Why would someone want to read this?* The answer should be: *Because it touches their lives in a certain way.* How will the new fire codes affect businesses in town? How many businesses, and at what cost? Who will be hurt by the crackdown on unlicensed pets? How much will the new school addition cost? Who will pay for it, and who will benefit?

Your readers want to know how the story impacts them. They also want to see the bigger picture. How have these issues played out elsewhere? Have other communities or states changed their fire codes in the same way? How many? What effect did the change have in those places? How does the cost of the school addition compare with that of similar projects in other districts? If your district is paying more or less than other places, taxpayers should know why.

Use Details and Specifics

Don't say: Some towns in the area have adopted the optional meals tax. Name the towns. Don't say: Police have stepped up patrols in several neighborhoods following an increase in reports of various crimes. Name the neighborhoods. Detail the types and frequency of the crimes. These specifics provide important information to help your audience understand the dimensions of the story. Say how many pieces of equipment are fighting a fire. Describe the mood of a demonstration; tell your audience exactly what people were chanting and what their signs said. You are the eyes and ears of your audience. Offering compelling details gives them the sense they are there with you.

Avoid such waffle words as *several, few, some* and *many*. Use specific numbers whenever possible. Substitute specific nouns for general pronouns such as *they, them* and *it*. Vague words make for vague stories.

USE VOICES

Quotes and sound bites from the people you interview add a reality to your stories. These voices show how real people are affected and let your audience hear people's responses and reactions in a conversational language that breaks up the recitation of facts and figures.

But don't get carried away with quotes. A story requires much more than stringing together other people's words. A good quote (or sound bite) is a simple sentence or two that provides a personal insight or evokes an emotion or a detail. An overly long quote or audio clip slows your story.

Think about ways of paraphrasing parts of longer quotes. For example, here's a quote from a story about a new anti-bullying law:

"We believe that the preventive law makes great strides forward," said Superintendent Margaret Bouvier, "but there is still an enormous amount of work in implementing those plans, keeping up with the training that's needed, making sure we are adequately addressing the issues and not under- or over-addressing anything."

The quote has lots of information — presented in the dialect of bureaucratese. When read out loud, it could leave you gasping for air. Most people speak in run-on sentences; the audience needs our help in sorting them out. You can't change a quote, but you can paraphrase the complex parts to make the message clearer:

Superintendent Margaret Bouvier supports the new anti-bullying regulations but says officials must keep up with training and other issues that will develop as the plan goes into effect.

"We believe that the preventive law makes great strides forward, but there is still an enormous amount of work in implementing those plans," she said.

Avoid one- or two-word "orphan quotes." These are annoying for editors and readers. Using quotes around common words is like putting a hat on a dog: it doesn't look right, and it isn't necessary.

Example: Riley said he was "very angry" about the new regulations.

You have no reason to use the quote marks. Nothing about Riley's expression of mood requires that we quote it exactly. If Mr. Riley had something more unique to say *(Riley said he was "wicked steamed" about the new regulations)*, then quote marks are necessary to indicate his own special language.

Beware of Jargon and Cliché

Good journalists are experts at translating the specialized language spoken in their beats. Emergency personnel, government officials and school administrators use terms you probably hadn't heard before you started reporting. As you spend time on the beat, you'll learn to communicate with your sources using their words and how to translate their jargon and overly formal language into everyday language your audience will understand.

If the officials at a hearing keep talking about *technology-enabled pricing for toll lanes*, don't pass that mouthful along to your audience. Keep asking for an explanation until you understand they are really talking about Easy Pass lanes that allow drivers with transponders to zip through tollbooths that charge them automatically.

Sometimes politicians and bureaucrats spout long strings of euphemisms to obscure a blunt truth they'd rather not say. So patients in mental hospitals become *mental health consumers;* torture is *enhanced interrogation methods* and a revealed lie is an *inoperative statement.* Reporters must always be on guard not to become co-conspirators in this corruption of language.

You should be vigilant about your own bad language habits, particularly the tendency to fall into cliché. News stories unfortunately echo with unimaginative phrases that reporters use over and over. In the world of bad journalism, a candidate *throws his hat in the ring* at a *hastily called news conference*, rescuers *sift through the rubble*, and people become *concerned citizens*. These phrases slip into our stories out of habit. Avoid this tendency by taking a tip from the writer George Orwell: *"Never use a metaphor, simile, or other figure of speech you are used to seeing in print."*

The best way to keep these embarrassments out of your stories, especially under the pressure of deadline, is to write conversationally. Think of how your friends and family, would respond if you told them the city council is looking at *revenue enhancements* (rather than taxes and fees) to balance the budget or that you plan to call the parking department to *express your displeasure* (complain) that your car was ticketed or that you will *take under advisement* (think about) a request that you wash the dishes. They would probably laugh at you for sounding ridiculous.

Tell a Story

Even the most routine piece should be more than a list of facts and figures or a recitation of events. Nearly every story can have a plot, characters and background that should hold your audience's interest from beginning to end. This can be a challenge when you're covering a council meeting or school board hearing with a range of agenda items. That's where some proactive reporting can make a difference. Get the agenda and find someone in the community who is affected by the major topic to be discussed at the meeting. You can use this person's example to frame the story, showing the impact and history of the issue through his or her opinions and experiences. If the story doesn't lend itself to this kind of narrative, don't simply transcribe the meeting in a chronological order. Decide what's important to your audience. You can have another imagined conversation with your friends. What would you tell them, in order of importance? Think of the details that would interest them and how you would show them that they should care.

These techniques don't work every time. Sometimes a short, factual story is all your audience needs and all the subject deserves. The trick is knowing when it's appropriate to aim for something more. Some stories make the front page or the top of the website because the subject is so compelling. Others get there because the reporter has written his or her way up to the top spot.

Find an Ending

Most reporters spend too much time on beginnings and not enough on endings. If readers have stuck with you through the story, you should reward them for staying with you to the end. You have as many options for endings as you do for ledes. You can use a quote that offers a personal perspective while summarizing some point raised in the story. You can offer information on the next step this story is likely to take. When is the next hearing on the issue? When are test results expected? When will the accused be arraigned? What you should not do is bring up a new idea at the end or let your story end without some conclusion.

Edit Your Work

Even if the hounds of deadline are baying in the background, you still need to take time to review your final version. Does the story answer all the questions you had when you set out to report it? Is the copy clean? Are you sure you've checked the spellings of the names; have you caught all typos and style errors in capitalization, punctuation and grammar? However good your story might be, its credibility — and yours — won't be helped if it is riddled with simple mistakes.

Here are a few things to check to make sure you haven't sabotaged all your hard work.

Check Organization and Continuity

Try to look at your final version with the fresh eyes of a reader, viewer and editor. Does the story raise any unanswered questions? Do the explanations work? Does it flow — are there any rough patches that would slow down readers or turn them away? Do you help readers move from one idea to the next? Do you offer enough examples? Most important: Will someone new to the subject be able to understand the core issues?

Is your story balanced? Do you present all sides' positions and rebuttals? You don't have to count paragraphs or screen time to assure everyone gets equal exposure — some positions take longer to explain than others. But make sure you haven't left out any important debate points. Are all claims, data and other information attributed to the right sources?

Copy Reading

Don't expect others to find your errors. Your name is on the story; it's up to you to make sure your copy is flawless. Don't rely on your computer's spelling and grammar checks to catch all your errors. Many glitches can slip through. Both *affect* and *effect* are legitimate words; spell-checker won't help you if the wrong word is in your copy. The same is true for typos. Spell-checker won't catch *Untied States*.

Writers use different techniques to edit their own copy:

▶ *Slowly read the text out loud.* Using speech to supplement sight can turn up typos and grammar errors, such as tense and number agreement, that your eyes alone may miss.

▶ *Reread the story from the bottom up.* If you've been writing and rewriting a longer piece, the text may seem so familiar that it begins to blur together in your mind. Walk away from the story for a bit; then go to the last sentence and read up to the top. This takes the story out of familiar context. It allows you a fresh look at each sentence.

▶ *Go back and start over each time you find a mistake.* Each mistake you find in the copy suggests more errors may be lurking above or below. Both this technique and the bottom-up drill require time and patience. But if you have the time, give it a try.

judgment call

First, Fast (and/or) Accurate

The 2011 shooting deaths of two St. Petersburg, Fla., police officers illustrate a question every journalist struggles with: How do you balance the rush to be first against the risk of being wrong or doing harm — especially when you're competing with traditional and new media.

The public learned many of the first details in the St. Pete shootings from a local resident's tweets and a radio shock jock who broadcast calls from people at the scene. Police officers were among the callers to the station, which electronically disguised their voices. They identified the shooter, his wife and brother and were the first to say two officers had been killed.

A local cable channel identified the dead after learning their names from the local police benevolent society, even as police officials asked for more time to notify the families. The cable channel stopped using the names, but the newspaper continued to run them on its website.

With so much information coming from so many media, the pressure to be first with a story is greater than ever. Beating the competition earns you and your organization praise, prestige and bragging rights — if you are *right*.

Being first but *wrong* can carry long-term consequences. Reporters and their organizations face criticism and even legal action if they name the wrong suspect in a criminal case. They can earn the scorn of their community if they identify an accident or crime victim before the family is notified. The notoriety of reporting something wrong or the guilt of causing unnecessary anguish will stick to you much longer than the celebrity of being first.

Corrections don't absolve you of guilt. Even if you change your initial report misidentifying someone in a criminal case, that mistake can linger in the minds of your audience and on the Web forever. The person you wrongly identified could carry that burden for the rest of his or her life.

It is better to err on the side of caution. Take a big deep breath before you rush out a report. Don't be stampeded by what others are saying. Trust your own instincts and judgment. Are you sure of your source? Can you get confirmation from the public information officer or a high-ranking official? If she won't go on the record, make a case for her off-the-record guidance. Tell her what you want to report; explain that you face great pressure to use the information but you don't want to embarrass yourself or others. If the source knows you, she may give you a nod or a shake of the head as a way of confirming or denying your information without putting herself at risk.

Your editors should be involved in the decision. But remember, it's your name on the story. Remember the old saying: When in doubt, leave it out. You will damage your credibility much more by being wrong than by coming in second in the race to be first.

This chapter concludes the skills section of the *Field Guide* with the hope you have picked up tips and techniques to help you with any subject you cover as a reporter. Now it's time to apply those skills to the specific beats discussed in Part II.

BEATS

PART II

CHAPTER 5

COPS AND CRIME

C rime shouts out from the front page in the morning and leads the local broadcast at night. It sits atop the center column of websites throughout the day. Movies, television shows and some selective statistics reinforce the notion of crime's omnipresence. The U.S. Department of Justice's aggregations of the numbers are often quoted: 25 million Americans fall victim to some type of crime each year; a quarter of those crimes are violent.

People are understandably concerned about safety in their community and want all the information they can get. That is the job of the reporter. It is not an easy task.

Covering the world of law enforcement requires careful study. The police have their own language — a dizzying vocabulary of procedures, legal jargon and slang.

Police have their suspicions about outsiders, particularly the media. Detectives investigating a case and street cops trying to control a situation see reporters as a distraction and, possibly, a threat to their work. Many departments carry a culture of grievance about journalists who have interfered with a case, reported misinformation or written stories that have cost careers. Breaking through the "blue wall" of police silence requires patience, skill and perspective.

Reporters must develop connections with officers while keeping an emotional distance from their subjects. Police officers are interesting people doing difficult work. It can be easy to lose your objectivity when officers exceed or abuse the powers they are given to enforce the law. The public image of cops as heroes is counterbalanced by reports of

from the beat

POLICE

Ruben Rosario
St. Paul Pioneer Press

As a newbie covering Brooklyn crime for the New York Daily News, Ruben Rosario learned by trial and error what it took to cover the nation's largest police department. Years later, as an editor and columnist with the St. Paul Pioneer Press, Rosario still remembers the education process of seeing his first crime scene or interviewing a hostile police officer.

"It's often the entry level reporters who are sent in to cover the cops," he says. "On the surface, it doesn't seem that hard. The police department gives you some press releases, or you look at the police log and write down what happened. But you learn that you have to take it a little deeper."

Taking it deeper can be hard. Police are reluctant to talk to reporters, especially less experienced ones who don't know the beat. And any reporter, even a knowledgeable one, can be viewed as a distraction.

"The last thing a cop wants to see is a reporter showing up while he's trying to do his job," Rosario says. "Your challenge is to get them to talk with you when they don't want to."

Rosario offers these suggestions:

▶ **Learn everything you can.**

Immerse yourself in law enforcement and policing, no small task considering the thousands of laws and regulations police enforce each day.

"You need to familiarize yourself with police procedure," he says. "If you don't know what you're covering, you're going to shortchange the public."

▶ **Be thick skinned.**

Your sources may love you or hate you depending on the stories you write. Remember you are writing for your audience, not your sources.

"There are going to be times when you're patted on the back and other times when they curse you," he says. "The most important thing is that they respect you."

▶ **Get close, but not too close.**

You can get more information if you spend time with police away from the station.

"You hang out with them, bend elbows, play billiards and racquetball," he says. "A good reporter will get them to understand that we're in the information business, same as them. We're like homicide detectives — we're only as good as the information we get."

abuse and corruption. Americans are suspicious of authority; most of us glance in our rearview mirror when we drive by a squad car. In the middle of this ambivalence stands the reporter.

Police reporters need perspective about the crime they report on every day. They face the temptation to sensationalize on the public's fears, yet for all the attention crime receives, it is important to remember that crime rates in the United States have been falling for the past two decades. Homicide rates peaked at 9.8 per 100,000 in 1991. By 2009 the rate was down to 5.4 per 100,000. The decreasing numbers are seen in nearly every other type of violent crime.

Covering the police is a busy beat, with a long list of story possibilities, ranging from traffic accidents to multiple shootings. You will write about community relations efforts and bank robberies, muggings and criminal mischief, missing children and murders. It is a beat without regular hours; crime is an unscheduled event. Breaking stories must be reported with quick accuracy and written with skill and care — you should always take care not to portray someone who has been arrested as guilty

Some stories will go beyond the first-day report; a single incident can turn into a compelling narrative that takes days or months to report. The Seattle Times wrote a series that took a deeper look at the slaying of four police officers in a suburban coffee shop, writing about their lives and the long criminal record of their assailant. It won the paper the 2010 Pulitzer Prize for breaking news reporting.

Such stories are the payoff for all the hurdles and hard work of the police beat. You will get the opportunity to produce narratives of drama, suspense, tragedy and triumphs populated with riveting characters. These are the stories that will attract attention and comment.

COPS BEAT ▶ PEOPLE

A police beat reporter relies heavily on sources; they can be hard to come by.

The big stories — the murder and mayhem cases, the allegations of fraud and brutality — do not unfold before the public eye. Police officials are necessarily guarded about criminal investigations. They have a case to solve; too much publicity can endanger an arrest or conviction. Officers are also hesitant to speak with journalists because of station house mythologies about a reporter who ruined a good officer's career by writing a story that accused him of some misdeed.

But developing sources within a police department isn't a hopeless task. The job can be done through honesty, consistency and patience. A good reporter will try to break down that wall with personal connections. The first step is to know the players in your department and to develop relationships with them.

Department Spokespersons

The size and skills of police department information offices vary among jurisdictions. Larger law enforcement agencies may have a number of public information officers (PIOs) answering phone calls. Smaller agencies may have no official spokesperson. The duty may rotate among the officers or even the rank and file. More likely, everyone will defer to the chief.

A PIO's job is to provide details about cases and to shine the image of the department for the public. Most will understand you are a professional doing your job. But don't mistake them for your close friend. The PIOs' loyalties are to their departments; they may see their job as controlling the flow of news. They may not want to reveal information about a case. It's your job to convince them they should.

Police Commissioners

Larger cities often have a police commissioner or superintendent. Some also have police commissions made up of elected or appointed officials who have a hand in determining department policy and budget issues. Knowing the commissioner or commissioners provides insight into the inner workings of the department. These high-level officials probably won't know all details of high-profile criminal investigations.

Chiefs

The police chief is the department's commanding officer. He or she is responsible for the day-to-day operations of the department. Access to the chief depends on the size of the department. You may be able to develop a relationship with the chief in a smaller city; it will probably be harder to maintain regular contact with a big-city chief. You should still try. A good relationship with the department's leader sets an important tone. If the chief will talk to you, other officers will feel more comfortable to do the same.

from the source

Stephanie Slater
Boynton Beach Public Information Officer

When Stephanie Slater, the public information officer for the Boynton Beach, Fla., police, encounters reporters who don't know anything about police work, she keeps calm by recalling her days as a fledgling police reporter.

"They gave me the police beat with no prior experience," she recalls. "I had to learn along the way."

Slater covered the cops for seven years. When the police did a poor job of getting information to the media following a gang shooting at a shopping mall, she told the command staff that the department's media relations system was hurting its public image. She even suggested that the police department consider hiring a full-time public information officer instead of making media relations a police sergeant's secondary responsibility. The chief was so impressed that he offered her a job. "After writing about law enforcement for so many years, I realized I had a passion for it," she says.

Many reporters are as inexperienced as she was; they often have additional duties in shrinking newsrooms; they don't have the time to learn the beat or check in regularly. Slater says her first contact with some reporters comes when they call desperate for details of a breaking story.

"It becomes adversarial when a reporter I haven't heard from for months wants information right away," she says.

Slater has this advice:

▶ **Get to know your department.**

Spend as much time at the department as you can.

"Go for a ride-along, listen to the radio and learn the 10 codes. Familiarize yourself with all things relating to police work."

▶ **Call me often.**

A few minutes on the phone on a regular basis can make a big difference.

"I'd rather they call me every day even if I can only say I don't have anything. It shouldn't be only for breaking news."

▶ **There *is* such a thing as a stupid question.**

Police flaks can find it frustrating when a reporter calls with a question about a case that was answered on the press release the reporter is citing.

"There's nothing more obnoxious than when a reporter calls and asks you questions that are answered. It gives you a bad impression."

COMMAND STRUCTURE

POLICE DEPARTMENTS ARE QUASI-MILITARY organizations with a command structure based on rank. The police chief is at the top; in many departments, officers with the rank of captains command various divisions, from detective bureaus to traffic offices and individual precinct houses. Lieutenants often serve as watch commanders, supervising the patrols out on the streets. As in the military, sergeants are the glue of the command structure; they oversee street operations from the field and run front desks at station houses. This hierarchy repeats itself in the various special units where detectives hold ranks from captain to detective.

State police are often organized along a broader military hierarchy. Ranks can range from colonel and major down to corporal and private.

The information you get from sources in the command structure usually matches the degree of rank. Higher-level officers will know more and perhaps be more forthcoming; lower ranks have less of an overview of the department but may have a greater understanding of their beat than their superior officers.

Patrol Officers

The rank-and-file police officers are likely to be wary of a new reporter. They have a natural caution about journalists that is often heightened by warnings from their superiors about speaking with the media. This makes sense from the command point of view; superior officers don't want a cacophony of police voices showing up in newspaper and website stories.

But it is important to cultivate contacts among the patrolmen and -women. They have detailed knowledge of what is happening out on the street and in the station houses. They have insight on the effects command decisions are having on their jobs. They are usually familiar with union activities, including grievances and contract negotiations. Knowing street officers can be handy at a crime scene. They may provide you with a quick set of details about the case much sooner than higher-ranking officers.

Many police departments have community relations officers who cover very specific geographic beats. Their job is to talk with the people in their neighborhoods and attend

LAW ENFORCEMENT AGENCIES

I T IS IMPORTANT TO UNDERSTAND how different law enforcement agencies cooperate — and sometimes conflict. The lines of authority can become blurred. State authorities get involved in small-town murder investigations. Federal investigators may take over larger cases. Local investigators can feel shunted to the side. Such situations offer opportunities to reporters. When federal investigators won't talk, contacts you've made in local departments provide information, especially if they feel their glory is being stolen.

Here is a look at the different agencies you're likely to cover.

MUNICIPAL DEPARTMENTS

The federal Bureau of Justice Statistics' 2007 census found 12,575 local police departments with at least one full-time officer. These departments had 580,749 full-time employees, including an estimated 463,000 sworn officers — nearly two-thirds of all the law enforcement officers in the nation.

In smaller departments individual officers do a little bit of everything, responding to citizen calls about rowdy behavior on the streets and domestic disputes in homes. They investigate minor crimes, including burglaries and vandalism. They direct traffic, ticketing motorists who violate ordinances and regulations. Larger departments assign officers to community policing, building better relationships with neighborhood residents.

Municipal departments are organized into geographic divisions with uniformed officers assigned to districts or precincts. The department's size also determines whether uniformed officers patrol by themselves or with a partner. Many departments that used a partner system have cut back to single officer patrols to save money. Whether they patrol alone or in pairs, these officers keep an eye out for traffic violations and suspicious activities. They also respond to dispatcher calls. All their actions are noted on daily logs.

Larger departments may have separate offices for homicide, burglary, robbery and sexual crimes. Vice detectives investigate gambling, prostitution and drug trafficking.

Municipalities may have other separate police agencies to patrol public transportation systems, public housing and parks.

COUNTY SHERIFF DEPARTMENTS

Sheriff departments employ the second-largest group of law enforcement officers; one in four of the nation's law officers work for sheriffs. A 2008 census by the National Sheriffs'

Association counted 3,085 sheriff's offices and departments across the country. They included small rural operations and major departments; the Los Angeles County Sheriff's Department is the nation's seventh-largest law enforcement agency.

Sheriffs are chosen by voters and wield significant political influence in smaller, rural counties. In more populous states, they often have a secondary role of staffing courts and running county jails.

County law enforcement officers are called sheriff's deputies, deputy sheriffs, sheriff's police, or sheriff's officers. These officers often have the same duties as a municipal department's officers, from patrolling county roads to investigating homicides and other major crimes.

STATE LAW ENFORCEMENT

State police officers, sometimes called state troopers or highway patrol officers, enforce motor vehicle laws and regulations on state highways. These departments are maintained by every state except Hawaii.

State law enforcement supplement local municipal departments, providing state crime labs and police academies. State police working for a state attorney or the attorney general conduct major statewide investigations. Other state officers work with special units, such as water patrol, canine search and rescue departments, special weapons and tactics (SWAT) and emergency response teams. Some states maintain a "resident trooper" in smaller towns without local police departments. These troopers may be the only law officers in the area.

State police detectives help smaller municipal departments investigate major crimes and work with interagency task forces to combat organized crime, drug rings and fraud.

States have fish and game wardens and park rangers to enforce fishing, hunting and boating laws. These officers patrol recreational areas, conduct search and rescue operations and investigate cases of illegal hunting and crimes against the public in forests and recreational areas.

CAMPUS POLICE

Many cities have colleges and universities with their own sworn police departments, which means their officers have the authority to investigate crimes, make arrests and even use deadly force. Other colleges may have only security departments whose personnel patrol campus without full police authority.

community meetings. You are likely to see these officers on a regular basis. They can be a great source of information you may not get from the official spokespeople.

Developing relationships is all about trust. You'll need to show the beat cops that when they speak to you confidentially, you will use the information in a fair and honest way. Don't take everything they say as the gospel. Like everyone, cops like to gossip. But if you speak to a number of officers, you can start piecing together a picture of an individual investigation or a developing issue within the department.

Police Unions, Associations, Criminal Justice Experts

Police chiefs and patrol officers have national and state associations. Both groups can provide comment on and context to local policing issues. Union organizations for patrol officers and various levels of officers also are good sources.

Academic experts at criminal justice colleges are another good resource. If you're looking for an outsider's perspective, think about reaching out to faculty at a local school or one of the nationally recognized criminal justice departments. These include John Jay College in New York, Northeastern University in Boston, Florida State University and the University of Pennsylvania. The American Society of Criminology, www.asc41.com, is an organization of academics, professionals and interested parties that offers analysis of crime issues.

Other Resources

Other crime reporters are a terrific source. A number of organizations track crime and policing trends and offer reviews of what other reporters have been doing. One such group is the Criminal Justice Journalists, http://crimjj.wordpress.com, which is composed of reporters who cover crime, courts and prison beats. This website contains a primer on covering crime and justice issues. The group also maintains a database of crime stories and other information resources at its News Center, http://cjj.mn-8.net/.

The Institute for Justice and Journalism, www.justicejournalism.org, offers analysis of tricky subjects including reporter bias, the use of racial identifications in crime stories and the impact of crime scene stories on television news.

COPS BEAT ▶ Places

You will be at a big disadvantage if the only times the police see you are for sensational crimes or departmental scandals. You must make the effort to get out of the newsroom and into the station houses, ride in the squad cars and walk the streets the cops patrol. You'll need to find the time — even if it's just once a week — to get out among the patrol officers and commanders who will be important sources when that big story breaks.

Navigating the Department

- [ ] Learn the geography of your department.
- [ ] Familiarize yourself with the command structure. Meet with the chief, commissioner and public information staff.

- [ ] Visit headquarters and the stations. Go for ride-alongs out of each station.
- [ ] Visit the bars and restaurants frequented by police.

You may cover a police department that has one station and a couple of patrol cars. Or you could be in a larger city with a number of precinct houses and a complex network of patrol areas. Many departments offer maps that show coverage areas in grids. These maps are invaluable to new reporters looking to understand the landscape of their beat.

Locate the police stations. Make a list of the command structure and different units that work out of those houses. Who are the captains, the watch lieutenants, the desk sergeants and the patrol officers assigned to those different areas?

Making the Rounds

Although visiting headquarters and the district stations should be a daily routine, chances are you won't have that luxury of time. The telephone and Internet are your next best options. Make regular calls to the PIO; the department may put the daily logs on its website. But you should still try to make on-site visits. You don't have to stay that long. Pop in when you can so people remember what you look like.

Headquarters Stop by the public information office to ask about some of the trends you've been seeing in the daily logs. Ask if the department is doing any public service campaigns, such as driver's safety or fraud against elders, which could produce good stories. Visit with the police commissioner and the police chief if only for a few minutes. Come armed with questions you think may play into some of the stories you're working on. Gather threads of conversations you may be able to use in the future.

Precinct Houses/District Stations You can usually check the daily logs here. Look for the cops you've made contact with in the past. Get to know the desk sergeants. Visit with other units in the house, such as traffic enforcement or the detective bureau. Don't take up too much of the officers' time, but let them know you will be a regular — a known commodity.

FEDERAL AGENCIES

THE U.S. DEPARTMENT OF JUSTICE DEPARTMENT is the chief law enforcement agency in the nation. The Federal Bureau of Investigation (FBI) is the lead agency in Justice. Its agents enforce more than 200 federal laws related to national security, such as espionage and terrorism, organized crime, criminal gangs and drug rings. FBI agents also investigate bank robberies, kidnappings, cybercrime and public corruption. Federal agents have extraordinary powers to conduct their investigations, including court-authorized wiretaps.

The FBI has 56 field offices in major cities and 400 smaller offices — called resident agencies — in other municipalities. The agent-in-charge is usually a well-known figure who often calls news conferences to announce results of major investigations. Even if you are a small-town reporter, it is important to get to know the head FBI agent and the office's PIO.

Other federal agencies operate in your state or even in your city. U.S. Drug Enforcement Administration (DEA) agents investigate the production, importation and sale of illegal drugs. Bureau of Alcohol, Tobacco, Firearms, and Explosives (ATF) agents enforce federal firearms and explosives laws. They help investigate bombing cases and the use of illegal weapons. As the name implies, they also investigate violations of federal alcohol and tobacco tax regulations.

The Department of Homeland Security has law officers in several different agencies under its jurisdiction. These agencies include:

- ▶ **Border Patrol** guards the nation's borders against illegal entry and smuggling of illegal goods. The Border Patrol works in coordination with Customs and the U.S. Department of Agriculture to guard against the importation of potentially contaminated agriculture products.
- ▶ **Immigration and Customs Enforcement (ICE)** enforces immigrations laws and monitors imports and exports.
- ▶ **The U.S. Secret Service,** better known for protecting the president, also investigates counterfeiting, currency violations and credit card fraud.
- ▶ **Federal air marshals** provide security against attacks on U.S. aircraft, passengers, and crews.
- ▶ **U.S. marshal offices** provide security for the federal courts, transport criminals and hunt escaped fugitives. Marshals also protect witnesses in federal cases.

Other federal agencies have police and special agents. Included in this list are the U.S. Postal Service, the Bureau of Indian Affairs Office of Law Enforcement, the Forest Service, and the National Park Service.

Most departments allow, and even encourage, reporter ride-alongs. Take advantage of the opportunity. Spending the night in a patrol car with an officer is invaluable. You can learn about the neighborhood, the department and the individual officers. Ask questions. Listen more than talk. Hang out with the officers back at the station at the end of their shift. Try to do ride-alongs out of each station house. You probably won't be able to get many stories from the night's experience, but the time spent will pay off in the insights you will get and the camaraderie you will develop with the patrol officers.

Hangouts Find the bars and restaurants where the police hang out after their shifts. Spend some time there developing relationships. Be prepared to begin a conversation with some general question that could lead to more chitchat. Don't persist in questions about the department. Find a common-ground subject, such as sports, children or dogs. The idea is to get the police officers to feel more comfortable around you. It may not feel that comfortable at first, but if you can become accepted as a regular, you may find yourself invited over to the pool table or challenged to a game of darts. Again, you shouldn't expect to generate a lot of stories from these visits. Simply be yourself and ask lots of questions. A good listener is almost always appreciated.

COPS BEAT ▶ Documents

You will find easy access to volumes of data on the activities of your city's police. Nearly all departments produce daily crime logs that detail the calls police answered and the actions they took. Departments aggregate these daily logs into monthly and annual reports that show the number and types of calls they answer, the crimes they solve (and don't solve) and even the race of the drivers that they stop.

These data can reveal crime patterns in various neighborhoods and how they may be changing over the years. What are the fluctuations in the murder rate? Have burglary, robbery and incidents of domestic violence climbed along with unemployment rates? Is a spike in the number of serious assaults in a specific neighborhood an indication of a growing drug or gang problem? Many departments now produce street maps that show the frequency and types of crimes superimposed over a street grid. This is valuable information to share with your audience on a permanent location in your website.

The data also can show the effectiveness of your police department. What is the closure rate on murder cases? On violent robberies? What percentage of cases was referred to the district attorney's office for prosecution? Police logs should show response time. When did a call come in, and when did police arrive at the scene? Does the response time differ depending on the neighborhood? Do the more affluent sections of your city see police arrive quicker than an inner-city section?

Similar data from thousands of departments around the country are collected and analyzed by federal agencies. The results can be used to compare your department with regional and national averages.

Less dramatic data can make for significant stories. What was the average pay among officers last year? How did it compare with the previous year's? You might find that the top salary went to a lower-ranking cop who worked special details and lots of overtime. How many officers are out on disability? What is their compensation costing taxpayers?

Sometimes the records themselves are a story. A sudden decrease or increase in the number of burglaries or robberies shouldn't just be reported; it needs analysis. When St. Louis police announced a big reduction in property crime, the St. Louis Post-Dispatch found the drop wasn't due to better policing but rather to a change in the way crimes were counted. In the past, when someone went down the street, breaking into cars, each break-in was counted as an individual crime. But under new FBI crime reporting rules, the break-ins were counted as one crime. The police weren't purposely fudging the numbers, but they didn't explain that the counting process had changed until questioned by reporters.

Not all records are public. Certain reports are preliminary assessments of a criminal case. These reports may name people as possible suspects who will later be cleared. Revealing their names could forever taint their reputations.

Public record disclosure laws vary among the states, but all walk a line between the public's right to information and a person's right to privacy. This tension is summarized by the Los Angeles Police Department's public records law site: *"The law requires law enforcement agencies to provide information the public has the right to know and at the same time, to withhold information if the release would jeopardize an individual's right to privacy."*

Where to Find the Documents

Data and documents reside at all levels of law enforcement — from the police logs at the local station house to aggregated national data out of the Justice Department in Washington, D.C.

You should check the information at all levels. The precinct logs offer a daily snapshot of what's happening in your area. The national figures offer insight into how the duties of your community's police compare with those of similar municipalities' police. First, let's start at the local level.

Logs A time-honored routine in covering the cops is the stop at headquarters, or individual precinct houses, to see the daily log. The log details what calls police officers handled over the past 24 hours. These entries catalog incidents from serious crime to complaints of public urination. If officers make an arrest, the logs provide information about the suspects and the charges filed against them; details can include name, age, occupation and address.

Few log items merit stories. Some newspapers and websites run the logs as daily features. The bizarre or unusual (a real example: a woman summoning officers to a McDonald's to complain they were out of Chicken McNuggets) might produce a lighthearted brief. More serious crimes or police action will warrant detailed stories.

But perhaps one of the best things about the police log is the chance it gives reporters to develop wider-ranging stories. A scattering of calls about teenagers getting high on aerosol whipping cream cans may lead you to a story about the rise in the number of young people finding dangerous new ways of intoxication. The logs provide for conversations that may veer into more interesting subject matter. You might notice the occasional report of someone flashing young women and, in speaking with the officers, learn that this person is doing the same thing in a neighboring precinct or the next town over.

The Internet offers an alternative to physically making the rounds. Many departments now post the logs on their websites. That's a good thing for the public. People can go online to see what criminal behavior has been reported in their neighborhood and what local police have been doing about it. Web-based police logs are a time saver for busy reporters. But something may be lost in the convenience of the Web. If you rely too heavily on your fingers instead of your feet, you'll be denying yourself those important face-to-face interactions that can lead to better relationships and tips.

The best advice is to use these web-based logs when time is short, but try to make the time at least once a week to visit the cop shop for some real-time conversation.

▶ ▶ ▶ BEAT BACKGROUNDER ◀ ◀ ◀

READING A POLICE LOG

HERE ARE THREE EXCERPTS from a daily log posted on the Internet by the Derry, N.H., Police Department that provide a range of the kinds of calls police face during a shift. (Source: www.derry.nh.us/Pages/DerryNH_PoliceLogs/I0162B197.1/10-18-10.pdf.)

As you can see, the report begins with a call number, followed by the time of call. The reason for the call is listed as "Assist Other Agency." In this case it was to help the Derry Fire Department. The section marked "Narrative" gives the details: Firefighters were called about smoke in a building.

The name of the police dispatcher is listed, followed by the names of the three officers who responded to the call. The listing shows the times they were dispatched, the times they arrived and the times they cleared the scene.

Derry Police Department

Dispatch Log From: 10/18/2010 Thru: 10/18/2010   0000 - 2359   P

For Date: 10/18/2010 - Monday

Call Number	Time	Call Reason	Action	Priority	Duplicate

0-21474   0046   Phone - ASSIST OTHER AGENCY   Services Rendered   3
Call Taker: Dispatcher Jonathon S Pickering
Location/Address: BYPASS 28
          ID: Patrol Brian K French
                  Disp-00:46:47   Arvd-00:48:07 Clrd-01:01:27
          ID: Patrol James M Ciulla
                  Disp-00:46:47   Arvd-00:48:35 Clrd-01:01:26
          ID: Sergeant Frank Stoncius
                  Disp-00:46:48   Arvd-00:48:06 Clrd-01:01:26
    Narrative: 10/18/2010 0048 Dispatcher Jonathon S Pickering
                  10/18/2010 0048 called in as smoke in building, assisting
                  DFD

    Narrative: 10/18/2010 0101 Dispatcher Jonathon S Pickering
                  10/18/2010 0101 problems with furnace, clear

0-21475   0138   Phone - NOISE COMPLAINT   Quieted on Request   2
Call Taker: Dispatcher Jonathon S Pickering
Location/Address: LINLEW DR
          ID: Patrol Stephen E Clark
                  Disp-01:39:09   Arvd-01:46:21 Clrd-01:53:40
          ID: Patrol Brian K French
                  Disp-01:39:10   Arvd-01:47:08 Clrd-01:53:39
    Narrative: 10/18/2010 0153 Dispatcher Jonathon S Pickering
                  10/18/2010 0153 loud music, turned down on request

0-21476   0157   Initiated - MV CHECK   Vehicle checked   1
Call Taker: Dispatcher Jonathon S Pickering
Location: TRINITY CHURCH
          ID: Patrol Brian K French
                                            Arvd-01:57:00 Clrd-01:58:01
    Vehicle: Reg: NH 2602358

0-21477   0216   Initiated - MV STOP   Summons Issued   3
Call Taker: Dispatcher Jonathon S Pickering
Location/Address: MAPLE ST + E BROADWAY
          ID: Patrol Stephen E Clark
                                            Arvd-02:16:00 Clrd-02:37:26
          ID: Sergeant Frank Stoncius
                  Disp-02:26:35   Arvd-02:26:36 Clrd-02:37:26
    Vehicle: Reg: TM NH 936941

0-21478   0611   Initiated - MV STOP   Warning Issued   3
Call Taker: Dispatcher Jonathon S Pickering
Location/Address: W BROADWAY + CLARK ST
          ID: Patrol Stephen E Clark
                                            Arvd-06:11:00 Clrd-06:18:48
    Vehicle: Reg: TL NH T310812
    Narrative: 10/18/2010 0616 Dispatcher Jonathon S Pickering
                  10/18/2010 0616 NH 2942335

0-21479   0634   Initiated - MV STOP   Warning Issued   3
Call Taker: Dispatcher Jonathon S Pickering
Location/Address: W BROADWAY + CENTRAL ST
          ID: Patrol Stephen E Clark
                                            Arvd-06:34:00 Clrd-06:39:37
    Vehicle: Reg: MA 38AE84

0-21480   0723   Phone - SUSPICIOUS ACTIVITY   No Action Required   2
Call Taker: Dispatcher Jill A Priestley
Location/Address: BOYD RD
          ID: Patrol David Michaud
                  Disp-07:24:35   Arvd-07:28:18 Clrd-07:49:26
                  Patrol Jonathan M Imperial

The next call was for a noise complaint. Officers were dispatched at 1:46 a.m. and 1:47 a.m. The loud music was "turned down on request," and the officers left six minutes later.

The final log entry details the arrest, transportation and jailing of a man charged with criminal threatening. Four officers were dispatched. The suspect, whose name, date of birth and address are listed, was taken into custody. He was transported to police headquarters, placed in a cell and brought before a magistrate, who set bail. The suspect was then transported to jail. Note that the official arrest document number is listed; a curious reporter could access the public record to learn more about the case.

Derry Police Department

Dispatch Log From: 10/18/2010 Thru: 10/18/2010 0000 - 2359 Printed: 10/25/2010

Call Number	Time	Call	Reason	Action
10-21474	0046	Phone -	ASSIST OTHER AGENCY	Services Rendered

Call Taker: Dispatcher Jonathon S Pickering
Location/Address: BYPASS 28
   ID: Patrol Brian K French   Disp-00:46:47 Arvd-00:48:07 Clrd-01:01:27
   ID: Patrol James M Ciulla   Disp-00:46:47 Arvd-00:48:35 Clrd-01:01:26
   ID: Sergeant Frank Stoncius Disp-00:46:48 Arvd-00:48:06 Clrd-01:01:26

Narrative: **10/18/2010 0048 Dispatcher Jonathon S Pickering**

called in as smoke in building, assisting DFD problems with furnace, clear

10-21475	0138	Phone	NOISE COMPLAINT	Quieted on Request

Call Taker: Dispatcher Jonathon S Pickering
Location/Address: LINLEW DR
   ID: Patrol Stephen E Clark Disp-01:39:09 Arvd-01:46:21 Clrd-01:53:40
   ID: Patrol Brian K French   Disp-01:39:10 Arvd-01:47:08 Clrd-01:53:39

Narrative: **10/18/2010 0153 Dispatcher Jonathon S Pickering**

loud music, turned down on request

10-21490	1223	Phone -	ARREST Made	

Call Taker: Dispatcher Jill A Priestley
Location/Address: PINKERTON ST
   ID: Patrol Jeffrey M Dawe   Disp-12:23:57 Arvd-12:27:01 Clrd-12:51:11
   ID: Sergeant John T Cooney Disp-12:24:01 Arvd-12:27:03 Clrd-12:34:56
   ID: Patrol Andrew J Faucher Disp-12:24:10 Arvd-12:27:05 Clrd-12:35:02
   ID: Patrol Brian J Landry   Disp-12:49:09 Arvd-12:49:11 Clrd-13:00:18

Narrative: **10/18/2010 1234 Dispatcher Jill A Priestley**
ONE IN CUSTODY 10/18/2010 1234

Narrative: **10/18/2010 1235 Dispatcher Jill A Priestley**
ENROUTE WITH ONE 10/18/2010 1235
Narrative: **10/18/2010 1238 Dispatcher Jill A Priestley**
OFF AT PDHQ 10/18/2010 1238
Narrative: **10/18/2010 1242 Dispatcher Jill A Priestley**
IN WITH KYLE GERRISH DOB 080992 OF 8 SHELDON RD DERRY NH FOR
CRIMINAL THREAT 10/18/2010 1242
Narrative: **10/18/2010 1300 Dispatcher Jill A Priestley**
PLACED IN CELL#3 10/18/2010 1300
Narrative: **10/18/2010 1326 Dispatcher Jill A Priestley**
BAIL SET AT $1,000.00 CASH PER LAPOINTE 10/18/2010 1326
Narrative: **10/18/2010 1546 Dispatcher Christine D Carlson**
10/18/2010 1545 Transporting subject to Brentwood at this time
Refer To Arrest: 10-1077-AR
Arrest: GERRISH, KYLE
Address: 8 SHELDON RD DERRY, NH
DOB: 08/09/1992
Charges: CRIMINAL THREATENING

Campus Crime Colleges and universities that receive federal funding must provide information on campus crime. Under a federal law known as the Clery Act (1998), named after a murdered student, campus police or college security departments must provide data on crime incidents on or near campus. (See this chapter's Resources section for how to find the data on a particular school.) The U.S. Department of Education oversees compliance with the act and can impose fines up to $27,500 against schools that don't keep or provide the data. Federal officials can even keep noncompliant schools from participating in federal student financial aid programs. If your assignment takes you to campus and the officers refuse to cooperate, be ready to invoke the Clery Act to get the information.

Crime Statistics Local police logs and other records provide a good source of information about how well your department is doing. You can put that into context by using the cornucopia of data available from the U.S. Department of Justice and the FBI.

The Justice Department's Bureau of Justice Statistics offers news releases, studies, reports and statistical tables on a range of subjects from police activities to crime rates

Region and jurisdiction	All causes	Homicide	Drug/alcohol intoxication	Suicide	Accident	Illness	Other/ unknown
All States	2686	1553	317	289	182	139	206
Northeast	369	206	49	33	20	40	21
Connecticut	13	12	0	0	0	0	1
Maine	9	4	1	2	1	0	1
Massachusetts	25	7	10	3	0	4	1
New Hampshire	7	5	1	1	0	0	0
New Jersey	44	24	7	3	3	3	4
New York	142	72	17	13	10	23	7
Pennsylvania	113	75	9	10	4	8	7
Rhode Island	11	4	4	0	1	2	0
Vermont	5	3	0	1	1	0	0
Midwest	472	326	38	41	31	17	19
Illinois	100	67	5	11	6	6	5
Indiana	33	33	0	0	0	0	0
Iowa	25	16	0	6	2	0	1
Kansas	27	17	3	2	2	1	2
Michigan	90	59	11	7	7	4	2
Minnesota	23	16	2	0	3	1	1
Missouri	16	10	2	4	0	0	0
Nebraska	11	8	0	0	1	2	0
North Dakota	7	2	2	3	0	0	0
Ohio	97	66	12	2	7	3	7
South Dakota	5	5	0	0	0	0	0
Wisconsin	38	27	1	6	3	0	1
South	907	455	121	112	74	48	97
Alabama	10	6	1	1	0	1	1
Arkansas[a]	4	0	2	0	0	1	1
Delaware	8	7	0	0	0	0	1
District of Columbia	12	7	1	2	0	1	1
Florida	277	157	24	6	28	6	56
Georgia	/	/	/	/	/	/	/
Kentucky	11	11	0	0	0	0	0
Louisiana[a]	23	14	2	1	2	3	1
Maryland	/	/	/	/	/	/	/
Mississippi[a]	3	1	0	2	0	0	0
Northa Carolina[b]	57	19	6	9	13	3	7
Oklahoma[b]	39	31	1	6	1	0	0
South Carolina[c]	10	3	2	0	2	0	3
Tennessee[a]	7	1	2	0	1	0	3
Texas	380	153	77	77	22	30	21
Virginia	59	42	2	8	3	3	1
West Virginia	7	3	1	0	2	0	1

Figure 5.1   Bureau of Justice Statistics study on jail deaths

Source: http://bjs.ojp.usdoj.gov/content/dcrp/tables/dcst06let8.cfm

Murder

by State, Types of Weapons, 2009

State	Total murders[1]	Total firearms	Handguns	Rifles	Shotguns	Firearms (type unknown)	Knives or cutting instruments	Other weapons	Hands, fists, feet, etc.[2]
Alabama	318	229	196	1	32	0	29	40	20
Alaska	22	13	1	0	0	12	4	3	2
Arizona	328	197	164	10	10	13	61	53	17
Arkansas	171	107	54	5	5	43	21	38	5
California	1,972	1,360	1,022	45	49	244	291	214	107
Colorado	167	94	55	6	6	27	23	30	20
Connecticut	107	70	51	0	2	17	17	14	6
Delaware	41	31	20	2	0	9	6	1	3
District of Columbia	144	113	80	1	1	31	17	9	5
Georgia	543	378	323	17	19	19	56	97	12
Hawaii	21	8	4	2	1	1	3	4	6
Idaho	22	5	3	0	0	2	3	9	5
Illinois[3]	479	386	360	5	8	13	39	48	6
Indiana	293	209	136	8	14	51	34	40	10
Iowa	34	11	3	1	3	4	8	6	9
Kansas	118	85	38	9	0	38	14	11	8
Kentucky	170	112	90	5	6	11	22	27	9
Louisiana	486	402	330	20	11	41	32	37	15
Maine	26	11	4	0	0	7	6	6	3
Maryland	438	305	297	2	6	0	58	57	18
Massachusetts	169	93	47	2	1	43	40	29	7
Michigan	625	437	239	25	19	154	47	112	29
Minnesota	72	38	35	1	1	1	14	8	12
Mississippi	151	105	83	9	6	7	22	15	9
Missouri	381	276	170	8	11	87	40	50	15
Montana	28	19	9	2	5	3	4	2	3
Nebraska	40	23	22	1	0	0	8	4	5
Nevada	156	91	66	1	3	21	25	27	13
New Hampshire	10	4	1	0	0	3	3	2	1
New Jersey	319	220	189	3	6	22	44	36	19
New Mexico	144	78	54	2	3	19	24	29	13
New York	779	481	117	8	13	343	166	109	23
North Carolina	480	335	243	17	20	55	49	64	32
North Dakota	9	3	1	1	1	0	0	3	3
Ohio	502	311	193	2	9	107	52	95	44
Oklahoma	225	125	104	10	4	7	45	25	30
Oregon	83	41	9	2	10	20	21	19	2
Pennsylvania	658	468	373	13	11	71	66	100	24
Rhode Island	31	18	0	0	0	18	6	5	2
South Carolina	286	197	115	4	12	66	28	41	20
South Dakota	11	4	0	1	2	1	5	1	1
Tennessee	461	295	200	13	22	60	45	92	29
Texas	1,325	862	661	55	58	88	197	153	113
Utah	37	25	15	0	5	5	8	2	2
Vermont	7	0	0	0	0	0	4	1	2
Virginia	347	229	108	8	7	106	41	55	22
Washington	169	101	75	16	4	6	35	14	19
West Virginia	76	38	20	2	3	13	19	13	6
Wisconsin	144	95	65	3	9	18	22	13	14
Wyoming	11	8	7	0	0	1	1	1	1

Figure 5.2   FBI uniform crime statistics chart on murder weapons

[1] Total number of murders for which supplemental homicide data were received.
[2] Pushed is included in hands, fists, feet, etc.
[3] Limited supplemental homicide data were received.

Source: http://bjs.ojp.usdoj.gov/content/dcrp/tables/dcst06let8.cfm

Mark Puente
Cleveland Plain Dealer

Mark Puente came to journalism later in life; he went back to school to be a reporter after driving a truck for 14 years. His decision benefited many: his family, his newspaper and the citizens of Cleveland. But one person probably regrets Puente's career move: the former sheriff of Cuyahoga County, Ohio.

Puente had been on the cop beat for 18 months when a regular contact came to him with a tip.

"My office was in police headquarters. People knew who I was, and I was approached by a source whose brother was a deputy," Puente says. "He was someone I dealt with three or four days a week."

The source was angry. He told Puente that the sheriff had just laid off 18 employees while promoting his niece, his son-in-law's best friend and a drinking buddy from the VFW Hall.

The tip came on a slow day, so he pursued the story. Within time he was able to get hiring and promotion records from the sheriff's department and details on campaign contributions — some through Freedom of Information Act (FOIA; 1966) requests and others through his sources in the county.

The records showed the sheriff promoted the three people, but the paperwork didn't indicate his relationship to them. Puente called the sheriff's department on a Friday. The PIO denied the charges and then said a news conference would address the issue on Monday.

Puente didn't wait for the story to go public. He knocked on the sheriff's door Saturday morning.

"The sheriff went through the roof," Puente recalls. "He was 74; he had been sheriff for 32 years. He told me no damn reporter was going to knock him out of office."

With the sheriff's reaction in his notebook, Puente had what he needed for the story. It ran Sunday on the front page. "It started a lot of good outrage," Puente says.

The sheriff was among the outraged. At the Monday morning news conference he whacked Puente in the head with his cane on his way to the podium.

Puente got in many more telling whacks. People called with tips. Records turned up to show department employees were expected to send their boss checks on his birthday and Christmas. A former mistress provided taped conversations with the sheriff telling her how to lie to investigators.

Puente wrote 17 stories, many based on public records. Together, they told a tale of long-time corruption in the sheriff's department and gaps in a system that allowed such wrongdoing. The final stories detailed the sheriff's resignation and eventual conviction on corruption charges.

Puente credits his contacts within county government for his success.

"The people who wear shirts and ties, the high-ranking administrators, they want to put the spin on everything. It's the low-ranking people who were affected by the sheriff's rule who helped out with the story."

POLICE

behind the beat

Puente won local, state and national awards for his work and was nominated for a Pulitzer. But he was most touched when he walked through the sheriff's office the day after the sheriff resigned.

"Before, the staff wouldn't make eye contact. They were afraid," he says. "After he resigned, people came up to me with tears in their eyes. One woman got up from her desk and hugged me. No award will ever beat that."

Puente has these suggestions for young cop reporters:

▶ **Treat everyone the same.**

Visit offices as often as possible. Talk with everyone. Friendliness and interest in all employees pays off.

"It's a challenge to get public employees to tell me things they shouldn't," he says. "What I simply do is treat them all with respect and I guess they saw me as a friend."

▶ **Don't let anyone outwork you.**

The clear example of this dictum was Puente's unwillingness to wait for the sheriff to hold a news conference to address the charges.

"I wanted to make sure I stayed out front of the story," he says. "If you have a beat, you should own that beat."

and prison populations. You can navigate the website or call the bureau to find data related to a local story. For example: You have a case where someone died in custody. A quick check of the website finds a study of jailhouse deaths in 2003–2006. The deaths are categorized by cause and broken down by regions and states.

The FBI's Uniform Crime Records is another treasure trove of information about crime and policing. The bureau collects data from 18,000 law enforcement agencies around the nation and then analyzes and collates them by various categories. Any new police reporter should go to the main page, www.fbi.gov/stats-services/crimestats, and begin digging around. It's interesting to see what kind of information you can find. For example, on page 71 is a chart detailing murders, categorized by the weapons used and broken down by states.

COPS BEAT ▶ STORIES

A police reporter sees story possibilities every day. Police logs provide material for spot stories about individual cases; over time the collection of reports can point to trends in crime and policing. Conversations with your contacts can lead you to stories that are developing on the street or inside the department.

Motor vehicle accidents involving injuries, deaths or significant property damage will require stories, as will complex multicar accidents that tie up traffic for hours. Although simple property crimes, such as smashed windows or car theft, probably won't top news, you can note them on your website as an item in a police log box.

Look for noncrime stories. Monitor your municipality's budget discussions as they relate to police department funding. Police union negotiations can produce a vigorous public debate over the need for safe streets versus the way to pay for them. Pensions are another volatile issue. Police contracts often include generous benefits and an earlier retirement as reward for years of hazardous duty. This can create mixed feelings among your audience about paying for benefits not available to regular taxpayers.

Ideas can come from outside your coverage area. Read up on national law enforcement issues; monitor the Bureau of Justice Statistics website for reports on policing issues that may relate to your department. Track crime reporter blogs and journalism association websites to see what kinds of stories are being published around the country.

Perhaps the best source is your own imagination. Ask yourself questions; be curious. Jerry Mitchell, a reporter for The Clarion-Ledger of Jackson, Miss., became interested in the history of civil rights murders in the 1960s and began researching the cold cases. The result was a series of stories that led to the arrest and convictions of several members of the Ku Klux Klan involved in 30-year-old murders. Reporters with the East Valley Tribune of Mesa, Ariz., decided to look into the sheriff department's aggressive campaign against illegal immigrants. They found the focus on that issue affected other policing duties, including a slower response time to crimes, a dropping arrest rate and rising overtime costs. The staff won the Pulitzer Prize for local reporting. A story in the Philadelphia Daily News about a drug informant's role in more than 200 arrests grew into a series that raised questions about the actions of a narcotics detective and the validity of hundreds of cases. One man facing a life sentence was released from jail as a result, and the News won a Pulitzer.

These award winners have one thing in common: the willingness of the reporters to ask questions and dig deeper. They had no magic formula. All it took was time and effort to pore over files and interview sources. This kind of success is available to anyone who puts in the effort.

Imagination and creativity are important factors in your day-to-day writing as well. Think of ways to portray incidents of crime and violence that go beyond a simple recitation of the facts. Edna Buchanan, a crime reporter for the Miami Herald, earned a Pulitzer Prize for turning routine gun-and-run stories into compact narratives. Consider how she handled the shooting of an unruly customer at a fast-food restaurant. In the hands of another reporter, the story could have been a couple of paragraphs detailing the who, when and where of a homicide. Instead, Buchanan assembled the facts into a tale of human foible and tragedy.

> *Gary Robinson died hungry.*
>
> *He wanted fried chicken, the three-piece box for $2.19. Drunk, loud and obnoxious, he pushed ahead of seven customers in line at a fast-food chicken outlet. The counter girl told him that his behavior was impolite. She calmed him down with sweet talk, and he agreed to step to the end of the line. His turn came just before closing time, just after the fried chicken ran out.*
>
> *He punched the counter girl so hard her ears rang, and a security guard shot him — three times.*

Covering Cases: Big Stories

reporting checklist

- ☐ Monitor police calls on case.
- ☐ Find responding officers.
- ☐ Find scene commander.
- ☐ Identify victims, suspects who have been arrested.
- ☐ Take pictures, videos.
- ☐ Call on your sources.
- ☐ Check court records.

Although it is an unfortunate saying, the idea of "if it bleeds, it leads" often sets the criteria for which crimes and investigations you will cover. News can be defined as events that are less than usual. Murder is a dramatic, unusual event — so are armed robberies, sexual assaults and arrests involving large quantities of drugs.

Perhaps the most significant and challenging police stories involve a serious crime followed by a high-profile investigation. These are hard stories to report. The crime may not be discovered until hours after it has occurred. You may not be able to find witnesses; if you do, they may not want to speak with you. Neither will the cops. Officially, they don't want news reports to interfere with their investigation. Unofficially they may offer you tips that require work to verify. You likely will face competition from other media. A big murder case raises the stakes; everyone wants an exclusive story about possible suspects and other details of the crime. You can't let the heat of the moment overpower your journalistic sensibilities. Be thorough and careful in your work; don't report rumor or speculation. Identifying someone as a suspect prematurely can damage this individual's reputation for life. You risk damaging your reputation as well.

Here are the steps you will go through as a crime is reported, investigated and, perhaps, solved.

Responding to a Call The first you may hear about a crime will be on the police radio. Most news organizations monitor police calls from the newsroom. Private online services also track various police and fire radio frequencies and then forward reports to subscribers via text message or Twitter. Many police departments also send out Twitter alerts and post calls on their websites and Facebook accounts.

On Scene Get to the crime scene as soon as you can, but don't break any laws on the ride over. Chances are the action is over: the bank robbers have fled; the corpse has been discovered. But the sooner you get there, the easier it may be to speak with witnesses and officers. Those opportunities will fade as the crowd of media grows and higher-ranking officers appear on the scene to control the flow of information.

Find the Crime Scene Commander Try speaking with different officers on the scene to gather details. Eventually one officer or PIO will arrive to corral the media. He or she may be willing to provide some information. Other times the officer will refuse to share any details about the just-begun investigation.

Identify the Victim, Suspect, Details of the Crime Get the basics: What is the name of the victim or victims? Police may not release names until family is notified. If a neighbor or friend volunteers a name, be careful; you run the risk of identifying the wrong person unless it comes from an official.

Find out the details of the crime, the description of the suspect and the estimated time the crime took place. Some or all of those details may not be readily available.

Find Witnesses Speak with the people who have gathered to gawk. Someone there may have seen the crime or witnessed the discovery of the crime. Neighbors of the victim can provide background; someone may tell you about similar crimes that have occurred in the area. Take names and telephone numbers so you can reach these people in the future.

Put out inquiries on your Facebook and Twitter sites alongside of your reporting. Casting a wide net in the sea of social media may get you important information. But treat these public responses as simple tips. You must do your own reporting to verify what may be mostly speculation and rumor.

Pictures and Video Record any official statements given at the scene. Establish a sense of place: Even a simple shot of the home or business where the crime has occurred has value in illustrating the story. You may see more graphic images — an overturned car, a body lying under a sheet. You'll need to show some judgment about filming those grisly scenes. Before you become part of the public spectacle by taking pictures, ask yourself if those images will be used by your organization.

on the web

Following a Shooting

When U.S. Rep. Gabrielle Giffords and 19 other people were shot in a Tucson shopping mall in January 2011, news organizations large and small jumped on the Web to report the story. Within minutes after the suspected shooter was identified, reporters were able to find his Myspace and YouTube ramblings about government and religion, including a posting made shortly before the shooting saying good-bye to his friends. Online records revealed the suspect's past brushes with the law. Tweets from people who claimed to have gone to high school and college with the suspect helped flesh out a picture of a troubled young man.

Reporters were able share the evolving rush of details through blogs, tweets and online updates, providing their audiences with critical information at a time of anxiety over the implications of the shooting.

As the Tucson shootings illustrate, social media resources for police reporters populate the Web in growing numbers. You can find information about an incident and contact people who know the victim and suspect through Facebook pages and other postings. You can get tips from the scene of a crime through Twitter postings by witnesses and others with relevant information.

Many police departments now have their own blogs and Facebook pages that are updated regularly. Many post information on Twitter that is often more readily available than a police department spokesperson. For example, the Dalton, Ga., Police Department blog provides details of crimes and investigations, lists names and contact numbers for neighborhood patrol officers and even lists outstanding warrants for local residents.

You can also use these tools to get breaking news out to your audience. Media outlets are directing their audiences to pages that focus on crime. For example, a Washington Post blog called The Crime Scene provides news, features and reporters' perspectives on crime, policing and the courts. The Post also encourages readers to offer their reaction to news stories and to suggest ideas on how better to cover crime and justice issues. It doesn't require much time to set up such sites, and the feedback and interaction will improve your perspective and reach as a reporter.

But take note. The speed with which these tools help you get the information out carries risks. In the case of the Tucson shootings, the rush to the story led several major news organizations to report incorrectly that Giffords had died. Always temper the need to get the news out quickly with the absolute necessity of getting it right the first time.

on the web

Dalton Police Blog

June 13, 2011

DPD Arrests Pair in Theft From UPS Store

On Friday afternoon, the Dalton Police Department arrested Edward Michael Copenhaver and Margaret Katherine Carlisle on charges of misdemeanor theft by receiving in connection to an investigation at the Dalton UPS Store.

Copenhaver, 45, and Carlisle, 26, both of 1903 Middle Summit Drive in Dalton were arrested last month by the Alpharetta Police Department on charges related to the theft of Target gift cards that were supposed to be shipped from the UPS Store there to tornado victims in Tuscaloosa, Alabama. Copenhaver is part owner of both the UPS Store in Alpharetta and also the store in Dalton. Carlisle is one of his managers.

The Dalton Police Department was already investigating another report of missing money at the UPS Store at 1323 Walnut Avenue when the Alpharetta arrests took place. In March 2011, a Dalton property owner reported that cash payments for rent left by her tenants in a rent deposit box at the UPS Store had gone missing. While the investigation into this incident was proceeding, the pair's arrest in Alpharetta was reported by area media. Once those reports were broadcast, more Dalton citizens contacted the Dalton Police Department to report missing property that was supposed to have been shipped from the Walnut Avenue UPS Store.

One of those reports came from a resident who had a jacket arrive at his home in December 2010. The complainant hadn't ordered the jacket, and took it to the UPS Store to ship it back to the sender. After leaving the package with employees at the UPS Store, the complainant got a call from his son who said that he'd had the jacket shipped to the complainant's home as a gift for his daughter. The complainant returned to the UPS Store to try to get a tracking number on the package and was told that the employees had no idea what he was talking about. He contacted the company that shipped the jacket and found that the jacket had never been returned. After investigating the report, Dalton Police detectives executed a search warrant for Copenhaver's home on June 8th and found the jacket in a closet, still in the original packaging with the tags still attached. After taking the jacket as evidence, investigators obtained arrest warrants for Copenhaver and Carlisle on a charge of misdemeanor theft by receiving.

The Dalton Police Department is still investigating these incidents and further charges are possible. Anyone with any information on these cases can contact Detective Ricky Long at 706-278-9085, extension 168.

Posted at 10:35 AM | Permalink | Comments (0) | TrackBack (0)

Source: www.daltonpdblog.org

The Washington Post

TODAY'S NEWSPAPER
Subscribe | PostPoints

| NEWS | POLITICS | OPINIONS | BUSINESS | LOCAL | SPORTS | ARTS & LIVING | GOING OUT GUIDE |

SEARCH: Try Our New Search [go] | Search Archives

washingtonpost.com > Metro > Crime > Crime Scene

The Crime Scene
To Serve and Inform

Get D.C. Area Alerts | E-Mail Us | Twitter | RSS | Who's Who? | More Crime Coverage | More Local News

ABOUT THIS BLOG

What's The Crime Scene all about? Read our mission and tell us what you think.

Then meet the team behind The Post's crime and justice coverage.

SEARCH THIS BLOG

[   ] Go

RECENT POSTS

- Does crime follow the weather report?
- Gun found in D.C. jail may be part of 2003 scheme
- Man slated to be first in U.S. to get single-drug lethal injection
- Murder defendant's lengthy testimony frustrates his attorneys

Meet The Post's Crime & Justice Team

The reporters listed here often cover issues and jurisdictions outside the scope of their daily responsibilities. If you don't see what you're looking for below, e-mail us and we'll make sure it gets to the right person.

THE REPORTERS

Keith L. Alexander covers D.C. Superior Court. Contact Keith, get RSS alerts when he writes and read his archive.

Ruben Castaneda covers Prince George's County Circuit Court. Contact Ruben, get RSS alerts when he writes and read his archive.

Paul Duggan covers the District of Columbia. Contact Paul, get RSS alerts when he writes and read his archive.

Mary Pat Flaherty is a general assignment reporter. Contact Mary Pat, get RSS alerts when she writes and read her archive.

Maria Glod covers Maryland federal courts. Contact Maria, get RSS alerts when she writes and read her archive.

Tom Jackman covers Fairfax County. Contact Tom, get RSS alerts when he writes and read his archive.

Allison Klein covers Arlington County and Alexandria. Contact Allison,

Source: http://voices.washingtonpost.com/crime-scene/meet-the-crime-justice-team.html

Another caveat about the use of social media sources: You must verify the often-anonymous bits of information. Anyone can claim knowledge of an event or a person on the Web. In the case of the congresswoman's shooting, someone put up a fake Facebook profile of the alleged shooter that was circulated for a time before it was removed. Social media is a tremendous resource for finding information and individuals in the critical minutes and hours following a breaking crime story. But consider all that information as a preliminary "tip sheet." You must verify who these people are and where their information is coming from. Reach out and contact the people who are offering the information. Question them as to where their information comes from. Identify them if at all possible; if they want to remain anonymous, say so in your story. Don't simply parrot what you're reading on the Web.

Following the Investigation Serious crimes usually involve long investigations. Police won't want to share each new lead or tip with you. Your job is to get the details out to your audience. People will be fearful about the implications of the crime and hungry for details. You'll need to show good judgment. Some of the information you gather may be little more than gossip. Other details may be critical to an investigation; revealing them too soon may make it harder for police to make an arrest.

Call on Your Sources Don't rely on officials' statements or wait around all day for a news conference. Work your sources. That might include the uniformed officers who responded to the call and the detectives you've gotten to know from working your beat. Public information officers will provide the official version of the investigation. Some PIOs will go off the record if they feel they can trust you.

You can also try speaking with the prosecutor's office. It will probably have someone assigned to help police in the investigation. Sometimes the best sources are former assistant prosecutors and retired police who are still plugged into their former departments. Since they no longer have to worry about their position in the office, they may be more willing to go off record and tell you what they've heard.

But, as always, take care in what you use. Gather the information you can find; then get verification. With enough information you may see patterns developing. You can take that information and run it by the officials. They may not want you to write everything, but they don't want you to get it wrong.

Get the Background As the investigation unfolds, you should be collecting any information you can on the key figures — the victims, the suspects and, in some cases, the principal investigators. These details become an integral part of the ongoing story. Who was the victim? What life did he or she lead? What do friends and family have to say? Were there incidents leading up to the crime, or was this unexpected?

If police have arrested someone or are searching for a suspect, you'll want to report his background. Who is the suspect? What is his connection to the victim or the crime? What is his background, previous run-ins with the law? Speak with the suspect's family and friends. Get their side of the story. Police and prosecutors often start trying the case against a suspect even before he is brought to court. You should try to present the other side.

Stick to the Facts

Great caution must be taken when writing about suspects in a criminal investigation. Never exceed the official line. The police may identify someone as a suspect or a "person of interest" in an ongoing investigation. You can echo this if it is said at a news conference or in an official statement. You can't if a source gives you a name off the record. You face the possibility of libel charges if you accuse someone of a crime and then that person is never charged.

An example of this is the case of Richard Jewell, a security guard at the 1996 Atlanta Olympics who discovered a suspicious knapsack and helped evacuate the area before the bomb exploded. Three days after the bombing, The Atlanta Journal-Constitution reported that the FBI was treating Jewell as a possible suspect. Other media outlets picked up the chant, and Jewell's personal life was picked apart in newspapers and on network television. NBC News even reported that the FBI was close to charging Jewell with the bombing. As it turned out, Jewell was exonerated; another man was charged and convicted of the crime. Jewell sued NBC and several newspapers, settling with most of them out of court.

The lesson is never to get ahead of the official action on a case, no matter what the pressure is to beat your competition. You don't want to be sued. You don't want to damage your credibility as a reporter. But most of all you don't want to ruin someone's life. Public frenzy over a high-profile murder case could taint those even casually connected to the case for the rest of their lives.

The best practice is to stick to the facts of a case. If someone is *charged* with a crime, you can say so. You can also say what the person is specifically *charged* with doing. Details of those charges should always be accompanied with the qualifying words *alleged* or *accused*. Remember the basic tenant of our justice system: A suspect/defendant is innocent until proven guilty.

judgment call

Choose your words carefully. *The Associated Press Stylebook* says this about the word *alleged*:

▶ Avoid any suggestion that the writer is making an allegation.

▶ Specify the source of an allegation. In a criminal case, it should be an arrest record, an indictment or the statement of a public official connected with the case.

▶ Use *alleged bribe* or a similar phrase when necessary to make it clear that an unproved action is not being treated as fact. Be sure that the source of the charge is specified elsewhere in the story.

Arrest and Arraignment Once an arrest has been made, a court arraignment will detail the charges against the suspect, who will have a chance to respond. This may be the public's first look at the suspect. You will want to get a picture of the person. That opportunity may be limited to the "perp walk" from the police car to the courthouse. You may get another opportunity for a picture or video during arraignment. Check with court officials about the rules for cameras in the courtroom.

Warrants and Affidavits The arraignment of a suspect may offer good visuals, but the real story will be in the records. Police, working with prosecutors, must file detailed reports to justify the bringing of charges against a person. If authorities need a search warrant to go into the person's home or car, they must file paperwork detailing their reasons for seeking the warrant. They will also have to file a report detailing what they found in their search. Some of these records are sealed to protect the rights of the suspect and the integrity of the ongoing investigation. But you should haunt the court clerk's office in search of available records.

Outside Experts Seek out people who can discuss the investigation and the implications of the crime. Law enforcement experts such as criminal justice professors (often ex-cops themselves) can offer insight into the challenges of investigating a case and bringing it to trial. These experts can also comment on the nature of the crime itself. Does it reflect a trend? Is it representative of a larger societal issue?

Writing the Story

- ☐ Details of the crime
  - ☐ Who was the victim/victims?
  - ☐ When did the crime occur?
  - ☐ What exactly happened?
  - ☐ What was the significance?
- ☐ Details of the investigation
  - ☐ What evidence have the police recovered?
- ☐ Was a weapon used? If so, what type?
- ☐ Are fingerprints or DNA available?
- ☐ Where there any witnesses?
- ☐ Next steps
  - ☐ Who are the suspects?
  - ☐ Was there an arrest?
  - ☐ Was anyone indicted?

Most big cases will produce many stories. At the start you will write daily reports on the crime, its aftermath and the investigation. Some days you will report on significant developments. Other times the story will have few new details other than some official pronouncement on the status of the investigation. But each story needs to contain many of the same elements:

When did the crime occur? Where did it happen? What do police know? Who was affected? What is the significance of the crime? Was it an isolated incident, or is it part of a series of similar crimes? What evidence have police collected? Have police recovered a weapon? Did they find fingerprints or other evidence that could link the crime to a suspect?

These details may not come directly from news conferences or press releases. Some of them may be supplied by sources you can't name. Make sure you have some verification of these details before you use the information.

What have been the consequences of the case on the neighborhood? The city? Are residents more concerned about crime? Have they taken additional precautions?

What has been the impact of the case on the police department? Has it brought about new crime prevention initiatives? Has it encouraged better connections between police and the community?

Has the investigation led to new procedures within the department? Did investigators use new techniques? Has the case pointed out deficiencies in regular police activities or detective work? High-profile investigations can often point to the need for better, faster crime lab procedures. Is that the case here?

STORY SCAN: An Investigation/Arrest Story

Here is a 2010 story from the Terre Haute Tribune-Star–detailing the arrest and investigation into a "cold case" murder. It provides a good example of background, reaction and impact.

Arrest Made In Cold Murder Case

TERRE HAUTE — A convicted sex offender has been arrested and charged with murder and attempted murder in a 1979 cold case investigation recently reopened by Indiana State Police.

A simple lede to frame the multiple dimensions of the case. The lede could have become cluttered with names, dates and circumstances.

Richard L. Boswell Jr., 53, will make his initial appearance this morning in Vigo Superior Court 6 to face the allegation that he abducted and murdered 20-year-old Kathy Jo Baker in a rural area northeast of Riley on May 22, 1979.

An economical listing of the important details: the identities of the suspect and victim; the date and place of the crime; the anticipation of arraignment.

Boswell also has been accused of attempting to murder the woman's then 2-year-old son, Ryan Baker, by striking him in the head and leaving him for dead near his mother's body.

More details of the charges and the case.

DNA evidence preserved by ISP was used to connect Boswell to the murder, police said.

Announcement of Boswell's arrest was made Thursday afternoon in the office of Vigo County Prosecutor Terry Modesitt — in the presence of the mother, husband, sisters, niece and now 33-year-old son of Kathy Jo Baker.

A key detail — the use of new technology to solve an old case. This important fact might have gone better in the lede.

A framed photograph of a smiling, long-haired Baker sat on the table in front of Modesitt, Chief Deputy Prosecutor Rob Roberts, ISP Sgt. Joe Watts, Detective Tony Guinn and Detective Troy Stanton. Husband Kenny Baker told the media that the family had no comment to make following the press conference.

Good color details that show the emotional impact of the crime.

Important details of the investigation. The lag time in processing the DNA suggests follow-up story that asks why it took so long.

Details from the investigation. Attribution is important for such details.

The remaining sections of the story set up the history and details of the case.

Stanton said it is the ISP's practice to continually review cold cases, and it was in April 2008 that a new lead came up in the case. A DNA sample was collected from a suspect, and several items of evidence from the Baker case were sent to the ISP Laboratory for DNA analysis.

In March, almost two years after the DNA was submitted for testing, ISP detectives received lab results showing that DNA evidence found on Baker's clothing matched Boswell's DNA profile.

Boswell was interviewed on Aug. 19 at his Riley-area home, and confirmed to the detectives that he knew Baker through her brothers. He also told police he had assisted her with a lawn mower repair about one year before her death. That repair occurred at the same residence from which she was later reported missing.

Boswell also told investigators that at the time Baker went missing, he had friends who lived in the area of her home, and he commonly drove past that area in his yellow 1975 Pontiac Astre. A witness told police in 1979 that she saw Boswell's car in the area of the Baker residence on the day Kathy Jo Baker went missing.

On that day in May 1979, Kenny Baker contacted ISP to report that his wife and toddler son were missing from the home. A search of the area was conducted, but the mother and son were not found. Another police search of the area on the following morning did not locate them either. But around 1:30 p.m. that day, police learned that people fishing about a mile and a half north of the Baker residence reported hearing a baby crying in the woods on coal mine property the night before.

A search of that rural area led to Baker and her son, who had sustained a serious head injury. The child was taken to a hospital for treatment and recovered. Baker was pronounced dead at the scene, and her body was taken for an autopsy that determined the cause of death was strangulation and asphyxiation.

"DNA was a big part of this case," Watts said. "Kudos to the investigators on how it was properly packaged, properly held and properly maintained for 31 years."

Prosecutor Modesitt agreed that preservation of evidence is crucial in criminal cases, and that even 30 years in the future, additional investigative tools may be available to solve cold cases.

More indications that this case represents larger issues of murder investigation.

RESOURCES

Links

Crime Statistics

▶ Bureau of Justice Statistics, http://bjs.ojp.usdoj.gov

▶ FBI Uniform Crime Records, www.fbi.gov/stats-services/crimestats

▶ FBI Clery Act data, http://ope.ed.gov/security

Journalism Sites

▶ Criminal Justice Journalists, http://crimjj.wordpress.com

  ▶ The group also maintains a database of crime stories at http://cjj.mn-8.net.

▶ Institute for Justice and Journalism, www.justicejournalism.org

▶ Investigative Reporters and Editors, www.IRE.org

▶ Center on Wrongful Convictions, www.law.northwestern.edu/wrongfulconvictions

Law Enforcement Organizations

▶ Drug Enforcement Administration, www.usdoj.gov/dea

▶ FBI, www.fbi.gov

▶ National Association of Chiefs of Police, www.nacoponline.org

▶ National Sheriffs' Association, www.sheriffs.org

▶ U.S. Bureau of Alcohol, Tobacco, Firearms, and Explosives, www.atf.gov

▶ U.S. Customs and Border Protection, www.cbp.gov

▶ U.S. Department of Homeland Security, www.dhs.gov

▶ U.S. Marshals Service, www.usmarshals.gov

▶ U.S. Secret Service, www.secretservice.gov

Unions

▶ National Association of Police Organizations, www.napo.org

▶ International Union of Police Associations, www.iupa.org

Assignment Desk

Compare your department to nationwide averages using Justice Department and FBI data. What is the police-to-population ratio, and how does that compare with the average in your state and the nation? Get a roster of the special units within your department. Does it have a SWAT team? A computer crimes unit? You can compare and contrast the staffing of your department with that of departments around the country.

Sidebar Write a story that uses this comparative data. Get comments from local officials and national organizations such as the International Association of Chiefs of Police and the National Association of Police.

CHAPTER 6

FIRES AND
EMERGENCIES

Checklists

Beat Backgrounders

How do you cover the unexpected?

Major fires, emergencies and disasters come with little warning. Unlike other community beats, there are no agendas to detail what will happened. When an emergency strikes, there is often only chaos.

Many reporters — both newbies and veterans — have little experience covering such events. A fire story can be a challenge if you don't understand what is going on and what to ask. A major disaster can be overwhelming.

But you can find ways to prepare.

You'll likely cover a fire long before you're sent to a tornado or a distant earthquake. Covering these more routine calls will help develop the skills and contacts you'll need to handle a major storm, transportation accident or chemical spill. Responding to a fire can be an adrenaline-fueled experience. Facts must be gathered quickly and fed to your website's readers, who will be looking for information about the sirens wailing in the distance.

Stan Finger
Wichita Eagle weather writer

During tornado season, Stan Finger's workspace looks like a combination war room/radar site. As the Wichita Eagle's weather writer and emergency czar, Finger tracks storm fronts using weather radar and tweets and texts from official agencies and readers. He puts the information on his blog and the Eagle's website, as well as directing photographers and reporters to affected areas.

Finger and his newspaper's website need lots of eyes and ears. A widespread emergency or disaster cannot be covered by just a few reporters; it takes a community of officials, responders, citizens and survivors to assemble a comprehensive picture of what happened. Finger quotes a soldier who said that all he knew of the war was what he saw in front of him. Reporting on emergencies sometimes requires an army of reporters — both professionals and citizens.

"You need individuals to focus on tiny pieces of the tragedy," he says. "You need someone at the hospital, another person to go here, someone else to go there. You have to take what you see and what you're being told and weave it together in a compelling narrative."

Finger and his colleagues present the news in real time. He gathers reports from different sources, posting pictures and updates to alert people of approaching danger as the storm or tornado continues on its path. Finger takes care not to use unconfirmed information that could needlessly panic his audience.

"I never take what just one person is saying on face value. There can be a lot of noise out there," he says. "I don't report something I've seen on Twitter just once."

Finger has other advice:

▶ **Create a big picture with a mosaic of smaller vignettes.**

"Walk through the area and describe what it looks like, what happened to individuals. Share what people have to say."

▶ **Don't stop reporting when the emergency ends.**

"Ask where things stand, and keep asking those questions each day. The answers will change, and how they do will reflect how well/poorly the response and cleanup is going."

▶ **Think in the long term. You'll need to develop contacts for the weeks and months of recovery.**

"Take a lot of business cards with you. Tell people it's OK to call after they've had a chance to process all this."

When Steve Johnson heard firefighters were on their way to a home in one of the New Jersey towns he covers for Patch.com, he made a quick call to a fire dispatcher he knew. Within minutes he had the details on the Web: a sleepy resident, an unattended candle, fire started, daughter ran to neighbors, fire now out.

Soon after Johnson filed the story, a reader sent in a comment: "I smelled smoke and I knew you guys were on top of it."

"It was a good confirmation of how people rely on us," Johnson says.

People will rely on you much more in a large-scale emergency. Your website will become a vital community resource where people can follow developments and learn where to go for food and shelter or how to apply for aid. They can also add their own words and visuals to your coverage through social media sites.

Beyond reporting the facts, it will be your job to offer perspective. A fire, accident, extreme weather or other emergency leaves behind a trail of questions. Who was hurt? What are the social and financial costs? How did this happen, and what can be done to prevent this from happening again?

Getting answers to these questions will be much easier if you develop good contacts with your local emergency services officials and the state office of emergency management during the calm times, *before* an emergency strikes. Don't expect the officials and first responders to help you if they don't know you and you don't know anything about their jobs.

"The weakness I see in the media is that a lot of reporters don't understand the fire service," says Capt. Steve Ruda, head public information officer (PIO) for the Los Angeles Fire Department.

Ruda teaches a national fire academy course for PIOs titled "Someone's Got to Do It," a name that illustrates the reluctance many emergency personnel have about talking with reporters. "The preconception is that journalists are looking for something bad to write," says Ruda. "You have to build trust. Firefighters appreciate a reporter who takes the time to see what their job is like." That means writing about the other news coming from the fire and emergency services departments. Issues such as pay, pensions, layoffs and allegations of misdeeds by department personnel need to be reported — sometimes on a daily basis. The costs, policies and activities of these agencies can generate controversy and emotional debate. The municipal budget cuts that swept the country following the 2009 recession resulted in fire station closings and layoffs of emergency services personnel, creating concern among residents about the safety of their communities. Stories on these matters have a great following.

MORE EMERGENCIES, FEWER FIRES

THE NATIONAL FIRE PROTECTION ASSOCIATION recorded 3,010 civilian fire deaths and 1.3 million fires (one call every 23 seconds) in 2009. These events caused $12.5 billion in damages. Although impressive, these numbers have been steadily decreasing; the incidence of fires has dropped by over 20 percent since 1999 thanks to better fire codes and prevention programs. The number of deaths has decreased by similar percentages.

Many fires are routine: a smoky incident involving a pan of bacon and a forgetful cook or a space heater too close to the drapes. Few generate stories. But the routine can turn tragic without warning: the discovery of an elderly victim who fell asleep while smoking, the sudden collapse of a roof that kills or injures firefighters.

Fire departments handle more than fires. Their mission has grown to include hazardous materials (HAZMAT) calls and responses to transportation accidents and other emergencies. Many departments have greatly expanded their emergency medical services role. In 2009, for instance, Kansas City's fire department responded to 90,000 emergency medical calls and fewer than 2,000 structure fires, according to Kansas City Fire Chief Richard "Smokey" Dyer. Nationally, the breakdown is about 30 percent traditional fire calls and 70 percent emergency medical runs. Most of these emergency calls are for individual medical problems or accidents and don't merit much coverage.

As the number of fires and fire deaths drops, the incidence of floods, tornados, hurricanes and earthquakes has been growing. Through the 1990s the Federal Emergency Management Agency counted an annual average of 45.5 declared disasters and 7 declared emergencies. From 2001 to 2010 the average rose to 61 disasters and 16 declared emergencies per year. A majority of the declarations were due to severe storms and their related effects, such as tornados and floods. There is no clear explanation for the increase over the past two decades, but some climatologists have linked the frequency and severity of storms to evidence of global climate change. If this is the case, we can expect more events and more challenges for reporters around the nation.

EMERGENCIES BEAT ▶ People

The emergency beat is populated by a range of people from state emergency management officials to members of the local volunteer engine company. Most departments want information to come from the top — usually a PIO in the commissioner's or superintendent's office. Those officers aren't always available or willing to talk, so you'll need to develop both official and unofficial sources throughout the departments. Each contact offers a different perspective. The commissioner or superintendent can provide a global view of the department budget and policy. Fire chiefs can give you important facts at the scene of a fire or other emergency. Individual firefighters or emergency medical technicians (EMTs) can offer a minute-by-minute account of what happened.

You should get to know the people on the periphery of the emergency, such as the Red Cross, Salvation Army and other volunteer workers who assist people in times of trouble.

Department Spokespersons

Most professional departments have spokespersons or public information officers who deal with the media. These people are important contacts for the day-to-day routine of fire departments: the budgets, negotiations, purchases and planning. But the spokespersons may not be readily available during a fire or emergency. They may be inundated with other calls or waiting for reports from the scene. You can't wait for them to return a call. It is always best to go to the scene.

Fire Commissioners

Commissioners or superintendents — titles vary from department to department — top the organizational chart in larger cities. Elected or appointed, they are responsible for establishing budgets, rules and regulations. Some cities have a board of fire commissioners, a semilegislative body, often led by a top commissioner. Commissioners are important contacts for issues such as spending or disciplinary actions against fire personnel. They have less to do with a breaking story.

Chiefs

Larger departments may have a number of chiefs and deputy chiefs who supervise individual divisions or geographic units. Smaller departments may have just one chief. Fire chiefs usually are closer to the action, supervising units responding to a fire. Covering fires will be much easier if you get to know these chiefs before the alarm goes off.

from the source

Bob Khan
Phoenix Fire Chief

Bob Khan started his career riding a fire truck as a regular smoke eater. Then his career took a detour. He became a public information officer, developing the skills to present a favorable image of his department. The role helped boost his career; after holding several other jobs, he was appointed fire chief in Phoenix. He leads a department with 2,100 employees, 58 fire stations and a budget of $290 million.

Khan understands the importance of educated reporters. He started a training course to give journalists the experience of shrugging on heavy fire gear, driving trucks and fighting mock fires complete with theatrical smoke. He had them speak with the department's chaplain to hear what he had experienced during his career.

"They got to see what we see," he says. "They got a window into the firefighter's soul."

The training course fell victim to budget cuts and a shrinking number of public safety reporters. "There used to be a team of reporters that would hit a fire," Khan says. "Now it seems we have one reporter who looks at public safety for 3 million people."

Khan also notes a change in the type of coverage his department gets. He says that "gotcha stories" detailing the missteps and misdeeds of department personnel attract more reporters than the day-to-day stories of emergency services.

"There's always an inclination in journalism to get the story about somebody who fumbles the ball or makes a mistake doing something they shouldn't be doing off duty," he says. "It's more challenging to put the real face on the fire service." Here's Khan's advice to reporters:

▶ **Get to know the PIOs.**

"You can have a story any day as long as you make the contacts and have a knowledge of what you are writing about."

▶ **Invest time to understand the firefighters' job.**

"If I was a new reporter, I would ask to ride a fire truck and spend 12 hours to 24 hours in a firehouse," he says. "Ride along, drag some hose. Understand what it's like to work in 112-degree weather. We love it when we see someone committed to learn."

Emergency Management Officials

Officials with the Federal Emergency Management Agency (www.fema.gov) are an important source for information on preparation, response and recovery from weather and other disaster events. You should get to know the agency's regional officials. When FEMA is called in to a disaster scene, it will often help local authorities work with the media.

In addition to FEMA, each state has its own emergency management agency. Federal law requires states to form a state emergency response commission (SERC) that divides the state into planning districts and establishes local emergency planning committees. Get to know the state and local emergency planning officials. Find out who is on your local or regional emergency committee. Ask about state disaster plans and how they've changed over the years. Most state and local emergency organizations hold training exercises at least once a year. Covering these events will help you get to know the personalities and procedures central to any emergency or disaster response.

State Fire Marshals

Fire wardens or marshals are the top fire officials in the state. Their offices monitor the number, kinds and causes of fires around the state. State fire marshals often supervise or aid with arson investigations. They track the effectiveness of a fire department's response. This makes their offices valuable sources for stories that analyze fire trends in your area. The fire marshal's office is usually at the state capital, so making regular visits may be harder. But it is important to maintain good contacts with this office and to monitor its reports and findings.

The Blue Shirts

Rank-and-file firefighters and emergency services workers are important sources, offering a ground level view of what's happening within their department. They can provide specific details about a fire if they recognize you at the scene and feel comfortable speaking with you. They may request anonymity because they aren't authorized to speak for the department. Try to confirm the information higher up the chain of command.

The public's attitude toward firefighters can be complicated. Society generally holds them in the highest regard. They are the brave public servants who rush into burning buildings to save lives or, in less threatening circumstances, rescue cats from high tree limbs. The sacrifice of New York City firefighters on Sept. 11, 2001, established fire personnel as iconic American heroes. But firefighters can be the subject of controversy if they are thought to be taking advantage of a system that provides benefits not available to the rest of us.

Professional firefighters have strong union contracts that allow them to retire early or apply for disability compensation with full pay and benefits. The public's adoration of firefighters can turn to wrath when fire personnel game the system. Reporting such stories can be tricky; emotions run high on all sides of these issues.

OVERVIEW OF FIRE DEPARTMENTS

ACCORDING TO THE U.S. Fire Administration, only 14 percent of the nation's fire departments are staffed solely by professional firefighters. But these are major city departments that provide protection for 61 percent of the U.S. population. Seventy percent of fire departments rely solely on volunteers. The rest are a mix of volunteer and professionals.

MUNICIPAL DEPARTMENTS

Fire departments in larger cities have an organizational chart topped by the fire commission, followed by the chief. Assistant chiefs run units such as fire inspection and prevention, arson investigation and special operations. Firehouses, strategically located around the city, are led by assistant chiefs or fire captains and lieutenants and are staffed by firefighters who are on duty for multiple days. A typical schedule may be three days on followed by two days off. Smaller cities and towns may have a mix of professional and volunteer firefighters.

Professional firefighters face a rigorous selection and training process, usually through a civil service system that requires exams, education standards and tests of physical abilities. Many urban departments have firefighter unions that bargain over pay, hours and benefits.

COUNTY DEPARTMENTS

Less populated areas organize fire coverage under county government. This saves small towns the cost of running separate departments. The hierarchy can include a board of county fire commissioners, a top commissioner or supervisor and one or more fire chiefs. Firehouses, located around the county, may be staffed by full-time professionals and supplemented by volunteer firefighters.

VOLUNTEER DEPARTMENTS

Smaller municipalities and counties rely on volunteers who train at state fire academies and spend weekends brushing up on their skills. Volunteers are called to fires by phone, text or a town fire siren. They keep firefighting tools, helmets and other protective gear with them at all times. Some respond directly to the fire. Others rush to stations where fire vehicles are kept.

FIRE DISTRICTS

Some states allow unincorporated areas to organize into fire districts that rely mostly on volunteers. These districts, usually established within county lines, are governed by a board elected by district voters who are assessed a fire tax based on property values. Fire district officials can wield political clout and are followed closely by local residents.

Unions, Associations and Organizations

You can get background information, commentary and story ideas by tapping into national groups that represent firefighters and fire officials. The International Association of Fire Fighters, www.iaff.org, is a union that provides information on fire issues for its members and the media. Its staff can comment on contract negotiations and on-the-job issues for firefighters. The International Association of Fire Chiefs, www.iafc.org, offers the perspectives of fire department leaders with a focus on national issues and federal programs. The IAFC also maintains the related Volunteer and Combined Officer Section website for volunteer firefighters, www.vcos.org. All of these sites can add to your knowledge, but remember unions have their own agendas and points of view.

National groups can add perspective to local stories. The National Fire Protection Association, www.nfpa.org, has information about fire codes and safety issues. The U.S. Fire Administration, www.usfa.dhs.gov/index.shtm, analyzes statistics from departments around the country and can answer questions about federal programs that provide aid to local departments. The National Fire Information Council, www.nfic .org, has contacts with national, regional and state fire authorities.

Some local firefighters maintain their own websites and blogs, so do various state associations of firefighters, chiefs and emergency medical teams. These sites can be culled for contacts.

EMERGENCIES BEAT ▶ Places

You will need to spend time at your fire department's headquarters and stations to develop the contacts necessary to cover both administrative issues and emergency calls. Establishing relationships with the command structure, arranging for ride-alongs at different engine companies or simply hanging out with emergency services workers goes a long way toward understanding the beat and cultivating sources you'll need when stories break.

Navigating the Department

fire department checklist

- ☐ Study the fire coverage of your city or town; learn which station provides fire coverage for which neighborhoods.
- ☐ Learn the command structure and firehouse rosters so you'll know whom to look for during an emergency.
- ☐ Visit headquarters and the stations. Go for ride-alongs. Spend an occasional evening at each firehouse getting to know the firefighters and emergency personnel.

Locate each firehouse. Find out the types of trucks and the roster of firefighters assigned to the station. Keep a map in your computer that shows how the city divides fire coverage areas. This will help you to anticipate which engine company might be sent to a fire. You can also use the map to post locators for your stories.

Get out to the different locations, introduce yourself and spend some time with the firefighters. Find out where they train; it may be a local facility or a state fire academy. Ask to sit in on some classes.

Making the Rounds

rounds checklist

- [ ] Check incident reports on the Web, at headquarters or at individual stations.
- [ ] Make regular stops at fire headquarters to gab with the public information staff, the chief and even the commissioner.
- [ ] Rotate visits to the various firehouses.
- [ ] Make regular checks with state and local emergency management offices.

Establishing a regular routine of visits and phone calls will keep you on top of your beat. Calls or visits to the chief's office and fire stations can initiate conversations that lead to tips for good stories. A check of daily incident reports can offer a range of story possibilities. Visits to state and county emergency management offices will make your job easier should a disaster strike.

Headquarters Chances are you'll have reporting duties other than the emergency beat. Still, it's important to make a regular appearance at headquarters to maintain your contacts. Stop by the public information office; ask about details of the latest fire or investigation. The office may have the daily incident reports along with monthly and yearly compilations of the numbers. Ask if there are any safety initiatives or other public safety programs coming up that might make a good feature story. Visit with the command hierarchy, including the chief and/or commissioner. Don't expect to come away with a story; you're there to develop contacts and gather bits of information that may pay off later.

Firehouses Try to make regular visits to all the firehouses in your city, even if you get to each only once every few months. If you have a free night, stop by and hang out for as long as you think you are welcome. It may feel uncomfortable at first when firefighters treat you like the stranger you are. Persist. Talk to them about the job, their beefs, their close calls, their families. Ask about their equipment and what it does.

John Pepitone
Fox 4 Kansas City

John Pepitone has an advantage over other reporters when he covers an emergency call: His father was a Chicago firefighter for 30 years. Pepitone hung out at the station, slid down the fire pole and climbed over the equipment. "I knew a lot of his friends; I learned about their strong camaraderie and the lifestyle," he says.

As a reporter for Fox 4 in Kansas City, Pepitone mentions his father when he talks with firefighters. It can break the ice if they see him as someone who understands their job. "It's all about building relationships and gaining trust," he says.

Pepitone doesn't cover all emergency calls. The assignment desk often chooses whoever is available when it hears a fire call over the radio scanner. The chatter between the firefighters and the department's dispatchers usually makes it clear whether the call is newsworthy.

"When they [firefighters] pull up on the scene, they will report right away, 'We have flames showing. We have smoke showing.' That makes it easier to decide if we send someone," Pepitone says.

A reporter calls the department's public information office to confirm what was heard over the radio. That basic information may be posted on the TV station's website before a news crew arrives on the scene. Once there, Pepitone works with a producer to update the online story, including streaming video from his smartphone. If it's a big story, they may break into the station's broadcast with a special report.

Here are some emergency coverage tips from Pepitone:

▶ **Know whom to ask.**

Learn which officers are authorized, and willing, to talk. Some firefighters may not want to be identified. "You can have a conversation, but the minute they see the camera come out, you can see it's not going to happen," he says.

▶ **Be fair.**

Don't avoid less flattering stories. If you present all sides, your relationship with the department won't suffer. When a pumper crew was criticized for taking their fire truck out of their jurisdiction to see the captain's son pitch for his high school baseball team game, Pepitone explained in his story that crews must travel together in case they are called to a fire. His explanation earned him points.

"I treat them fairly and it doesn't seem to have hurt me much," he says.

With time, you will start to develop relationships; the station crew will get to know you — maybe even like you. Again, don't expect to generate a lot of stories from these visits. Simply be yourself and ask lots of questions. A good listener is almost always appreciated.

Once you're known to the various crews, you might be able to talk your way onto a fire call. Departments will generally allow this with advance notice. But if you're there when the bell goes off, try to ride with a crew. The experience will develop camaraderie and give you a better understanding of what it's like to be a firefighter or an EMT. And going on a call can be very exhilarating.

Emergency Management Offices All states have emergency management facilities that become command central during a crisis. You also may have county or regional emergency management offices, along with a city or town officer designated to handle emergency planning and response. These are often part-time jobs. Whatever the structure, get out to all these sites and meet the people who will be important sources in an emergency. Review their disaster plans. Attend their practice drills. They make for good stories and give you a glimpse of what to expect during the real thing.

EMERGENCIES BEAT ▶ Documents

The crush of daily emergency calls can obscure the bigger picture of what your fire department does and how well it performs. Fortunately, state and federal regulations compel fire departments to keep detailed public records. You can use these records to research and write meaningful pieces that go beyond individual fire stories.

The data can show if fires and other types of emergency calls have increased or decreased. You can see aggregate numbers for different types of emergency calls, resulting injuries and property losses. The data can show what is happening within specific neighborhoods. This paper trail offers answers to interesting questions: Do emergency calls increase during certain times of day or months of the year? Can you discern a pattern to suspicious fires reported over the past year? Does the fire department's response time change depending on the neighborhood? The answers can result in important stories.

Where to Find the Documents

Incident reports are the mainstay of fire and emergency department records. These can be found at headquarters, at fire stations or online. Records for all your state's municipalities should be available through the state fire marshal's office. Forty-two states file reports with the National Fire Incident Reporting System (NFIRS), which has over 900,000 fire incidents on its National Fire Database. This database, www.usfa.dhs.gov/statistics, allows you to compare your fire department's performance with 14,000 other departments.

U.S. Fire Administration Website

Source: www.usfa.dhs.gov/statistics

Incident Reports Incident reports usually include the type of fire or emergency, the time of alarm, the time emergency units arrived on scene, the time spent on the scene and the number of engines and personnel involved. Other details can include the fire's origin: Where did it start and what ignited it? The reports catalog injuries to rescue personnel and civilians. These data can help you to summarize individual incidents and provide big-picture context about the number and kinds of fire and emergency calls your department handles. You can map events to get a clearer idea of what areas of your town have more fire and emergency calls.

Make an effort to look at the reports as often as possible. Much of what you read will be the routine. A bulk of calls will be minor fires or EMT responses to run-of-the-mill heart palpitations, falls and other injuries. Not much story material there. Still, you'll never know what you'll find.

Interesting stories about the human condition can be tucked into the dry incident report. A boy gets his head stuck in a stair railing. A husband sets fire to the garage after

READING INCIDENT REPORTS

SOME DEPARTMENTS, SUCH AS PORTLAND, Ore., Fire and Rescue, post incident reports on their websites. Although brief, the reports provide a good overview of the fire department's day-to-day operations. Looking at the report, you can see that 1,017 of the week's total 1,319 incidents were medical calls, reflecting the general trend in municipal emergency services. Eighty-two were fire related; 220 fell into other emergency categories. Only seven were deemed major incidents.

Recent Blog Posts | **Media Invited to Clackamas County Water Rescue Consortium**

PF&R Incident Statistics: July 25 - July 31, 2010 - Printable Version - August 2, 2010 - 0 Comments

Total Incidents: 1319
Medical: 1017
Fire: 82
Other: 220
Major Incidents: 7 (further information below)

- 07/25/10 @ 1034 hrs, Commercial Fire, 9700 block of NE Sandy Blvd. Loss: $35,000, Cause: Motor Vehicle crash into building, vehicle caught fire damaging both.
- 07/26/10 @ 0649 hrs, Residential Fire, 14500 block of SE Rhine St. Loss: $56,350, Cause: Smoker's carelessness. One Civilian Injury reported.
- 07/27/10 @ 1809 hrs, Residential Fire, 14300 block of SE Woodward St. Loss: $5,000, Cause: Electrical Short.
- 07/28/10 @ 0735 hrs, Residential Fire, 4700 block of NE 62nd Ave. Loss: $12,050 Cause: Smoker's Carelessness.
- 07/29/10 @ 0009 hrs, Apartment Fire, 2700 block of NE Halsey St. Loss: $6,000, Cause: Under Investigation.
- 07/29/10 @ 1850 hrs, Residential Fire, 800 block of NE 67th Ave. Loss: $8,000, Cause: Use of heat gun to remove paint.
- 07/30/10 @ 0854 hrs, Apartment Fire, 13400 block of SE Division St. Loss: $5,000, Cause: Smoker's Carelessness.

Portland Fire & Rescue *We Respond: Always Ready, Always There*
August 2, 2010

Portland Fire Incident Report
Source: www.portlandonline.com/fire/index.cfm?c=50972&a=311303

The basic information is presented in a quick, compact format: date and time; type of incident; location; the dollar cost of the incident; a brief description of what happened; an assessment, if available, of the cause and, finally, any injuries.

Note that three of the seven incidents in the report list "smoker's carelessness" as the cause. This information could be used to develop an in-depth examination of how many significant fires and injuries are linked to smoking.

Some departments may offer this data in spreadsheet form that can be easily imported into your own searchable database. Having this data would allow you to cross reference details such as location, time and date to look for trends.

the zealous use of charcoal starter in the barbecue. A family is overcome by carbon monoxide fumes when a heavy snowfall blocks the furnace flue. These reports can be the basis for stories that entertain or offer important safety lessons.

Watch for trends. A rash of EMT calls for drug overdoses could indicate a new, dangerous type of street heroin. A number of house fires caused by space heaters could merit a story about the dangers of auxiliary heating units. Another story could look at how the combination of low temperatures and high oil prices has made for unsafe conditions.

Fire Inspection Records Commercial properties are subject to regular inspections by fire department personnel. The results of these inspections are documented in public records on file with the department.

These reports are generally routine. The inspector may list suggestions for the property owner. In rarer instances, the owner may face fines or even a temporary closure of the building until safety issues are addressed. These records become important after a major fire or other emergency. They can show if there were problems with the building. Check for violations or warnings. Do the files make reference to dangerous materials, an inadequate number of exits and signage? Is there a record of the building having a sprinkler system?

Personnel Records Data such as salaries and overtime pay also are available to the public, as are records of firefighters' disability claims. Many media outlets follow up on these claims to see if a firefighter's disabling injury is real. In one case, reporters discovered that a Boston firefighter receiving disability pay for what he claimed was a debilitating back injury was spending his time in a gym, competing as a body builder.

Emergency Plans Your local, county or state emergency management offices have planning documents on file detailing procedures for evacuation, response and recovery operations. These are scripts that emergency officials rehearse in regularly scheduled drills and follow in real emergencies. Federal and state laws require such plans to be reviewed and updated on a regular basis. Make sure your municipality or county is meeting those requirements. Get a copy of these plans. You may find stories to pursue on how people would be evacuated, where they would be sheltered, how emergency service personnel would respond and who would be in charge.

EMERGENCIES BEAT ▶ Stories

The emergency beat offers many kinds of stories beyond fires and trouble calls. Budget and personnel issues can foster debate over the need to cut spending versus the public's demand for safety services. The public also is sensitive about firefighters abusing privileges and their generous pension, medical and disability plans. You may get tips from the public about the improper use of time and equipment by firefighters. Care must be taken in reporting these allegations. Firefighters' special duties have to be balanced with the perception of special perks. It may anger citizens to see firefighters drive their engine to a supermarket. But it may be standard operating procedure for an engine crew to travel together if they are called to a fire while stocking up on groceries for the firehouse.

Look beyond your area for story ideas. Follow national fire safety and prevention issues. Does a major fire or emergency incident elsewhere warrant a story about how your department would respond to a similar emergency? Follow firefighting news and websites for developing trends and issues. Keep track of what is happening in your state capital and in Washington, D.C. Is Congress or the state legislature considering a law that may affect your department?

Most of the breaking stories on this beat will, of course, be fires. But you may also be called on to cover the rarer stories of large-scale emergencies or disasters such as flood-inducing rains, blizzards, tornados and hurricanes in coastal areas. Other emergencies include major evacuations caused by wild fires, explosions or chemical spills and transportation accidents such as a multivehicle accident, a train wreck or an airplane crash.

Whatever the story, you should be prepared for some emotionally wrenching experiences. You're likely to encounter frightened survivors and scenes of destruction. You may see severe injuries or even the dead. Some reporters thrive on the adrenaline-fueled challenge of reporting from such scenes. Others struggle with what they have witnessed.

You can't anticipate what you'll see when you go out on an emergency call, but you can prepare. Talk with other reporters about their experiences. Do the same with your sources: Firefighters and emergency medical technicians have plenty of war stories. They can give you a better idea of what to expect. Discussing your experiences with first responders will help put what you've seen and reported into context. That's important both for your craft and for your emotional well-being. Look for online disaster-coverage resources for reporters. One excellent site is the Dart Center for Journalism and Trauma at Columbia University (http://dartcenter.org).

Emergency and Disaster Stories

Major emergencies happen without warning. You won't have much time to prepare. You may get a heads-up about the approach of a weather-related emergency. But the hours before a storm hits are not the time for you and your organization to start thinking about how you will handle the story. Long-term planning for the worst is the best way to be ready.

Preparation Reviewing state and regional emergency response plans will help you develop your organization's own plan for crisis coverage. Such a plan should assign specific duties: Who will go to the scene, and what equipment should those people bring? Who will stay in the office working the phones? Who will check the hospitals and shelters? Just like the emergency agencies, you should review plans and do dry runs to familiarize each reporter with his or her duties.

Anticipate how things will play out. Which departments will respond to an emergency? If an evacuation is called, what is the route? Where will people be sheltered? What agencies will provide food, water, emergency supplies? How would the local Red Cross and Salvation Army chapters respond? Prepare a list of contact number, e-mails, and twitter feeds for the emergency management officials in your area.

Have the right equipment on hand to see you through the days — perhaps weeks — of an emergency. You will likely be without electricity. Water supplies may be tainted; supermarkets and gasoline stations will be closed. Don't count on Internet or cell phone connections. When the city of Greensburg, Kan., was hit by an EF5 tornado (the most severe category of tornado) in 2007, it leveled 95 percent of the town, taking out all electrical and cell phone services. Reporters had to run relays in and out of the stricken area to file reports.

Keep a "go" pack for emergencies. Include lots of batteries, water and nonperishable food. Get an adaptor you can plug into your car to power your phone and computer. Include a change of clothes, hand sanitizer and a pair of tall rubber boots in the event of flooding.

Evacuation Most disasters or large-scale emergencies will involve some form of evacuation. People in the path of a hurricane, flood or wildfire will be urged or ordered to flee. Those living in an area hit by an explosion or chemical spill will have to leave their homes. You can follow the migration via Twitter, but you will need to have someone on scene to speak with the people and to describe the movement of traffic. Police and firefighters may go door-to-door to make sure people have left or heard the warning. Tagging along with them will add insight and drama to your story.

Follow the evacuation to the school gymnasiums, stadiums or National Guard armories designated to receive refugees. Speak to the evacuees, making sure you have permission to enter the facility. If these are people fleeing an event that has already occurred, they can provide details of what happened. If they evacuated in advance of a threatening storm, the story of their journey to safety will offer your audience a sense of what the victims are going through. Make sure to collect contact information so you can follow up with these people when they are able to return home.

Interviewing Survivors

Interviewing survivors is never easy. People can suffer terrible loss in a disaster. Friends or family members may have died or been seriously hurt. Homes may have been damaged or destroyed.

People react differently. Some will refuse to answer questions; they may be angry or in shock. If people are reluctant, back off. Leave your card or contact information and ask them to call later if they change their mind. You will be surprised, though, by the number of people who *do* want to talk about what's happened. Reporters all have stories of the father, wife or child of a victim who talked on and on about his or her loved one. Speaking to a stranger can be a cathartic moment for people, a time to begin processing the awful thing that has happened and to let the world know what they have lost.

Be respectful of this moment without sensationalism or cynicism. Often the straightforward way to start the conversation is to simply ask, "Tell me who (this person) was." Listen to what is said. Don't interrupt. Don't rush the conversation. Sympathy always trumps deadline.

It is right, both morally and journalistically, to use what people say about their loss. The dead and injured are not simply numbers. They are the human side of disaster, and their stories — tragic or uplifting — need to be told. Many news organizations provide respectful biographies of the victims to dignify their deaths with descriptions of their lives. A fine example can be found in the months after the Sept. 11, 2001, attacks when the New York Times ran a series called "Portraits of Grief." These few paragraphs about each casualty honored the uniqueness of every individual.

Rely on the eloquence of those affected by disaster to provide other information for your audience. Ask the survivors what they'd like people to know. The answers can vary. You'll hear anecdotes of irony or heroism, complaints about the lack of emergency supplies or gratitude for the help extended by the police or fire department.

Finally, make sure you have your facts straight. Check details and quotes. Ask permission to contact them later. You may do a follow-up story that serves both them and your audience.

Social Media Social media sites can be a tremendous resource to find people, collect their stories and grasp the scope of an emergency or disaster. Check http://search.twitter.com to see if Twitter has established a hash tag or keyword for the event. Go to Facebook to see if new groups have formed around the event. Monitor YouTube and other video sites for postings you can link to or use to follow up in your reporting. New tools to harness the social media world are popping up every day. At this writing a service called Storify searches the Web and collects individual postings (including tweets, photos and video), to which you can add your own reporting.

You can also invite people to blog directly to your website, share their experiences and offer commentary, advice and help to others. When a blizzard paralyzed New York City in 2011, the New York Times created a blog called "You Probably Can't Get There From Here," collecting anecdotes from readers during and after the storm and providing practical tips about mass transit and which streets were (and weren't) plowed.

Be careful about using social media as a primary source. People may write about rumors as if they were fact, exaggerate incidents or make things up. Your job is to make sure you pass along good information. Always do your best to verify what you find online. When in doubt about its accuracy, leave it out.

Rescue Not everyone makes it out before disaster strikes. Residents may be isolated by floodwaters or blizzards. People may be trapped inside collapsed buildings or pinned inside their vehicles. The elderly and infirm may have no choice but to stay where they are. One of your jobs will be to monitor efforts to rescue these people.

Find out when emergency responders will go back into a disaster area to search for survivors. See if you can go along. The drama of rescue, told in pictures, video and words, adds another dimension to the ongoing story. If you can't be there, try to be at the assembly point, helicopter pad or emergency medical facility where the rescued will be taken. Speak with both rescuers and survivors. They will have important stories to tell.

Some of the rescued may be hospitalized. Check with the hospital administration a few times each day to get the numbers of patients and their conditions. Ask if the patients will speak with you. Their voices will lift your stories beyond a simple recitation of facts and numbers.

Recovery The story does not end when the floodwaters recede, the fire's embers cool or the ground stops shaking. The real story for most disaster survivors will be what happens in the months — even years — of recovery.

Look for what is being done, and not done, for survivors. Are they getting proper shelter? Food and water? Is it taking an overly long time to restore electricity and phone service? Look for instances of ordinary citizens providing help to the victims.

Survivors often have complaints about the lack of aid. You must balance their desire for rapid healing with reality. Some phases of recovery take time. FEMA, which provides low-cost loans and other monies to disaster victims, is often the object of harsh criticism. It can be frustrating to stand in a long line waiting to apply for aid only to learn you must fill out several forms and document your loss. Talk with these people, but make sure you get the government's explanation of when help will arrive. For context, compare the response with what's happened during similar crises.

Wait a few days or weeks for the dust to settle; then check with emergency officials to see what they think they did right and what they could have done better. If it was a natural disaster, was there enough warning to the population? If the emergency was manmade, you will need to investigate what happened, who may have been at fault and what steps are needed to avoid a repeat of the event. All this introspection and postmortem make for good stories.

Find a few families or neighborhoods hard-hit by the event. Follow their recovery. Writing about their individual struggles offers insight to the larger picture of a community on the mend or failing to recover.

Aftermath News archives contain many excellent examples of in-depth coverage of a disaster's aftermath. Look up the stories and series that followed Hurricane Katrina in 2005, the 2010 Deep Horizon spill in the Gulf of Mexico or the previously mentioned Greensburg, Kan., tornado. Communities hit by such disasters often take years to recover. Local news organizations such as the New Orleans Times-Picayune and national publications such as the New York Times regularly revisit disaster-ravaged communities to keep their audiences informed about what has happened in the years following the disaster. Studying the range of stories can give you a sense of what's possible.

Aftermath stories also look into causes and solutions. Manmade disasters, such as explosions, chemical leaks or major transportation accidents, must be investigated to determine what happened, who or what is to blame and what can be done to prevent a repeat occurrence. Serious transportation accidents are often examined by the National Transportation Safety Board, a federal agency. Explosions may come under the jurisdiction of the federal Bureau of Tobacco and Firearms. Check to see who is investigating and keep track of the case.

No one can be blamed for natural events such as storms or earthquakes. But you can look into the forces that brought the event about, whether predictions were accurate and timely and how well construction codes, warning systems and emergency response worked.

Disasters, whether manmade or "acts of God," are often followed by government review, lawsuits and even criminal cases. State and federal lawmakers may hold hearings on what went wrong. Builders may be sued for construction work that failed in a windstorm. Lawsuits may be filed against authorities for failing to provide enough warning of an event or for botching rescue and recovery operations. In the case of Hurricane Katrina, several police officers were prosecuted for murder in connection with the shooting of a civilian.

All these stories must be followed and, more importantly, explained. The background details of a lawsuit or investigation should go well beyond the public statements and news releases. It will be your job to help your audience understand the larger issues of these cases.

Fire Stories

Fires will be a more routine part of your beat. Most fire calls won't make much of a story. A small amount of smoke and flames and a quick response by engine crews are hardly worth more than a paragraph or two on your website.

But you will cover much larger, dangerous and costly blazes, so learn all you can about fires and firefighting methods. Check the Web for fire stories as examples of what you should do if a big fire breaks out in your town. Each fire is different, but the method of covering the story has common points you should study.

safety checklist

- ☐ Get to the scene quickly but safely; the fire isn't going anywhere.
- ☐ Stay out of the way. Don't block emergency vehicle routes with your car.
- ☐ Be aware of dangers such as moving trucks, smoke and hoses. Never straddle a hose.
- ☐ Whenever possible, stay upwind from the fire to avoid dangers and smoke.
- ☐ If possible, wear old clothes you can discard if exposed to smoke. Wear old shoes.

Getting There You obviously want to get to the fire scene as soon as you can. But don't mistake yourself for an emergency responder. You don't have a siren or flashing lights (nor can you legally operate them); you can't ignore traffic laws.

You may be stopped at a police roadblock. Explain politely that you are a reporter. Show your police ID if you have one. But don't get into an argument; that just wastes time.

SAFETY LECTURE

Emergency scenes can be chaotic places filled with smoke, water, noise and potential dangers. As a "first responder" — one of the first people on the scene — you will be going into an unknown situation. Watch what firefighters and other emergency personnel do. They have the experience and training to react quickly to danger. Stay out of the way of rushing trucks and running firefighters. Watch where you walk. Debris, pools of water and fire hoses will be everywhere.

The most vivid memory of the first fire I covered was the lesson offered by a very large fireman who ran by, slowing just slightly to point to the ground between my legs. "Hey, moron," he said (actually he used a less polite word), "Watch out for the hose." Fire hoses can jump several feet in the air with an impressive force when water pressure changes. If you're straddling a hose when that happens … well, you get the picture. So always, as emergency responders are taught, maintain "situational awareness." Don't lose track of your surroundings as you interview or report. Make frequent 360-degree checks to be certain nothing bad — a cloud of toxic gas, a shower of sparks, an emergency vehicle — is bearing down on you. If you're covering a fire, try to position yourself so you can see what is going on from upwind of the event.

Always stand upwind from a fire. It's safer, you get a better perspective on the fire away from the path of the smoke and you won't smell like you've been curing in a smokehouse for the past three months.

Figure 6.1   Find a Safe Vantage Point

One last note: *Fires can be hazardous to your wardrobe.* Fire smoke, particularly from older homes and warehouses, will never leave your clothes. It has a nasty chemical smell so strong that you may have to undress before you go into your home. Shoes also take a beating from water and muck. The spiffy new clothes you wore to work, little knowing you'd be covering a pig farm fire, will be in great jeopardy. Store something sacrificial in your car or office: a pair of old jeans, a windbreaker and rubber boots.

If you can't get through the roadblock, find another route. Get as close as you can; then leave the car in any semilegal place. A press sticker on your car can help avoid delays and unpleasantries, such as tickets or towing. But don't waste time looking for a perfect spot. Getting to the scene is more important than avoiding a $25 parking ticket. Just leave the car and hope for the best.

Find the Incident Commander Look for the person in the white fire helmet. That signifies a command officer. If you see several white helmets, look at the labels with the person's name and rank.

Richard "Smokey" Dyer, the Kansas City fire chief, says reporters often are confused about whom to speak with. "In our department it is the incident commander who is in charge of the emergency scene," he says. "A higher ranking officer may come to the scene, but it is the incident commander who is ultimately in charge of the information."

Ask until you find the officer in charge. Whoever that may be, he or she will be your best source for information. All units report to the commander; the commander then coordinates the operation. Get a quick update on the situation, including injuries, deaths and rescues. Find out which hospitals are receiving the injured and let your organization know so someone can check on their conditions. Keep going back to the commander for updates. Never interfere with firefighters or rescue personnel while they are doing their jobs.

Check the Scene Make note of how many pieces and types of equipment are on scene. (See *A Reporter's Guide to Fire Equipment*, Appendix 2.) See if other departments have responded in mutual aid.

CALLS AND ALARMS

FIRE ALARMS AND OTHER EMERGENCY CALLS can be monitored on radio scanners in your newsroom or you can subscribe to services that follow the calls and issue updates via e-mail and Twitter. A growing number of departments file real-time reports on their websites, Facebook pages and Twitter.

However the information comes in, you'll need to understand the jargon of numbers and codes. We've all heard or read about firefighters battling a three-alarm blaze or struggling for hours to contain a five-alarm fire. But few of us know the difference. The explanation is simple: It depends.

Fire departments respond to fires under the system of alarms. Generally, more alarms means a bigger fire — the number of alarms refers to the number of firehouses called to respond to an emergency. But a three-alarm fire is different in Appleton, Wis., than it is in New York City. Larger cities have bigger firehouses, which hold multiple trucks and rescue vehicles. Smaller cities have one or two trucks assigned to a station. So a three-alarm fire in New York could marshal a dozen fire engines while the Appleton three-alarm might bring out just three trucks. Learn what the codes mean for your department. The National Fire Incident Reporting System website, http://nfirs.fema .gov, provides background to help you decipher departmental codes.

Mark the times each alarm is called. The time references will tell you how fast the blaze spread or how long it took to put out. Although your editor may be content with the simple mention of a two-alarm fire, you should be prepared to explain what that means.

Identify the Site Type and Location Is it residential? Commercial? Industrial? This is an important detail that will tell you if residents are at risk or if the building might contain dangerous materials. A fire at a food warehouse is a different story than a fire at a chemical depot. You can use the address to find important background information. Some towns maintain online tax records or local census data that can tell you who owns the building, who lives there or what the building is used for. If you are working with a news desk, the address can help it find more details, including inspection records or any previous incidents involving the property.

reporting fires checklist

- [ ] Find the chief on scene for a quick update.
- [ ] Check the scene to assess severity of the fire and the size of the response.
- [ ] Talk with witnesses and residents of the building.
- [ ] If you're filing for your website, take photos and video as well as posting info.
- [ ] Check back with your news desk to update, providing information about the location and where the injured have been taken.

Find Witnesses and Victims Approach the civilians on scene and ask if they saw what happened. Eyewitness accounts will add drama and color to your story. How did the fire break out? How did the people get out? Do they know anyone who was in the building? If anyone has an interesting story or seems knowledgeable, get a phone number you can call later for follow up. Update your story with each new piece of information.

Get Pictures and Video Chances are you will be asked to provide your website with sound, pictures and video. Fires and other emergencies offer dramatic visuals — raging flames, billowing smoke and firefighters in dangerous situations.

You will want video of the fire chief or officials in charge. You can shoot them answering questions. This can be done during your initial interview. But don't take too long. The commander will be busy. If you want to be creative, try to shoot him or her with the fire in the background. But you should do the maneuvering to get the shot; don't try to position the commander. A working firefighter will not have the patience to be posed for artistic value.

Use a wide shot to show the fire scene and give viewers a sense of dimension. Take some tighter shots of firefighters at work. Images of the fire equipment on scene will provide a sense of the effort to put out the blaze. You might also take some shots of bystanders and displaced residents. And you can record video or audio of interviews with witnesses and victims.

Don't make constant use of the camera; it's easy to become transfixed when viewing the scene through a lens and to lose perspective about the story. Once you get your first series of shots, go back to reporting. If the situation changes, make another round of images. If your website wants sound, you can use the audio channel on the camera, a simple digital audio recorder or your smartphone.

Consider other ways to illustrate the story. A map showing the location of the fire is easily done off the Web. A chart showing when the alarms were called provides visual information and another entry point for readers.

Tracking Fires

Fires are usually brief events that affect few people, with the exception of wildfires or the extraordinary fire that kills or displaces scores of people. Little incentive exists for news organizations or reporters to maintain regular blogs solely devoted to emergency departments. But you can find other sources on the Web. Fire departments, professional organizations and firefighters blog and tweet about fire topics. These sites can help you track issues and follow breaking news.

Many big-city fire departments maintain robust websites that offer real-time updates about fires and other emergency incidents. They tweet alarm calls to news outlets and stream live videos from fires that you can link to your organization's site. The departmental sites also provide feature material such as safety initiatives and community work performed by fire personnel. Portland, Ore.'s site has a regular feature on firehouse recipes for dishes such as sausage and sauerkraut.

These are terrific resources for overworked reporters. But don't become too reliant on them. Journalists have a responsibility to gather information that reflects what's truly happening. Fire department public relation staffs have a mission to boost the image of their departments. The two goals aren't mutually exclusive, but a good reporter always confirms what others are saying or showing.

Like many department sites, Chicago's offers a range of news and information. The page even has a link to a Freedom of Information Act form to request data from the department.

Less official sites also exist. Los Angeles Fire Department PIOs maintain their own website, with members of different shifts contributing each day. They include personal commentary, news about department personnel and links to local and national fire stories.

Chicago Fire Department's website

Source: www.cityofchicago.org/city/en/depts/cfd.html

⭐ ⭐ ⭐

🔊 Subscribe

| LAFD.ORG | News & Information | Breaking News | LAFD TV | Note |

📅 Sunday, June 12, 2011

Greater Alarm Fire in Sun Valley Quickly Neutralized

On Saturday, June 11, 2011 at 10:15 PM, 11 Companies of Los Angeles Firefighters, 4 LAFD Rescue Ambulances, 1 Arson Unit, 2 Urban Search and Rescue Units, 1 Rehab Unit, 1 Hazardous Materials Team, 2 EMS Battalion Captains, 5 Battalion Chief Officer Command Teams, 1 Division Chief Officer Command Team and a total of 92 Firefighters, all under the direction of Battalion Chief John Duca, responded to a Greater Alarm at 9797 North Glenoaks Boulevard in Sun Valley.

Even against the dark, night sky, a large plume of smoke could be seen enroute to the incident, indicating Firefighters were going to be engaged in a significant battle. First arriving companies confirmed a large outside fire at an auto salvage yard (DBA: Elite Auto). After making swift entry onto the property, Firefighters encountered additional concerns of not only downed power-lines, but also combustible metals, both of which present extreme hazards to personnel because of their volatility.

The command decision was quickly made to deploy large hose streams from both the ground and from aerial ladders in an effort to extinguish the stubborn blaze and to protect the adjacent occupancies from further damage. This large, outside fire burned so fiercely that two structures on the adjacent property (DBA: Elite Auto) sustained moderate damage.

Due to the strategic efforts of the command teams and an aggressive, sustained fire attack by nearly 100 Firefighters, the troops quickly gained the upper hand. The skillful firefight continued and the well-coordinated attack resulted in a knockdown in just over an hour.

The cause of the fire and its origin are under active investigation and the dollar loss is still being tabulated. There were no injuries.

Los Angeles Fire Department blog

Source: http://lafd.blogspot.com

on the web

Professional organizations, such as firefighters' unions and fire chiefs' associations, maintain their own websites. USfirefighters.net is a site by and for emergency responders that provides news categorized by state. Local, state and national fire associations also have sites. Some are listed at the end of the chapter.

Waiting Out the Incident After the initial rush of getting to the incident and reporting on the situation, you may find yourself waiting for the all clear. Fires move at their own pace. Some can be out in less than an hour. Others can take days to control. If it's a big fire that could spread to other buildings, you need to stay. Other situations are not so clear-cut. You have to balance your need to stay against the pressure to file your story. It's easier to stay if you have wireless capacity to file from the scene, or you can compromise and find a hotspot (Internet, not fire) near the scene where you can write and make calls while still monitoring the situation.

Writing the Story

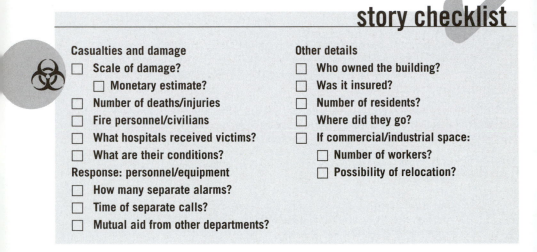

story checklist

Casualties and damage
- ☐ Scale of damage?
  - ☐ Monetary estimate?
- ☐ Number of deaths/injuries
- ☐ Fire personnel/civilians
- ☐ What hospitals received victims?
- ☐ What are their conditions?

Response: personnel/equipment
- ☐ How many separate alarms?
- ☐ Time of separate calls?
- ☐ Mutual aid from other departments?

Other details
- ☐ Who owned the building?
- ☐ Was it insured?
- ☐ Number of residents?
- ☐ Where did they go?
- ☐ If commercial/industrial space:
  - ☐ Number of workers?
  - ☐ Possibility of relocation?

Whether you stay or go, you will have to start filling in the corners of the story. Some of the questions grow in importance with the size of the incident. Here are the points all fire stories should include. Many apply to other emergency incidents.

Casualties and Damage Were there fatalities? Injuries? What was the damage? Is the building a total loss, or was the damage minor? Sometimes fire officials will make that assessment soon after the fire is out.

Who Owns the Building? Who occupies it? If information is not readily available, review tax and property records.

Was the Building Insured? Who held the policy, and when was it taken out? This information probably will have to wait for the follow-up story.

Was There a Sprinkler System? Also determine if there were smoke alarms. Did they work? Were they required? Such questions determine if there was a violation of regulations that could have led to more damage or loss of life.

Details About the Building and Occupants If it's a residence, how many people have been displaced? Where will they go? If the building housed one or more businesses, did they store flammable materials? How many employees will be out of work?

Follow-Up

Some important details won't be available immediately after the incident. Determining the causes and consequences of a fire or other emergency can take days. Here are some points to pursue for follow-up stories.

Cause The main question will be what caused the fire. The chief may have the answer, or witnesses may tell you what happened. Most fires are accidents that grow out of control. If no cause is obvious, arson investigators will be called. A ruling of arson makes for a bigger story, especially if there were fatalities or a significant financial loss.

Other Story Possibilities

Most fires and other emergency calls are unrelated events that carry little impact beyond the lives of those directly affected. Viewed as a group, however, they may have significance. Look for indications that a neighborhood is being plagued by a series of suspicious fires. How does the rate of fires compare with that of last year? You can also focus on a single incident. The story of one person badly burned in a fire, or of one family whose life is permanently changed, carries universal themes for your audience.

STORY SCAN: A FIRE STORY

Here's a breaking story that appeared on the Chicago Sun Times website that does a nice job of summarizing a complicated fire story.

Condo Fire Routes Hundreds of Disabled and Elderly Residents

The lede that handles facts beyond the who, what, where and why: the impact of the fire; in this case it is the fact that the residents included the elderly, disabled and college students.

Two women were hospitalized, hundreds were left on the streets, and others with physical ailments were tended to inside their homes following an extra-alarm electrical fire Sunday at a 200-unit downtown high-rise that houses elderly and disabled residents as well as college students.

Specifics of when and where — all attributed to a department spokesman. The reporter makes good use of the alarm sequence to describe the extent of the incident.

Emergency crews responded to the report of a fire about 12:15 a.m. at the 14-story building on the 170 block of West Oak Street, according to Fire Media Affairs Chief Kevin Mac-Gregor, who said the blaze was upgraded to a 4-11 alarm fire about 1 a.m. An EMS Plan 1 — which automatically sends five ambulances to the scene — was also called.

The flames were extinguished at 1:50 a.m. with at least 18 fire trucks and 120 firefighters and paramedics at the scene, MacGregor said. Initial reports indicated the fire began in several electrical vaults.

More details about the extent of the incident response. We also learn about a potential cause.

The 200-unit River North neighborhood building called Jenkins Hall is used for graduate and female undergraduates and married students at Moody Bible Institute. It is also Section 8 housing for elderly, disabled and low income residents, officials said.

Important details about the residents: The story carries slightly more significance because the elderly, disabled and college students lived in the building.

A thick cloud of smoke hung in the air early Sunday as fire crews attempted to ventilate the building and searched the building for other residents, careful not to kick in doors in case frail residents were still inside, officials said on scene.

Good descriptions help readers visualize the scene.

Some residents in wheelchairs, with canes or walkers, were escorted out of the building, although fire officials did not refer to these as rescues.

An 80 year-old woman suffering from exhaustion after climbing down multiple flights of stairs and an 85-year-old woman with shortness of breath were taken to Northwestern Memorial Hospital in fair condition, MacGregor said. No other injuries had been reported.

More details of injuries with the necessary attribution. Had the injuries been more severe, the information would be higher in the story.

The American Red Cross of Greater Chicago responded to the fire and assisted 99 senior citizens, as well as 65 students, according to Red Cross spokeswoman Martha Carlos.

Shelter for these residents was provided by Moody Bible Institute, but the Red Cross provided some breakfast, water, blankets, cleanup kits and toiletries for those affected by the blaze, Carlos said.

Follow-up details on the fate of the residents.

Liz Essex, 84, heard the alarms and, with a bad back and knees and using a walker, escaped through a side stairwell from her 10th floor apartment, she said.

"Me and a lot of other people came downstairs holding onto the railing," Essex said.

"Some are too sick to get out."

An eyewitness relates her story, adding a human dimension. It might be argued this could have gone higher in the story.

Austin Wilson, a senior communications major at Moody Bible Institute, and his wife Kendall, both 22, live on the 14th floor of the building and were in their apartment when they said they smelled smoke then heard an alarm.

The couple ran down 14 flights of stairs with Kendall still clad in pajama pants.

More eyewitness accounts. A quote here would have added to the anecdote.

Fire crews used Ansul extinguishers, which is a dry chemical to combat electrical fires.

Traffic was rerouted to accommodate the emergency response, police News Affairs Officer Ronald Gaines said.

The story ends with some lesser, but still important details.

Resources

Links

Fire and Emergency Facts and Resources

► National Fire Protection Association, www.nfpa.org

► National Wildfire Coordinating Group, www.nwcg.gov/pms/pubs/glossary/information.htm

- ▶ National Fire Incident Reporting System, http://nfirs.fema.gov
- ▶ U.S. Fire Administration, www.usfa.dhs.gov/index.shtm

Journalism Sites

- ▶ Committee to Protect Journalists, Journalists Safety Guide, http://cpj.org/reports/2003/02/journalist-safety-guide.php
- ▶ Dart Center for Journalism and Trauma, http://dartcenter.org
- ▶ International Journalists Network crisis reporting toolkit and downloadable booklet on crisis coverage, http://ijnet.org
- ▶ International News Safety Institute, http://newssafety.org
- ▶ Investigative Reporters and Editors storm and disaster resources, www.ire.org/inthe news_archive/hurricane.html
- ▶ Knight Digital Media Center, www.knightdigitalmediacenter.org/news_blog/comments/20100209_covering_disasters_trauma_new_resources_for_journalists

Professional Organizations and Blogs

- ▶ International Association of Firefighters, http://www.iaff.org
- ▶ International Association of Fire Chiefs, http://www.iafc.org
- ▶ The IAFC also maintains the related Volunteer and Combined Officer Section website for personnel at volunteer departments, www.vcos.org
- ▶ National Association of Emergency Medical Technicians, www.naemt.org
- ▶ International Association of EMTs and Paramedics, www.iaep.org
- ▶ National Emergency Management Association, www.nemaweb.org
- ▶ International Association of Emergency Managers, www.iaem.com
- ▶ U.S. First Responders Association, www.usfra.org

Weather Coverage

- ▶ Accuweather, www.accuweather.com
- ▶ American Meteorological Society, http://www.ametsoc.org
- ▶ National Oceanic and Atmospheric Administration, http://noaa.gov

Assignment Desk

See how your department stacks up against national norms. Does it have more or fewer personnel per capita than the average department? More or less equipment? How does the number of fire calls compare with the national number?

Sidebar Use this comparison of local and national data to write a story. Get comments from local officials and someone with a national organization to add perspective on the subject. That might be the U.S. Fire Administration or the International Association of Fire Chiefs or other fire protection and professional organizations.

CHAPTER 7

COURTS

Covering the courts is one of the most important duties in journalism. The framers of the Constitution believed an open justice system was essential for a free society, and they saw a free, unfettered press as the public's eyes and ears in court proceedings. This journalistic responsibility goes beyond the sensational murder cases or the celebrity trials of athletes, politicians and actors. The daily business of the district and municipal courts needs to be watched to keep the judicial system honest and to assure people that their rights are protected.

But don't let all this talk of weighty responsibility overshadow an important fact about the court beat: It can be tremendous fun. Every kind of human drama — and occasional comedy — plays out in testimony, evidence and the dry language found in affidavits and other filings. A domestic violence case contains elements of a love story gone wrong. A malpractice suit offers insights into how routine childbirth can spin horribly out of control. The arraignment of a would-be burglar turns into a comic tale when police testify how he got stuck in the chimney of a pizzeria. A sharp eye and deft touch can turn such material into memorable stories.

Linda Deutsch, The Associated Press' top trial reporter, originally wanted to write about the entertainment industry. Instead, she wound up covering more than three decades of high-profile cases from the

from the beat

Linda Deutsch
Associated Press trial reporter

AP's Linda Deutsch addresses fellow reporters after acting as pool reporter for a jury tour of a murder scene.

Linda Deutsch will always take the time to help a reporter new to the court beat.

That may be because of an experience she had as a young AP reporter helping with a trial in federal court. She had just come into the courtroom and sat listening while the lawyers discussed a motion regarding mandamus.

"I turned to the reporter next to me and said, 'Who's Mandamus?'" The reporter patiently explained that mandamus was not a person, but rather Latin for "We command," referring to a court order that compels a lower court or a government officer to perform mandatory duties, such as providing information specific to the case.

That was Lesson No. 1 for Deutsch: "You can't be afraid to ask stupid questions."

Deutsch has no secret formula for success, just hard work, perseverance and the willingness to ask about what she doesn't understand. Here are some of her suggestions for reporters starting out on the court beat.

▶ **Ask your fellow reporters.**

"Trial coverage is not so hugely competitive. There is rarely a scoop in the courtroom," she says. For that reason, journalists reporting on a trial often cooperate, sharing notes on testimony or quotes from news conferences. "You can't be everywhere in the building at once. You have to be able to go to your colleagues."

▶ **Ask the court clerks.**

"You need to know the clerks of the judge," she says. "They can help you learn about how the filing system works, where documents are and how you get them."

▶ **Ask the lawyers.**

When Deutsch was assigned to cover the criminal case against the captain blamed for the massive 1988 Exxon Valdez oil tanker spill in the Gulf of Alaska, the first thing she did was find his lawyer. "I told him I don't know anything about maritime law," she says. "He was so excited to have someone interested in his specialty that he sat me down and explained everything. Lawyers want you to understand what's going on. It's to their advantage."

Charles Manson murder spree and the O.J. Simpson murder trials to the death of Michael Jackson. Deutsch says movies and other fictional versions of trials don't compare to what she has encountered in courtrooms.

"The real thing is so much more interesting than the imitations of justice you see on the screen," she says. "You know you are writing about real people and you know something is going to happen to them — and that something horrible has happened to get them into court."

Writing a trial story that is fair, accurate and interesting is challenge enough. Now reporters face the added task of blogging live from the courtroom. These blogs create a virtual spectators' gallery where participants can follow the trial, comment, lament, question and vent in real time. Trish Mehaffey, a court and crime reporter for The Gazette of Cedar Rapids, Iowa, blogs about cases as they unfold before her in court. In addition to her real-time reporting, Mehaffey moderates an online community of interested citizens, gavel groupies and lawyers who contribute to the trial's running commentary.

"For me it's proof that this way of covering trials is working and that I am creating a community," Mehaffey says. "It really becomes an educational tool for all of us."

This virtual courtroom community can be seen as an extension of the openness the Constitution's authors had in mind; they would be happy with the way new media allows for more public participation. If Thomas Jefferson and John Adams were here today, they'd be blogging about it.

COURT BEAT ▶ People

The court system has many players, from the courthouse employees to the lawyers, defendants, plaintiffs, victims and families. You will encounter them when covering a trial or making your rounds. Getting to know who they are and understanding that each has a particular point of view are essential to covering your beat.

Lawyers

Lawyers have different specialties, many that rarely involve stepping inside a courthouse. Reporters on the court beat deal mostly with litigators, the lawyers who present cases in court. Litigators include lawyers who represent plaintiffs and defendants in civil cases, but you'll probably spend more time with the defense attorneys and prosecutors who face each other in criminal cases.

Some lawyers specialize in criminal law; others are generalists who take on various types of clients, including criminal defendants. Law firms volunteer attorneys for pro bono work in criminal cases; states also have public defender offices that provide legal counsel to defendants who can't afford to pay a lawyer. Public defenders either work directly for a government public defender's office or as private attorneys paid by the government. The state provides these services under the 1963 decision Gideon v. Wainwright, in which the Supreme Court ruled that the Constitution's Sixth Amendment requires all criminal defendants have adequate legal representation.

Prosecuting attorneys represent the government in criminal cases. Prosecutors who work in state courts carry different titles, ranging from attorney general — the state's top prosecutor — to state's attorney, district attorney, county attorney and county prosecutor. Prosecutors' offices usually cover geographic divisions, often by county. In most states the office is headed by an elected official who hires other lawyers to serve as assistants (assistant district attorney, assistant state's attorney). In some places specially trained police officers serve as prosecutors in local courts.

The federal government is represented by United States attorneys. The nation is divided into 93 United States attorney districts in the 50 states plus the Virgin Islands, Guam and the Northern Mariana Islands. U.S. attorneys are appointed by the president with the approval of the Senate, and they serve as the top federal law enforcement officer in their jurisdiction. These officials supervise lawyers, investigators and other staff who pursue criminal and civil cases for the federal government.

Whatever their title, lawyers have at least one thing in common: They are *advocates*. That means their job is to represent the interests of their clients. You may develop a good relationship with a defense lawyer or prosecutor, but never consider them your friends, and never assume that what they say is the uncontested truth.

Anything a lawyer says about a case is for the benefit of the people and institutions the lawyer represents. Remember this when you think your winning personality or great journalistic skill has wrested some secret from a lawyer.

Some lawyers, such as Harland Braun, talk to reporters to present their side in the so-called "court of public opinion." Media coverage can boost a lawyer's public profile. For private attorneys that means more business. For prosecutors it can mean job security and perhaps a launching pad for higher office. For some it is the simple pleasure of celebrity.

But don't expect lawyers to talk with you all the time. In certain situations lawyers may consider silence the safest way to hide their strategy from the other side; others are reticent because they've been burned by a reporter who got something wrong. Whatever is behind the silence, you must continue to reach out to these lawyers. Make the simple case that you want to write a balanced story and — an important point — that you want to make sure you don't say something factually wrong that would hurt their client.

Sometimes lawyers are ordered not to talk. Judges can issue a gag order prohibiting both sides from commenting about a case. This usually is done to limit information before a jury is chosen or to cool public emotions in a highly sensational case. A lawyer could face a contempt of court citation for blabbing. In these situations, lawyers may offer to talk to you if you agree not to attribute the information to them. Although courts can't constrain you from publishing what you've learned, the judge may want you to identify your source.

Harland Braun
Defense Attorney

Defense lawyer Harland Braun isn't shy about using the media to sell a client's case. The tactic has served him well defending actors, politicians and police in high-profile trials. Braun knows that reporters need to find a focus for stories about complicated, sensational cases. He's only too happy to offer that focus.

"You don't want to give the press a chance to choose the story," Braun says. "You want to set up the story that serves your client best."

When he represented actor Robert Blake, the star of the old television detective show Baretta, who was charged with killing his wife, Braun portrayed the victim as a bad person who had angered many people.

"We spent a year before the trial convincing the public that his wife deserved to die," says Braun. "The idea was to impress the public that there were a lot of people out there that wanted to kill her."

Braun dropped out of the case before Blake was acquitted. The actor was later found liable for the death in a civil case.

Braun believes that prosecutors also use reporters. The difference, he says, is a matter of subtlety. Because prosecutors represent the government, they can't appear to seek the spotlight. They work behind the scenes, going off the record to direct reporters to evidence and legal filings that support their position. Defense attorneys can be more straightforward, calling news conferences to spin the case.

"To say you're not going to try a case in the press is like saying you're not going to show up the first day of trial, because the trial starts the first day the prosecution starts leaking evidence," Braun says.

Although Braun returns all reporters' calls ("They don't like to be ignored, and I may need them later"), he is selective about the order of callbacks. The first calls go to news organizations with the largest audiences. Then he calls reporters who ask smart, informed questions.

"One of the most aggravating things for me is to have to deal with reporters who have no idea about what the facts are," he says.

This situation requires some judgment on your part. Is the information you've been given off the record crucial enough to risk your own contempt of court citation for refusing to say where you got it? And, perhaps more importantly, are you sure that this whispered information isn't merely a ploy by the lawyer to spin public perception of the case?

In many instances, you'll need to speak with lawyers outside the case to get a neutral opinion on the issues, progress and tactics of a trial. Other times you'll want a lawyer's help to interpret a judge's ruling. Develop a short list of attorneys you trust for quick deadline consultations. But don't rely on them exclusively. Seek out lawyers who specialize in the area of law in question. Talk to a criminal lawyer about a murder trial; find a family law specialist to comment about a divorce or child custody case.

You can find the right attorney by asking your local bar association for the name of an expert. Another good resource is Martindale-Hubbell's website (www.martindale.com), which provides a directory of attorneys from around the country, including their age, education and contact information. Many state bar association websites list lawyers by specialty.

Academics

Law professors are another source for legal comment. They can be helpful in interpreting issues of law and putting the case you're covering into a larger context. Again, talk to a professor who specializes in the type of law relevant to the case. Most law schools publish online source lists to help you find the right professor. Or call the school's public relations staff to speed the process.

Judges

Judges have different titles — municipal, district, appeals and so forth — that speak to their roles and stature. Some states elect judges; others appoint them. Some judges run their courtrooms with an iron fist; others are easygoing and quotable. All judges have one thing in common: They won't talk to you about the case over which they're presiding. This is not a personal choice. The canons of ethics prohibit judges from speaking about their trials. Elected judges may bend the rules a bit because they want to remain in the voters' eyes. Appointed judges, especially those appointed for life, will be less responsive.

Some judges have duties outside the courtroom. Chief judges serve as administrators, supervising the operation of the court and its employees. They hire and fire. They oversee large budgets and lobby to get more money from the state to run their courts. These issues can provide rich material for courthouse reporters.

It's important to make contact with the judges who figure in your story or beat. There are different ways of reaching out. You can do a profile on the judge or interview her about some aspect of her background or her court that doesn't involve the case at hand. At the very least you should ask for a few minutes to introduce yourself. A face-to-face moment with a judge helps him see you as a responsible professional who cares about your work.

This rule applies to the judge's secretary and clerk. Getting to know them often helps speed their response to a question you might have on an issue.

Court Personnel

Perhaps your most important relationship will be with the court clerks. They are the gate-keepers, schedulers and institutional memory of the courts. All suits, motions, affidavits and other important paperwork come through their offices. Clerks can make your job easier. They can dig out files related to a case, tip you to new filings and draw on their long experience to lend perspective to a story. But clerks who don't know or like you can make life much tougher. They make you jump through bureaucratic hoops by requiring that you request files by case number, a procedure that takes precious time. They can be sticklers for procedure, leaving out important documents if you fail to make a specific request. So it is important to be on good terms with the clerks. *Don't* demand special treatment. *Do* thank them for everything they do for you. If you need to find documents that require some searching, show you are aware of what you're asking for and explain why it's important.

Also take time to establish good relations with the bailiffs and other court officers who act as traffic cops in the courthouse and the courtroom. It will make your life easier, especially when you have to go in and out of courtrooms. The bailiffs and officers will understand you are just doing your job and will generally try to accommodate you, especially if you become a familiar figure.

COURT BEAT ▶ Places

courthouse checklist

- [ ] Learn where the various courthouses are and what jurisdictions they cover.
- [ ] Learn security rules about banned items such as recorders and cameras.
- [ ] Know the specific name of the office you're visiting.
- [ ] Make regular contact with the administrative judge, the court clerk and the clerk's staff.

The first task for a court reporter is to understand the geography of the beat. State courts are usually arranged under county or administrative districts. That often means various courts (district, superior, and so on) are in the same building. Federal courts are housed separately. Make sure you understand which court handles the different cases you'll be covering. Then visit them all.

Navigating the Courthouse

Your first stop at the courthouse will be security. Court proceedings generate anger and passion, so the public must go through metal detectors and searches. If you are on a regular beat, it may be possible to get an identification card that allows the guards to wave you through. Check with the administrative judge's office, or the bailiff's office.

Learn the rules about bringing in cameras, audio recorders, laptops and even cell phones. Federal rules generally prohibit any electronics in the courthouse. You may have to check your devices at the door. Individual judges make distinctions; a growing number allow reporters to blog from the courtroom. State court rules vary. Many states grant judges broad discretion in deciding what they will allow in their courtrooms. Other states put restrictions based on the kind of case being heard. At this writing Alabama requires all parties to a case to consent to electronic coverage. Alaska and Virginia bar recording devices in sexual assault cases. The Radio Television Digital News Association offers a listing of the state-by-state rules on its website: www.rtdna.org/pages/media_items/cameras-in-the-court-a-state-by-state-guide55.php?g=45%3fid=55.

Because these rules are in constant flux, it's best for you to always ask what you can and can't bring before you leave for court.

Familiarize yourself with the courthouse layout. A single courthouse may be home to both the district and superior courts clerks. You'll need to figure out the location and hours of the different offices. Make your questions specific: don't just ask for "the clerk's office"; include the court name and the name of the judge in your query.

Making the Rounds

Covering trials is only a small part of the court beat. The day-to-day mission is to report on what's happening within the courts. Someone — a plaintiff, prosecutor or defense lawyer — may announce a new and newsworthy lawsuit, a criminal charge or some new action in a case. A judge may issue a long-awaited ruling. The sources you've spent time cultivating may tip you to a filing made without fanfare. The message here is don't sit and wait for the news to come to you. You've got to go find it.

A successful courts reporter does a lot of walking, talking and listening. Poke your head in the clerk and administrator's offices. Catch the corridor conversations with lawyers and prosecutors, the court officers and secretaries. You don't have to do this daily; make your rounds every couple of days once you figure out the rhythm of the courthouse.

STATE AND FEDERAL COURTS

THE FEDERAL GOVERNMENT AND THE STATES have separate but parallel legal systems. Cases under federal jurisdiction involve laws passed by Congress and regulations created by the executive branch under the authority of the president. State courts have jurisdiction over laws passed by the state legislature and regulations created under the governor's administration. Most criminal violations are tried in state courts, although criminal convictions can be appealed to federal courts if there is a constitutional issue involved.

States organize their courts in different ways. Names and terms may be different (for example, New York trial courts are called supreme courts, while the high court is the court of appeals); most states have a high court, an appellate division and district courts. Many states also have a municipal court system that handles a bulk of minor civil and criminal offenses such as traffic violations within city jurisdictions.

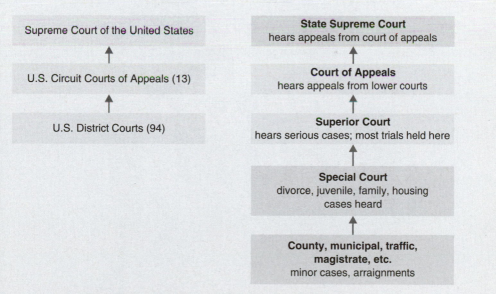

Figure 7.1   The Federal Court System, The State Court System

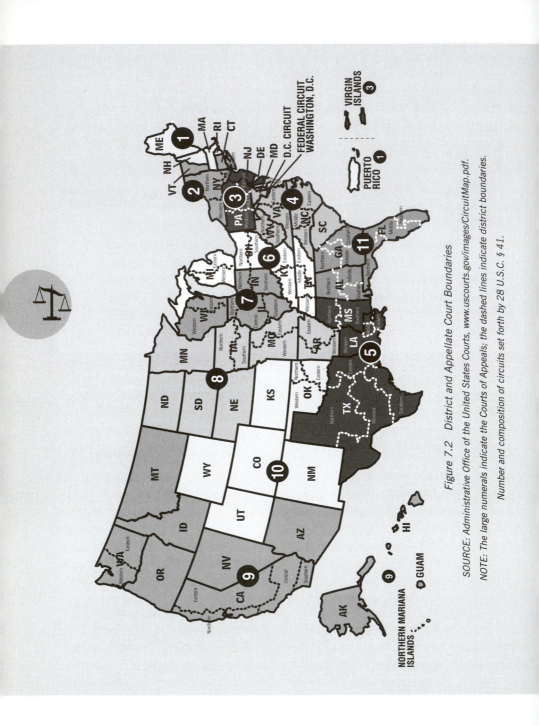

Figure 7.2   District and Appellate Court Boundaries

SOURCE: Administrative Office of the United States Courts, www.uscourts.gov/images/CircuitMap.pdf.

NOTE: The large numerals indicate the Courts of Appeals; the dashed lines indicate district boundaries.

Number and composition of circuits set forth by 28 U.S.C. § 41.

Special state and municipal courts handle issues such as small claims, bankruptcy, and housing. There are family courts and juvenile courts. Probate courts preside over estates, trusts and wills. States and cities are creating a new range of specialized courts to relieve the caseload on traditional courts. These new courts (also called problem-solving courts) focus on such areas as domestic violence, drug offenses and mental health. West Virginia has a homeless court; Dallas and Houston have veterans' courts.

Federal criminal cases cover charges such as kidnapping, bank robbery, flight across state lines and crimes on federal lands, such as military bases and Indian reservations. Federal courts have jurisdiction over crimes that cross state boundaries, kidnapping, criminal organizations, drug trafficking and tax and financial securities violations.

Federal civil cases involve companies and individuals from one state suing someone in another state over financial issues. If Company A of Wisconsin is suing Company B of California, they will go to federal court if the financial damages at stake exceed a federally established minimum. Both federal criminal and civil cases start in one of the 94 U.S. District Courts. Cases can be appealed to one of 12 U.S. Circuit Courts of Appeals that have jurisdiction over geographic regions. A 13th court of appeals in Washington, D.C., handles cases that fall under national jurisdiction, usually issues involving the government. The appeal process does not consider the facts of a case. Rather, these panels look solely at issues of law, previous rulings and court procedure.

The U.S. Supreme Court uses the same criteria in considering appeals. The Supreme Court also takes appeals of certain state court decisions. The nine Supreme Court justices consider only a fraction of the appeals, choosing cases that raise significant questions of statutory or constitutional law.

The Clerk's Office Start your rounds with the clerk's office. Ask if anything new or interesting has been filed, and browse the documents of pending cases. Ask for files by name, for example, "Can I see what's new in the Simpson case?" If the case is more obscure or if the clerk's office is less than cooperative, you'll be asked for the case number. You can find it online or look it up on the docket at the clerk's counter. Searching for a case number can sometimes be frustrating if each filing in one case is given a separate number. Don't be afraid to ask the clerks for help, even if they seem unwilling. They are paid to serve the public, and you are there as the public's representative.

Judges, Lawyers and Others Your rounds should include a stop at the top administrative judge's office. Check with the staff to see if any general orders have been issued to the other judges or court officers. If you can, stick your head in the judge's office to say hello, or make an occasional appointment to discuss court issues. Polite persistence in your courthouse rounds helps you develop important relationships.

Although lawyers have offices outside the courthouse, you're likely to run into many of them in the building's corridors and cafeteria. Don't hesitate to start a conversation, even about something as trivial as the weather or last night's game. Chat up the court officers; listen for hallway gossip. By making the rounds, you become a familiar, reliable face. That can pay big dividends if the courthouse crowd sees you as a conduit to the public.

COURT BEAT ▶ Documents

Nothing official happens in a courthouse without paperwork. Orders are written, warrants and decisions are issued, affidavits and pleas are filed. All these actions generate a stream of paper that, with very few exceptions, is available to members of the public and the media. It used to be harder to find these documents. You would have to wait in line at the clerk's office and hope you had the right information to hunt through the numerous files. But with more and more documents available online, citizens and their reporter representatives no longer have to wait.

Covering a case does not mean simply covering the trial; the trial is the last step in a long succession of legal maneuverings. You'll need the documents to follow that action. The criminal case document trail begins with police reports, filings of charges and evidentiary materials. Various motions are made to the court by prosecution and defense lawyers before the trial. Civil cases begin with a written complaint, writ or petition by the plaintiff. The defendant usually responds with his or her own filing. What follows is a blizzard of paper that can include company records, depositions and legal arguments based on rulings of earlier cases. This volley of motion and countermotion can last years. Much of it is procedural and doesn't warrant a story.

Where to Find the Documents

Unless a judge rules otherwise, all documents in a case are public record. You simply have to find them. Many states offer databases of rulings, pleas and other filings that can be searched by such Boolean connectors as *and, or,* along with names of the defendants and plaintiffs, the lawyers and the issues of the case. An example: if you're looking for documents relating to a case in which Sam Jones is charged with fraud, you would type: "Jones" *and* "fraud" *and* "district court." As search systems become more sophisticated,

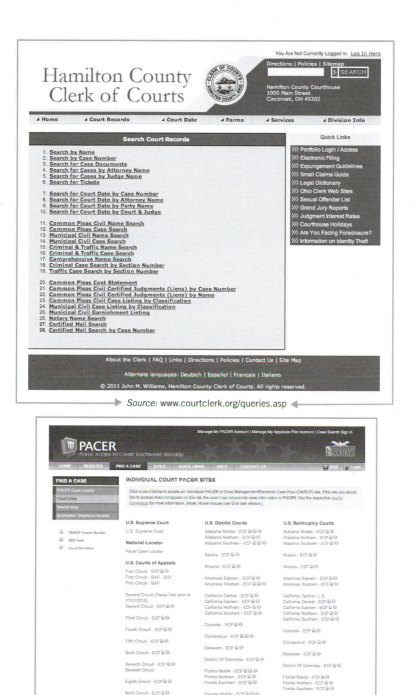

Source: www.courtclerk.org/queries.asp

Source: www.pacer.gov/psco/cgi-bin/links.pl

you may not need the connectors. Most websites offer instructions on how to search. You can also search these databases by docket number. Some courts have made it even easier to find a case. For example, look on page 131 to see a website from Hamilton County, Ohio. You can see the website offers various ways of searching for a case, from the name of the defendant, the case number, the lawyers in the case and the judge's name.

Documents within the federal system can be found on the PACER federal website (see page 131).

As you can see, a national cache of legal documents is at your fingertips. PACER and some state and county sites require you to apply for a login; some charge fees. Check with the court administrator if you have a question about accessing material.

Another advantage of online records is the ability to share them with your audience. Providing links to the document gives your audience the option of going deeper into a story. If the defense files a 10-page affidavit arguing against the inclusion of a videotape confession that you can only summarize in a story, put a link to the entire document in your story, giving readers the choice to read further. Keep a link to all the documents relevant to a case on your news organization's website, with a brief description of each filing. If only paper records are available, scan them in.

A warning: it can take days for a document to appear online. Don't expect a search will find everything filed that day. Checking with the clerk is always your best bet. Despite the convenience of the Internet, it's still important to spend face time in the clerk's office. The staff knows more about what's going on than will ever appear on your computer screen.

Following the Courts Online In addition to posting documents online, some courts have their own blogs that include trial schedules, postings of recent rulings and chatty pieces about courthouse changes and new employees — and in some cases, profiles of new employees.

Here's one from Clark County, Nevada, the jurisdiction for Las Vegas, on page 133.

Some courts maintain Twitter accounts; if you sign up to "follow" a court's Twitter feed (such as http://twitter.com/illinoiscourts), you'll be instantly informed about new rulings or calendar postings. Other states, such as Missouri, will e-mail or phone interested parties when new material is filed in a case.

Courts are also covered by a variety of other bloggers, from attorney associations to individuals with an interest in, and sometimes a grudge against, the court system. The nonprofit blog watching Washington state courts carries the slogan "*reading the opinions so you don't have to.*" These sites are excellent sources for documents, background and story ideas. But remember that any blog is only a starting point. Confirm whatever you see on the Web with the court — especially if the blog belongs to an individual or group with a strong point of view.

Source: http://clakcoutycourts.us

Source: www.courts.mo.gov/casenet/cases/charges.do

Source: www.wasupremecourtblog.com

How to Use the Documents

Court documents may seem imposing at first glance, but after you read a couple, you'll see they are fairly easy to figure out. This simple divorce petition filed by pop star Britney Spears, for example, offers several bits of useful information. The petition lists the date of filing, the name of Spears' attorney and some details of the couple's separation and property. These details open the door to other lines of inquiry. Perhaps the most important detail is the case number — the key to finding subsequent documents.

Most court filings are much longer than a one-page petition. Despite the size and formal language, they're usually straightforward and can make for riveting reading. Filings, especially a judge's ruling, include a case summary followed by the facts and legal precedents regarding the case. The summary provides immediate details of a ruling; this is what you can quickly put on your website after reading the first few pages. You can use more details for later versions of your story.

If you are unsure about anything in a document, don't guess. Take the time to find a lawyer who can interpret the legalese. Seek out a member of the local bar or one of the

ATTORNEY OR PARTY WITHOUT ATTORNEY (Name, State Bar number and address):
Laura A. Wasser, Esq. (SBN 173740)
WASSER, COOPERMAN & CARTER
Professional Corporation
2029 Century Park East, Suite 1200
Los Angeles, CA 90067-2905
TELEPHONE NO.: (310)277-7117   FAX NO. (Optional):
E-MAIL ADDRESS (Optional):
ATTORNEY FOR (Name): Britney Spears

FILED
LOS ANGELES SUPERIOR COURT
NOV 07 2005
JOHN A. CLARKE, CLERK
BY ___ PADILLA, DEPUTY

SUPERIOR COURT OF CALIFORNIA, COUNTY OF LOS ANGELES
STREET ADDRESS 111 North Hill Street
MAILING ADDRESS 111 North Hill Street
CITY AND ZIP CODE Los Angeles, CA 90012
BRANCH NAME CENTRAL DISTRICT

MARRIAGE OF
PETITIONER: BRITNEY SPEARS
RESPONDENT: KEVIN FEDERLINE

PETITION FOR
[X] Dissolution of Marriage
[ ] Legal Separation
[ ] Nullity of Marriage
[ ] AMENDED

CASE NUMBER: BD455662
*Case being assigned to Judge Gordon

1. RESIDENCE (Dissolution only) [X] Petitioner [ ] Respondent has been a resident of this state for at least six months and of this county for at least three months immediately preceding the filing of this Petition for Dissolution of Marriage.

2. STATISTICAL FACTS
   a. Date of marriage: 10/6/04
   b. Date of separation: 11/6/06
   c. Time from date of marriage to date of separation (specify):
      Years: 2   Months: 1

3. DECLARATION REGARDING MINOR CHILDREN (include children of this relationship born prior to or during the marriage or adopted during the marriage):
   a. [ ] There are no minor children.
   b. [X] The minor children are:

Child's name	Birthdate	Age	Sex
Sean Preston Federline	9/14/05	13 months	M
Jayden James Federline	9/12/06	8 weeks	M

   [ ] Continued on Attachment 3b.
   c. If there are minor children of the Petitioner and Respondent, a completed Declaration Under Uniform Child Custody Jurisdiction and Enforcement Act (UCCJEA) (form FL-105) must be attached.
   d. [ ] A completed voluntary declaration of paternity regarding minor children born to the Petitioner and Respondent prior to the marriage is attached.

4. SEPARATE PROPERTY
   Petitioner requests that the assets and debts listed [ ] in Property Declaration (form FL-160) [ ] in Attachment 4
   [X] below   be confirmed as separate property.
      Item   Confirm to
   a) Miscellaneous jewelry and other personal effects   Petitioner
   b) Earnings and accumulations of Petitioner from and after the   Petitioner
      date of separation
   c) There are additional separate property assets and obligations
      of the parties, the exact nature and extent of which are not
      presently known.

NOTICE: You may redact (black out) social security numbers from any written material filed with the court in this case other than a form used to collect child or spousal support.

PETITION—MARRIAGE
(Family Law)

---

attorneys involved in the case. Remember, it is more important to get it right than get it first, as one cable television reporter learned when he tried to interpret the U.S. Supreme Court ruling on the 2000 presidential election recount in Florida. Thumbing through the lengthy ruling on air in real time, the reporter first said the ruling was in favor of Democrat Al Gore. He was wrong — the court had decided for George W. Bush — and the reporter spent many embarrassing minutes fumbling with a correction.

Sealed Records

Sometimes judges will seal the records of a case. Reasons vary. It might be done to protect the privacy of the accused or accuser. If a case is settled out of court, both parties may make the sealing of the records part of the agreement to avoid publicity

READING A DECISION

THE EXCERPTS BELOW COME FROM A 41-PAGE Florida Supreme Court ruling reversing the death sentence of Victor Caraballo, who was convicted of murder. In the first page, under the heading Overview, the court wrote:

" ... *Caraballo was convicted of the 2002 first-degree murder, kidnapping, robbery and sexual battery of Ana Maria Angel. . . . because of error that occurred in the penalty phase we reverse Caraballo's death sentence and remand his case to the trial court for a new penalty phase.*"

That is the lede: the court has reversed the death sentence. You can send out a quick story with this flash, noting that the case will now go back to a lower court for a new penalty hearing. The ruling then goes on to detail the facts of the crime, the investigation and the trial. The reason for the court's ruling — the defense's contention that the jury should not have been allowed to hear a doctor's testimony about the defendant's mental capacity — is detailed in the final third of the document. After explaining legal precedents and Florida statute, the court notes on page 38 why it has thrown out the death sentence.

"*Thus, the admission of Dr. Garcia's testimony interfered with the jury's ability to conduct a proper evaluation. . . . Consequently, there is at a minimum a reasonable possibility that the admission of Dr. Garcia's testimony, which attacked the credibility of evidence offered by Caraballo as mitigation, affected the jury's determination of whether it should recommend a sentence of life imprisonment or death. Therefore, the error was harmful.*"

This reasoning would be high up in your story, right after you offer some details of the case.

Source: www.floridasupremecourt.org/decisions/2010/sc07-1375.pdf

and embarrassment. Whatever the motivation, we, as journalists, generally oppose such actions in our role as agents of the people and their right to know.

If a judge seals the records, consider challenging the decision using your state's public records laws or, for federal courts, the Freedom of Information Act. The Society of Professional Journalists is a strong advocate for open records. The society's website, www.spj.org/opendoors.asp, can be of great help in figuring out laws and strategies.

If a judge orders records to be sealed or, in rarer instances, orders the public out of a courtroom during the sensitive testimony of a child or some other witness, you should politely make your objections known, then seek out a First Amendment attorney versed in

Michael Rezendes
Boston Globe

Boston Globe Spotlight reporter Michael Rezendes had spent six weeks developing a relationship with the lawyer representing Geoghan's victims. When the Globe went to court to unseal the records, the lawyer gave Rezendes an important tip.

"He saw we were serious about pursing the story, so he told me there was a way to get some of the information without waiting for the court to decide on our petition," Rezendes said.

The lawyer had found a way to legally slip excerpts of the archdiocese's records, which showed that church officials were aware of Geoghan's abuse, into the lawsuit's public files. Rezendes looked for the excerpts. And looked. After three searches, he determined the material was missing. The Globe's lawyers quietly won an order requiring the church to refile the documents. Those excerpts from the church's Geoghan files formed the backbone of the first story in the Globe series, which ran on Jan. 6, 2002.

As the newspaper's investigative team worked on those files, the plaintiffs' lawyer received Geoghan's psychological records from the archdiocese and decided to file them immediately. But that created a problem: Once the documents were filed, competing media outlets would also have access to them. So Rezendes arranged for the plaintiffs' lawyer to file the documents late on a Friday afternoon. Rezendes would copy the files just before the court closed, spend the weekend poring over them with the Spotlight team, which would then write a second story, to be published Monday, Jan. 7, before any other reporter was aware of the files.

It wasn't that easy. When Rezendes went to get the files, the clerk refused to release them; she was unaware of the ruling putting them in the public record. The clerk insisted on getting a judge's approval. As the clock ticked toward the end of the day, Rezendes and a fellow reporter went with the clerk to consult with a judge, who balked at releasing them. Finally, Rezendes had the ruling faxed to the judge, who then relented.

Rezendes dashed to the courthouse copying room shortly before the 5 p.m. closing to find the copy room clerk with her coat on. "It will have to wait till Monday," she said.

"I thought the top of my head was going to blow off," Rezendes recalls.

Rezendes maintained his cool. He begged. He pleaded. He thinks he may have gotten on his knees. "I've seen other reporters yell at bureaucrats and try to assert their authority. I never, never do that," he says. "You get more with honey and respect."

The woman took off her coat and helped Rezendes and his colleague make copies. The story was published on Monday, the second in the long series of stories that resulted in the resignation of Boston's cardinal, a multimillion-dollar settlement with abuse victims and a national reaction to clergy abuse that caused major changes in church policy.

Rezendes says the episode illustrates the importance of sources and records. "I would have never gotten the documents if I hadn't established the relationship with the lawyer," he says. "I also believe you have to be very, very persistent in looking for documents."

open records and open court law. Your news organization may have one on retainer. You can also seek help from the local civil liberties organization. Often, a judge will relent when faced with such a challenge or be overruled by an appeals court.

A case in point is The Boston Globe's coverage of the sexual abuse scandal within the Boston Catholic Archdiocese (see page 137). After the courts sealed the records in 86 civil cases brought by victims of the Rev. John J. Geoghan, the Globe's editor, Martin Baron, pushed to have the files opened while his reporters pursued other means of unearthing information about the abuses committed by Geoghan and other priests. The Globe prevailed; the Geoghan files were opened, setting a precedent that triggered the release of records on other priests accused of sexually abusing minors. The stories of those priests led to the resignation of Cardinal Bernard Law and a $30 million settlement with more than 500 victims. The case encouraged victims in other states and countries to come forward. The Globe won a well-deserved Pulitzer Prize.

COURT BEAT ▶ Stories

Think of possible story ideas as you make your rounds. Judicial appointments or elections make for important stories about who is sitting on the bench. Most courts are overworked and underfunded, which means you can find stories about the backlog of cases and the impact on those awaiting justice. Look for trends. Have the number of plea bargains increased? Are judges increasing jail time and fines in violent crimes but cutting back punishment in victimless crimes such as drug possession?

Although the day-to-day of the courthouse routine will take up much of your time, covering trials will challenge and engage you the most. Trials are dynamic, complicated stories written on deadline. They will also be the stories you will be most judged by.

Covering Trials: Preliminary Stages

A trial story doesn't begin with the first day of testimony. Many steps take place before a case goes to trial. Each of these steps should be followed; information about an important case often comes out at these hearings and court filings. What follows is the usual sequence for criminal trials.

Arraignment Hearing A defendant, represented by counsel, is officially charged before a judge and enters a plea. The judge also determines bail. The judge at arraignment is not likely to be the one who presides over the case. The arraignment is often the public's first glimpse of the accused — either standing in the courtroom or making the "perp walk" into the courthouse.

CIVIL AND CRIMINAL CASES

LEGAL CASES ARE DIVIDED into two separate types: civil and criminal. The cases proceed along parallel lines, but with some major differences.

Civil cases are brought by plaintiffs, the term for an individual, group or business with a financial grievance against another party. The party being sued is the defendant. In some cases the person filing the complaint is called the petitioner; the defendant is called the respondent.

In civil cases companies sue other companies over contract disputes. Individuals sue over financial damages or personal injuries, as in a medical malpractice case. The government brings action against individuals and businesses accused of violating civil laws and regulations. The government or specific officials can be plaintiffs or defendants.

Cases involving high-profile names or issues of public interest, such as lawsuits against tobacco companies, attract the most attention. These cases are often announced by the plaintiffs. But checking civil court filings can reveal significant stories lurking in the files. One charge of malpractice against a hospital may not be a big deal; a number of similar suits filed over time can indicate a problem with patient care.

Civil cases can take years to go to trial with a long sequence of motions and discovery requests. The two sides may fight over the admissibility of evidence. After all that maneuvering, civil cases are often settled out of court. If there is a court verdict, the losing side can appeal to a higher court.

Criminal cases are brought by government prosecutors against individuals accused of causing violent harm (assault, battery, rape, robbery, manslaughter, murder) or financial injury (extortion, burglary, fraud). Punishment can include jail and fines. Many cases never go to trial; in a plea bargain the defendant pleads guilty to a lesser charge to avoid a harsher sentence.

Criminal trials are preceded by a series of pretrial steps that can include arraignment, preliminary hearings and grand jury sessions. Most cases are tried within days, but more serious charges such as murder can take months of preparation.

Some criminal cases continue after the verdict. Defendants can appeal their conviction by raising legal issues about their case. If the appeals court decides the conviction was flawed, it can order a new trial or send the case back to the trial court to review the sentence. The prosecution cannot appeal if the defendant is found not guilty. The Constitution's double jeopardy clause protects against repeated prosecution on the same charge.

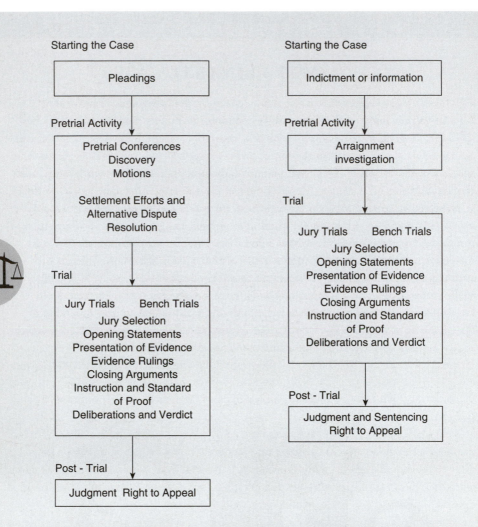

Starting the Case

| Pleadings |

Pretrial Activity

| Pretrial Conferences
Discovery
Motions

Settlement Efforts and
Alternative Dispute
Resolution |

Trial

| Jury Trials   Bench Trials
Jury Selection
Opening Statements
Presentation of Evidence
Evidence Rulings
Closing Arguments
Instruction and Standard
of Proof
Deliberations and Verdict |

Post - Trial

| Judgment Right to Appeal |

*Figure 7.3   How civil cases move
through federal court*

Source: Federal Judiciary Center

http://www.fjc.gov/federal/courts.nsf/autoframe?Open
Form&nav=menu4b&page=/federal/courts.nsf/page/6CE
BFD17E88FFCF68525682700561C5B?opendocument

Starting the Case

| Indictment or information |

Pretrial Activity

| Arraignment
investigation |

Trial

| Jury Trials   Bench Trials
Jury Selection
Opening Statements
Presentation of Evidence
Evidence Rulings
Closing Arguments
Instruction and Standard
of Proof
Deliberations and Verdict |

Post - Trial

| Judgment and Sentencing
Right to Appeal |

*Figure 7.4   How criminal cases move
through federal court*

Source: Federal Judiciary Center

http://www.fjc.gov/federal/courts.nsf/autoframe?OpenFo
rm&nav=menu4b&page=/federal/courts.nsf/page/6CEB
FD17E88FFCF68525682700561C5B?opendocument

Preliminary Hearing Many states begin criminal proceedings with a preliminary hearing to determine whether there is sufficient evidence to bring charges. These hearings can resemble one-sided minitrials where the prosecution presents evidence to prove there is probable cause that a crime was committed by the defendant. The defense can cross-examine witnesses and argue for dismissal of the case. The judge can drop charges if the evidence isn't there. This is an important stage to cover. The judge can also order that the defendant be examined by a psychiatrist to establish whether he or she is competent to stand trial. You can use all these details to follow up on the story.

Grand Juries About half the states, and the federal system, require a grand jury, a collection of citizens (traditionally 23) who hear evidence and vote out an indictment if they determine that probable cause has been established. In the other states, a judge makes the determination in preliminary hearings described above. Grand jury hearings are closed to the public to protect the accused. Reporters often wait outside the hearing room or find other ways to get information about the proceedings. Do this with great caution. You can be held in contempt of court if you are seen as interfering with the process, such as approaching grand jurors for information.

If the preliminary hearing or the grand jury determines there is evidence to proceed, a formal indictment is issued against the accused. It contains most of the information presented to the grand jury or preliminary hearing.

Other Pretrial Activities More business takes place before a trial starts. Defense attorneys can challenge the inclusion of evidence gathered by police by alleging the defendant's constitutional rights were violated. In the case of a sensational crime, the attorneys might seek a change of venue to move the trial to another jurisdiction where there has been less publicity. Both sides will file discovery motions to learn what evidence, witnesses and other factors the other side might present. In discovery, the prosecution must disclose more information than the defense, including all evidence that tends to exonerate the defendant. The defense need not disclose anything that might be incriminating.

Other motions, affidavits, and evidentiary hearings are likely. During this sequence the prosecution, defense or even the judge may try to close the proceedings to the media. It is your right to challenge such an attempt. Rise from your seat and ask the court's permission to speak (your fellow reporters should join with you). Note your objection and ask the judge for time to allow the media to consult an attorney and file a formal objection. Even if the judge denies your request, you are now on record and can officially appeal the ruling.

Covering Trials: Courtroom Action

pretrial checklist

- [ ] Check all files related to the case.
- [ ] Get the witness lists presented by the prosecution and defense.
- [ ] Meet the prosecutor and defense attorney. Make regular contact with them.
- [ ] Find out about media seating in the courtroom. You often have to make an official request to get a courtroom seat when covering a big trial.
- [ ] Sit on the aisle so you can go in and out to file if laptops are barred from the courtroom.
- [ ] Get the list of proposed jurors. You can use the information to contact jurors after the trial.
- [ ] Find out if there is a service that can provide a transcript of the day's proceedings.

Most trials take a day or two, but you'll likely cover cases involving more serious charges or complicated issues. Those trials can take weeks, sometimes months. Preparation for the long haul is essential.

Get the witness list. It will offer insight on how the trial will proceed. Although not everyone on the list will be called to testify, it provides a preliminary cast of characters. Reach out to the lawyers on both sides. In a criminal trial, the prosecutor's office generally has someone assigned to deal with the media. Get to know this person and make regular contact before the trial. Defense attorneys and lawyers in civil cases don't usually have press people, but they may be eager to present their client's case before the trial.

The Courtroom A courtroom is usually set up the way you've seen it on television or in the movies. The judge sits on the bench, an elevated podium facing the courtroom. The witness stand is next to the judge, also facing the courtroom. The court reporter, who records a real-time transcript of the trial, sits underneath the bench, alongside the court clerk, who manages the flow of paperwork and evidence. Juries, ranging from six to 14 members, sit perpendicular to the judge on one side of the courtroom. The bailiff, who enforces courtroom decorum, sits next to the jury. Lawyers for the defense and prosecution (or plaintiffs in a civil trial) sit at tables facing the judge and witness stand. A low railing usually separates the attorneys from the public.

The media generally sits among the spectators. In high-profile cases, a certain number of seats are reserved for the media. Make sure you get your request for a seat with the

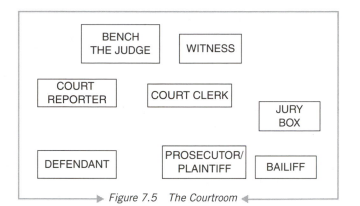

Figure 7.5   The Courtroom

judge's clerk or court administrator's office well before the trial begins. If you have a choice, the best seat is located in the middle of gallery on the aisle. This allows you to hear and view the proceedings and courtroom reaction. It also allows you to make a quick exit to update your story or blog if you're not allowed to type in the courtroom. Be aware that you may lose your spot if you leave.

What You Can Bring It's a mixed bag as to whether you will be allowed to bring your own recording device into the courtroom. Federal court rules ban all electronic devices — even cell phones — from the courthouse, but individual judges make exceptions. State courts generally allow one video and one still pool camera in the courtroom to provide feeds to all the media organizations covering the case. Make sure your organization is on the list (usually maintained by the court administrator or some committee formed by the journalists covering the trial) to get content for your website. State courts generally allow photographers and reporters to have cameras and recorders outside in the hallways. It is up to you to know what the rules are and to push for greater electronic access. (See "On the Web," p. 145, for more.)

Taking Notes It's not a bad thing if you can't use an audio recorder; searching for the right quote can slow you down on deadline. Note taking keeps you focused on what's happening; otherwise, it's easy to let your attention drift during long days of technical testimony. So take lots of notes. The trick is developing techniques that will speed the review process once it comes time to write your story. Review the tips in Chapter 1.

A growing number of jurisdictions offer same-day online transcripts. These are a terrific backstop to check your notes. But never count on the transcript being posted in time for your story. Technology will always fail, especially when you're relying on it most.

Jury Selection Trials are heard by juries or a judge. In most instances the defendant can make that choice. Jury trials begin with voir dire, a process to ensure that members of the jury are fit to serve. Potential jurors are asked if they have any personal connections with any of the players (the lawyers, defendants or their alleged victims in a criminal case or the two sides in a civil case). Jurors are also asked if they have an open mind about the outcome.

The judge will dismiss a potential juror if it is obvious he or she doesn't fit those criteria. Each side can argue for dismissal of a potential juror for the same reasons. Each side also gets a set number of peremptory challenges to dismiss a potential juror without giving a reason. The process can be a long one, particularly in a case that has received significant publicity. Watching jury selection is like witnessing a game of chess: It's slow and the lawyers' strategies aren't necessarily obvious. Look for patterns in the process. Is one side favoring a type of juror (young, old, male or female)? Both sides may employ jury consultants to help pick a jury. But don't get hung up on strategy; speculation about jury selection fades once testimony begins.

Jury selection stories should highlight the issues that are driving the two sides to pick or reject jurors. Potential jurors are often questioned about their attitudes toward crime and the police. They are asked if they or relations have been affected by crimes similar to the one they may be asked to decide. Here is an example from a jury selection story for a case involving an office shooting rampage. Note the quick summary of the process and the economical presentation of what the jury looks like:

A total of 161 prospective jurors were individually questioned over the course of four days. Because of the projected length of the trial, the judge decided to select a total of 16 jurors (several of whom would be chosen at random at the end of the case to become the alternates). Ultimately, seven men and nine women were selected.

The jurors included:

▶ a music store employee

▶ an employee of Home Depot

▶ a hospital speech pathologist

▶ an accountant

▶ two nurses

▶ a technical support manager for a biotech business

▶ a worker at a nonprofit organization that distributes clothing to the needy

Many of the jurors had previously served as jurors in other trials or on grand juries; several also knew people who suffered from Asperger's syndrome or ADHD. And one of the nurses — who was later selected to be the jury's foreperson — told the court that her mother-in-law had been murdered in 2004; the person charged with that murder subsequently pleaded not guilty by reason of insanity (after he allegedly stopped taking his prescription medications).

Courts are protective of jurors' identities and privacy. Don't name jurors during the trial. Refer to them by their age, gender and profession, and, in cases where it may be relevant, by race. Contacting jurors during the trial is strictly forbidden; it presents the possibility of tainting the verdict. Simply saying hello to a juror outside the courtroom can earn you a contempt of court citation. Jurors can be interviewed only *after* a verdict is reached.

Blogging a Trial

As rigorous as the daily trial story can be, some reporters are taking on the added task of blogging from the courtroom, using laptops and smart phones to send real-time updates of testimony and courtroom drama. The Citizen Media Law Project at Harvard's Berkman Center for Internet & Society says the policy for trial blogs varies from courtroom to courtroom. Federal criminal court rules are usually interpreted as prohibiting live blogging from courtrooms during trials. Some states permit laptops in courtrooms; some don't. Still others don't address the issue at all. As mentioned, the Radio Television Digital News Association keeps track of individual state rules. Check its website: www.rtdna.org/pages/media_items/cameras-in-the-court-a-state-by-state-guide55.php?g=45%3fid=55.

Because Iowa's law is silent on the question, Trish Mehaffey, the courts reporter for The Gazette of Cedar Rapids, blogs regularly from state courtrooms. However, the first trial she blogged was a federal tax and mail fraud case that had high community interest. Mehaffey got permission to blog after making a direct appeal to the judge.

"I sent him an e-mail explaining why I wanted to cover it," she says. "I explained how it was important to the public and he told me I could do it."

A few hundred people followed the blog at first, but the audience grew into thousands, including citizens with connections to the case. But when the case moved into federal appeals court, Mehaffey was not allowed to bring her laptop into the courthouse. Instead she had to run to the parking lot and blog from her car during breaks in the appeal.

San Francisco Chronicle reporter Henry Lee had a similar experience when he covered the murder trial of an Oakland, Calif., entrepreneur accused of murdering his wife.

Lee says most California judges won't allow live blogging, but he approached the trial judge in the courthouse hallway and made a personal request. "He knew me and knew my reputation and felt comfortable," Lee says.

Lee, who does Sudoku puzzles in the courtroom during lulls in other cases, was kept busy in this one, updating the Chronicle's website every few hours and writing a summary story for the overnight website and print edition. Mehaffey also has responsibilities to her blog, the online site and the newspaper. Each task requires a different focus.

"The paper is looking for a second-day lede," she says. "Online is looking for what happened that day."

Live courtroom blogging takes up most of their time as they file a running account of courtroom action while moderating real-time comments filed by blog followers. The commentators can range from average citizens to legal experts. Lee says the trial lawyers would review his blog each night to see the case through the eyes of the jury. Mehaffey said a presiding judge took a look at her blog from the bench. "It freaked him out that it was in real time," she says.

Lee calls the interactivity of live blogs both "the beauty and the horror of it."

"You'd get good comments and some bad ranting and ravings. I'd have to say 'thanks for your comment' and then delete it."

Court beat blogging isn't limited to real-time courtroom coverage. Court reporters also blog on less immediate subjects. The Wichita Eagle features a blog called "What the Judge Ate for Breakfast," which takes a deeper look at past and future cases and issues (http://blogs.kansas.com/courts).

Live blogging requires special skills. Here are some tips from voices of experience:

▶ *Be prepared to multitask.* You have to type in testimony while watching the reactions of the jury and other courtroom players. "Make sure you master touch typing," Lee advises

▶ *Don't try to be simply a stenographer.* Note the important points as they come up. "Summarize some key points every couple of paragraphs," Lee says.

▶ *Don't expect to understand all the legal issues;* take advantage of legal pros following the blog. Mehaffey had lawyers and mental health experts jump on the blog to explain the complexities of an insanity defense. "Be honest," she says. "If you don't understand something, say so."

daily trial story checklist

- [ ] Lead with the new details of the day. Were there new revelations in the testimony? A contradiction or confirmation of earlier testimony? A new strategy by the lawyers?
- [ ] Focus on the significant issues. Don't lead with a dramatic moment, such as a spectator creating a disturbance, unless it is relevant to the course of the trial.
- [ ] How does today's action relate to the case as a whole?
- [ ] What did the opposing lawyers offer in rebuttal to the evidence?
- [ ] Give readers a sense of being in the courtroom. Describe the tone and demeanor of the lawyers and witnesses. Use examples to illustrate your point.
- [ ] Restate the issues of the case (Jones is accused of beating his wife with a frozen turkey during a pre-Thanksgiving argument that got out of hand).
- [ ] What is at stake? Prison time? Fines?
- [ ] What court is hearing the case?
- [ ] What happens next/tomorrow?

Trial Proceedings Trials begin with opening statements by the prosecution and defense. Note the word *statements*. A common mistake is to call these presentations "opening arguments." Lawyers are prohibited from "arguing" in their openings; they must keep to the facts in presenting an outline of the case from their perspective. These statements often reveal their strategies for the trial. Some states allow defendants to postpone opening statement until the prosecution has presented its case.

This example from the New Orleans Times-Picayune uses the defense and prosecution openings to frame the case in a compelling narrative that asks the question the jury will face: Was the baby alive or dead?

> *Clara Craig quietly labored alone for 12 hours in her grandmother's small Bunche Village home before delivering a baby girl on the morning of Feb. 10, 2009, in the sheets of her own bed, without alerting any of her relatives in*

the next room. Five hours later, a police officer plucked the tiny body from the waters of Lake Pontchartrain in Kenner, where Craig had placed her, about 5 feet from the rocky shoreline.

There's no question how the infant came into this world or how she came to be on the lake's murky bottom.

But a jury of nine woman and three men will be asked to decide a key element in Craig's second-degree murder trial, which got underway in Jefferson Parish's 24th Judicial District Court on Tuesday: Was the infant alive or dead when Craig placed her in the water?

"The evidence will show that this baby was born alive," Assistant District Attorney Laura Schneidau told jurors during her opening statement.

Craig's defense attorney, Morris Reed Sr., told jurors the baby never showed any signs of life. He said Craig was panicked about the expense of burying the child, but didn't want to just put the baby in a garbage bin.

"She thought she was burying a child in the water," he said.

After opening statements the prosecution — or in civil trials, the plaintiff — presents the case against the defendant. In criminal cases, that includes the presentation of evidence, such as fingerprints, DNA tests, weapons, records and other items that link the defendant to the crime. The prosecution will call witnesses, including law enforcement officers, forensic specialists, eyewitnesses and other people who support the prosecution's case. In civil cases the evidence is a bit drier. Expert witnesses may testify about financial practices and business dealing. In medical malpractice a parade of paid medical experts will provide dueling opinions.

You can use testimony to build a narrative of what the prosecution (plaintiff) claims to have happened. Always qualify these points; testimony and evidence are not proof of guilt; they are the prosecution or plaintiff's attempt to show guilt or culpability. Attribute every statement to the witnesses. Write how the other side disputes the testimony.

Challenges to that testimony happen on cross-examination. After the prosecution/plaintiff presents a witness, the defense has its own set of questions, usually to blunt what was said in direct testimony and to raise questions about what the witness said or what the evidence really means. Cross-examination can be confrontational; if it is, you should note it in your story to give readers a sense of the mood in the courtroom. Remember the old axiom: Show, don't tell. Don't simply say, "In a confrontational cross-examination the witness said she was innocent." Give an excerpt of the back-and-forth between the lawyer and witness to illustrate what you mean:

> *Under sharp cross-examination by Asst. State Attorney Clarence Bailey, Smith admitted she was confused when she initially told police she had been to the victim's house earlier on the evening of the shooting. But she maintained she was innocent.*
>
> *"You told the police one thing, the grand jury another thing and now you're telling this court something else," Bailey said, raising his voice. "Do you expect this jury to believe you?"*
>
> *"Yes," she said, tears running down her face, "because I didn't kill Ralph."*

After the prosecution/plaintiff rests (finishes its presentation), the defense often will ask the judge for a directed verdict of not guilty, claiming the prosecution has failed to prove its case. This is a standard move that rarely succeeds. The defense may decide to rest and not present evidence or call witnesses if it feels the prosecution has failed to prove its case. That is also rare. Usually the defense follows the same procedure, presenting its own set of witnesses and evidence in the same sequence of direct examination and cross-examination. The defense can recall prosecution witnesses. When the defense rests, the prosecution is allowed to bring in rebuttal witnesses, a term for individuals used to contradict new allegations made by the defense.

Under our constitutional protections against self-incrimination, no defendant can be compelled to testify. It is up to the defendant and his or her lawyer to decide whether testifying, which would allow for a confrontational cross-examination by the prosecution, would help or hurt their case. If the defendant does not testify, the judge will tell the jury they should not consider it in their deliberations.

That is the bare bones of a trial. But within that outline are routines and delays that can fill up the day. One side can object to statements or testimony. The judge then rules on those objections. Sidebar conferences, among the lawyers and the judge, can take place before the judge rules. In more serious challenges, the judge may send the jury out of the courtroom, while each side makes its argument, or adjourn to his or her chambers for an in camera session. Sometimes court is adjourned so the judge can attend to other cases. These interruptions can take up the day, leaving you with little to write about.

Fair Trial and Free Press

Reporters, lawyers and judges struggle with the constitutional balancing act that weighs an individual's right to a fair trial against the public's right to know. The accused has the right to the presumption of innocence before and during the trial. It is the reporter's job to provide the details of a case as they become available. But a stream of sensational stories can threaten that presumption of innocence in the court of public opinion.

So where exactly do you draw the line between these dueling rights?

The American Bar Association and the Society of Professional Journalists (SPJ) have general guidelines. But each lawsuit and trial is different; it is hard to issue specific one-size-fits-all guidance.

The SPJ's Code of Ethics stresses that reporters should "minimize harm." Among the points to follow:

▶ Show good taste. Avoid pandering to lurid curiosity.

▶ Be cautious about identifying juvenile suspects or victims of sex crimes.

▶ Balance a criminal suspect's fair trial rights with the public's right to be informed.

The American Bar Association's Standards for Criminal Justice Fair Trial and Free Press (http://www.abanet.org/crimjust/standards/fairtrial.pdf) recognizes the need for an unfettered news media: "Absent a clear and present danger to the fairness of a trial or other compelling interest, no rule of court or judicial order should be promulgated that prohibits representatives of the news media from broadcasting or publishing any information in their possession relating to a criminal case."

The need for restraint and openness reads fine on paper. But the words pale when you are competing on a big story. The pressure is always there to come up with an exclusive and to post it as quickly as you can. It is hard to ignore sensational details reported by other media outlets.

No list can cover all instances you will face. But here are key points to remember:

▶ Be careful and specific. Stick to the phrasing of the official charges against a criminal defendant or the allegations made by a plaintiff in a civil suit.

▶ Include the defendant's side. Sometimes defendants won't talk to you. But try hard. Let the defendant know you want his or her side of the story.

Keep track of what's happening outside the courtroom during breaks and at the end of the day. Be ready to record interviews with the lawyers and family members that take place outside court. These courthouse steps interviews can become daily fare. Also look for opportunities to speak with people outside these staged gatherings. You'll get insights and quotes that other reporters don't have. Remember to apply your usual reporting standards: The fact that someone says something doesn't make it true. Always balance what this individual says with the other side's position.

After Testimony Ends After the defense and prosecution (plaintiff) finish their presentations and rebuttals, both sides deliver closing arguments, summarizing their points, interpreting the evidence and poking holes in the opposition's case. These can often be dramatic speeches that focus on the important parts of the case. Unlike the opening statements, these lawyerly speeches don't have to be based entirely on fact. As the name implies, arguments can employ all sorts of rhetorical flourishes to finesse an attempt to persuade the jury.

Closing arguments are followed by the judge's instruction to the jury. A judge's instructions can be the opposite of dramatic, often going into points of law as read in legalese straight from state or federal statutes. These points are often made at the request of the prosecution and defense. Although the language is dry, the instructions highlight the key issues facing the jury. In this example, drawn from an Alabama murder trial, the reporter uses the relevant portions of the judge's instructions to frame the legal issues faced by the jurors:

> Circuit Judge Charles Partin told jurors this morning that they must determine if Downs' death was homicide, as prosecutors allege, or suicide, as the defense maintains. If the jury believes the death was homicide, then jurors must determine if Nodine committed the crime and did so either intentionally or during the course of stalking her. The verdict form for count 1 contains boxes for not guilty, guilty of intentional murder and guilty of felony murder.
>
> Partin's legal instructions, which took a little more than an hour to deliver, included definitions of legal concepts like reasonable doubt, stalking and harassment.
>
> The murder charge is an all-or-nothing charge. Jurors do not have an option of convicting on a lesser-included offense like manslaughter or criminally negligent homicide.

Under Alabama law, prosecutors are not required to prove premeditation. The intent to commit murder, Partin told jurors, can form in a split second.

As is standard after trials, Partin also gave the jury instructions on how to evaluate evidence. He told them to use their common sense and to evaluate what weight to attach to witness testimony. He also told them that they do not have to accept the opinions offered by expert witnesses.

Partin also told jurors that he allowed witnesses to testify about statements that Downs made at or near the day of her death. Normally inadmissible hearsay, the judge said that he allowed such statements in evidence as an exception to that rule. Jurors are to consider those statements not for the truth of the matters at hand but to determine the victim's state of mind.

That question is important, Partin said, because the defense has raised the specter of suicide.

Waiting for the Jury After receiving its instructions, the jury goes into deliberation.

Courtrooms take on an odd atmosphere as the jury decides the case. You can often chat up the lawyers, families, even the defendant. These conversations may provide material for your stories as you wait for the verdict and help you to establish relationships you can call on after the verdict. Don't hesitate to talk with these people; they are often grateful for the distraction.

Many reporters and other courtroom "experts" try to divine the meaning of how long a jury deliberates. Some claim the longer it goes, the better it looks for the defendant. But anyone who has covered trials on a regular basis will tell you each case is unique. Length of deliberation often means nothing.

Sometimes jurors will send the judge a question to guide their deliberations or ask that certain parts of testimony be read back to them. The judge can reconvene court to answer those questions, which offer insight into what is being discussed in the jury room. You should seek outside expertise from other lawyers or law professors to interpret the significance of the questions.

Sometimes a jury can't decide. If just one juror fails to agree with the rest in a criminal case, the judge may declare a mistrial, which means the case must be retried for a new jury. Needless to say, few are happy with such an outcome. If it happens, contact jurors after they have been dismissed to find out details of the deliberations. Sometimes, jurors will meet with the media as a group to explain the deadlock.

verdict checklist: civil cases

- [ ] What were the claims against the defendant?
- [ ] Did the judge/jury set damages?
  - [ ] Compensatory?
  - [ ] Punitive?
- [ ] If damages were not set, when is the hearing date?
- [ ] How long was the trial?
- [ ] How long did the jury deliberate?

- [ ] Courtroom reaction
  - [ ] Plaintiff
  - [ ] Plaintiff's attorney
  - [ ] Defendant
  - [ ] Defense attorney
- [ ] Did the judge/jury issue a statement?
- [ ] If there was a jury, did any members speak to the media?
- [ ] Did you try to contact jurors?

verdict checklist: criminal cases

- [ ] What were the official charges?
- [ ] How many counts?
- [ ] Maximum sentence
  - [ ] Fines
  - [ ] Time served
- [ ] What is the sentencing date?
- [ ] How long was the trial?
- [ ] How long did the jury deliberate?

- [ ] Courtroom reaction
  - [ ] Defendant
  - [ ] Defendant's family
  - [ ] Victim's family
  - [ ] Defense attorney
  - [ ] Prosecutor
- [ ] Did the judge issue a statement?
- [ ] Did the jury speak to the media?
- [ ] Did you try to contact jurors?

The Verdict Once the jury reaches a verdict, the judge will summon the parties back to the courtroom. This often gives you an hour or two to prepare. It is a good strategy to write sections of background about the case before the verdict comes in. This will speed your ability to file a quick comprehensive story on the web that can be followed up with details of the reaction to the verdict. You should consider bringing in additional help to cover the reactions of the various parties who collect in separate press scrums outside the courtroom after the verdict. Having a camera and a recorder offers you a chance to illustrate the story and offer material to your website.

Criminal trial verdicts can be emotional events. The defendant's future is at stake; the verdict is also a cathartic moment for the victim and the victim's family and friends. You need to provide a description of the courtroom at the moment of the announcement. How did the defendant react? What did the attorneys and families of the defendant do? How did the victim, the victim's family and the defendant's family respond? Provide the details — the sights and sounds of the reactions — to give your audience a sense of what it was like to be sitting in the courtroom. Restate the details of the case, the charges, the key testimony and the consequences of the verdict. As noted, some of this can be written ahead of time. If the jury finds the defendant guilty, you must list the maximum sentence he or she faces and include the date that sentencing will take place.

Civil verdicts often lack immediacy and drama. If the case is decided by a judge, it may come as a written decision issued without the fanfare of a courtroom announcement. If you are anticipating a written decision, you should have contact information for all the parties. Also seek reaction from the legal and business community as to the impact of the decision. If it is a jury trial, the verdict will be announced in the courtroom; you can gather reaction on the spot. If the plaintiff wins, damages may be awarded with the verdict or after a later hearing. If damages are announced with the verdict, you'll need to explain how much was in compensatory damages and how much in punitive damages.

In both criminal and civil cases, you'll need to include any statements made by the judge, the defense and prosecution and the rest of the key players. It is a good idea before the verdict to ask, through the judge, if the jury would be willing to hold a news conference. Jurors may demur at first but be willing to talk individually or as a group in the hours or days after the verdict.

Covering Trials: Follow-Up

You will need to do a story that offers interpretation of the case and the verdict. Contact legal experts for comment on the tactics of the defense and prosecution and the broader legal issues of the case. Was the verdict unusual? What are the implications for future trials? How did the prosecution/plaintiff and defense succeed or fail in their strategies. What was key to the case? What evidence? Which testimony? What grounds could be used for appeal? Seek out members of the jury for comment if possible.

Penalty Phase Criminal case verdicts can be followed by a series of filings and hearings to determine the sentence. In capital murder cases, where the death penalty is an option, the jury may be asked to decide whether the convicted defendant should be executed or spend his or her life in prison. The penalty phase, even for lesser crimes, can involve another flurry of paperwork and dramatic courtroom presentation. Affidavits arguing for mercy are filed by friends and family of the convicted; the other side will argue for a stiff sentence. Psychologists and corrections officials will provide court-ordered reports on the convicted. The judge often hears personal statements from victims and victims' families about the impact of the crime. The defendant's family and friends can speak for leniency. All of this provides for dramatic, emotional stories.

In civil cases that find for the plaintiff, there can be postverdict hearings to present evidence about the amount of damages to be assessed against the defendant. There will be testimony about the costs connected with physical or financial injury, such as medical bills, lost investments or wages, property damage and other real losses. The judge or jury will be asked to decide the more contentious issue of the "pain and suffering" claimed by the plaintiff and punitive damages assessed as punishment for the defendant's actions.

Finally, some states require a separate trial for a defendant who has prevailed with an insanity plea. That trial is usually held before the same jury. Such verdicts are controversial and require careful, balanced reporting. Get reactions from both sides along with commentary from legal and medical experts.

The Sentence Defendants are often allowed speak to the court before the judge pronounces sentence. In some cases this will be the first time the public hears from the defendant, so interest runs high. The judge is also likely to offer an explanation about his or her decision on the sentence. Once the sentence is pronounced, you will face the same challenges you did with the verdict, including reactions from the defense and prosecuting lawyers, the friends and families of the defendant and the victims. You must also explain what the range of the sentence actually means. For example, someone with a 25-years-to-life sentence could apply for parole after 15 years.

Appeals A decision of not guilty brings criminal cases to an end. Once a defendant is found not guilty of a criminal charge, he or she cannot be tried again for the same crime. This is known as double jeopardy, a constitutional protection to keep the government from persecuting citizens by constantly prosecuting them. However, a defendant acquitted in a criminal case can be sued in civil court by relatives of the victim, who want to punish the defendant by seeking monetary damages. This happened in the case of ex-football star O.J. Simpson, who was sued by the families of the two people he was found not guilty of murdering in a criminal case. The families won in civil court, where plaintiffs have only to show that a preponderance of evidence suggests the defendant is responsible for the criminal actions.

Defendants found guilty in criminal court can appeal the verdict by challenging issues of law involving the trial. There can be claims the judge erred in a courtroom ruling, in instructions to the jury or by permitting the use of evidence or testimony that should have been excluded.

Civil appeals follow the same route. Appeals rarely succeed, but they can take years to make their way through the court system. Some cases that follow this path can become a continuing part of your career.

STORY SCAN: A VERDICT STORY

Here's a murder verdict story from the Philadelphia Inquirer that highlights the points discussed in the chapter.

Man Convicted for Fatal Beating of Infant Daughter

A straightforward lede that includes the verdict, details of the crime, the names of the defendant and the victim.

A Philadelphia jury yesterday found Tyrone Spellman guilty of third-degree murder and endangering the welfare of a child in the 2006 beating death of his 17-month-old daughter, Alayiah.

More of the case, attributing the allegations to the prosecution.

During the weeklong trial, prosecutors presented evidence that Spellman, 27, a devotee of Xbox-system video games, became enraged and hit the child repeatedly after she toppled and damaged the game player in the Brewerytown house he shared with his brother.

Prosecutors contended that the child's battered body was moved before EMTs arrived and posed near a barbell in another room to make the death look like an accident.

The jury's verdict, after eight hours of deliberations over two days, means that Spellman, who has three prior convictions on drug offenses in Pennsylvania and New Jersey, will face a maximum penalty of 23 1/2 to 47 years in prison, said Assistant District Attorney James Berardinelli.

Background on the verdict and what the conviction means. We learn the prosecutor's name, a detail secondary to the verdict and the crime.

Berardinelli, who had asked for a first-degree-murder conviction, said he was satisfied with the jury's decision.

Comment from the prosecutor.

Spellman was arrested in September 2006 after an autopsy indicated that the toddler's skull had been shattered by blows to the head.

Secondary details of the crime.

A summary of the defense's case.

Throughout the trial, defense attorney Bobby Hoof maintained that his client was innocent and tried to cast suspicion on the child's mother, Mia Turman, who had a history of neglecting the child, according to Department of Human Services reports Hoof introduced as evidence.

An early indication of a troubling outcome for the defense came about an hour after the resumption of deliberations yesterday, when the jury of seven women and five men asked Court of Common Pleas Judge Jeffrey P. Minehart the difference between first- and third-degree murder.

Blending of details and the judge's name.

First-degree murder is a malicious assault committed with the "specific intent" to kill the victim; third-degree murder is the death that occurs as the unintended consequence of that assault, the judge said.

Details of the judge's instructions.

In his closing argument Monday, Berardinelli urged the jurors to conclude that the series of blows inflicted on the child's head were done "with a wickedness of disposition . . . a hardness of heart and extreme indifference" to the impact that such a battering would have on the girl's 17-pound body.

Quotes from closing arguments summarizing the prosecution's case.

"That little baby's head cracked like a walnut," he said, urging the jury to return a verdict of first-degree murder because Spellman acted with reckless disregard for the consequences of his actions.

Insight on the jury's deliberation attributed to the prosecutor. This suggests the jury did not talk with reporters after announcing the verdict.

In a brief post-verdict conversation that he had with the jury forewoman, Berardinelli said, she told him that the panel came to the conclusion that Spellman acted "in a rage" but without intending to kill the child.

Resources

Links

Electronic Filing Rules

- ▶ Media Law Project at Harvard's Berkman Center for Internet & Society
- ▶ www.citmedialaw.org
- ▶ The Radio Television Digital News Association, www.rtdna.org/pages/media_items/cameras-in-the-court-a-state-by-state-guide55.php?g=45%3fid=55

Fairness Issues

- ▶ American Bar Association Fair Trial Standards, www.abanet.org/crimjust/standards/fairtrial.pdf
- ▶ Society of Professional Journalists, www.spj.org/ethicscode.asp

Lawyer Directories

- ▶ www.Lawyers.com
- ▶ Martindale-Hubbell, www.martindale.com
- ▶ Check for individual state bar association directories.

Legal Terms

▶ Black's Law Dictionary, www.thefreelibrary.com/Black's+Law+Dictionary,+8th+ed-a0126933970

▶ Federal Court Glossary, www.uscourts.gov/Common/Glossary.aspx

▶ dictionary.law.com

Open Records

▶ Society of Professional Journalists, www.spj.org/opendoors.asp

Statistics

▶ Federal Courts, www.uscourts.go /Statistics/FederalCourtManagementStatistics.aspx

▶ National Center for State Courts www.ncsconline.org/d_research/csp/CSP_Main_Page.html

Assignment Desk

Go to your state or federal district court and ask to see the recent docket of civil filings. Pick out two or three with interesting titles; then look at the case summaries (usually at the beginning of the document) to see what the case is about. Who is suing whom, and for what? What harm do the plaintiffs allege, and what are they seeking? What you're looking for is a case that would hold your audience's interest. Something people would want to talk about to friends or because it might touch on their lives. Cigarette smokers (and nonsmokers) will be interested in suit against a tobacco company. Parents will be interested in a suit filed against a school district. Piece together a narrative of the case from the filings and write a story explaining the case and why it is important. Look for details that help explain the legal issues. If you are unsure, speak with a law professor.

Sidebar Take the next step by interviewing the lawyers and, if possible, the plaintiffs and defendants in a case. Get their perspectives. What drove the plaintiff to file suit? What else did he or she try before suing? What are the plaintiff's goals? What does the defendant think? Was he or she surprised by the suit? A question such as "How has this case affected your life?" may bring a response that adds flesh and blood to an otherwise procedural story. Ask the lawyers whether this is similar to other cases. How do they see their chances? They will likely paint a positive picture, but you can ask them to be more specific. That's always a good way of getting deeper into a story. You can also make this a group effort; brainstorm the list of questions with classmates or fellow reporters. Don't be surprised if you have trouble getting people to talk. That's fine — rejection is part of a reporter's life. Still, it's always good to practice your interviewing skills.

CHAPTER 8

GOVERNMENT

When Carolyn Russell began her first term as a North Carolina state representative, a colleague gave her this advice: "You can vote any way you want to up here because the folks back home will never know."

That suggestion, quoted in an American Journalism Review story about the decline in reporting on state government, should anger any voter — and doubly anger any self-respecting journalist. A healthy democracy requires its citizens to know what their government officials are doing. It is the reporter's job to get that information out.

Important as this responsibility is, some journalists and their audiences view government stories as boring. The decline in daily newspaper circulation and local television news viewership has given rise to a conventional wisdom, supported by ratings and surveys, that readers are not interested in stories about local government. Many news outlets have cut back on coverage.

Whatever truth is in the surveys, we in the media are partly to blame for the lack of civic interest. Lazy citizens are the result of lazy reporters. Government stories that merely recite numbers and official talking points *are* boring. On the flip side, stories that rely on a stew of gossip and "gotcha" sensationalism raise the level of cynicism about government and lower public interest in governance.

Audrey Marks
The Magnolia

As an English major from Pennsylvania, Audrey Marks felt more prepared to discuss *Moby Dick* than annual budgets when she became a government reporter, first in Stillwater, Okla., then in Houston-area towns for a chain of weekly newspapers. She then graduated to direct other reporters for the chain.

It wasn't easy at first. She was viewed with suspicion as a newcomer — and an Easterner.

"I don't sound like anybody else out here," she says. "I had to win people over one person at a time."

She started by attending a Saturday workshop on the city budget. "It was really dry, policy-heavy stuff," Marks recalls. "During the breaks, people would come up to me and say, 'I don't know why you are here on a Saturday. You're young. You should be out enjoying yourself.'"

Marks persisted. "The biggest thing that was in my advantage was that I don't mind talking to people. I always look for a friendly face."

Her search paid off. The city manager's secretary guided her through the maze of City Hall offices and departments. A city councilor who served on the historical society became a reliable source after Marks chatted her up and did a story about the society.

"Because she would talk to me, the others on the council felt more comfortable about talking with me," Marks says.

Here are some tips from Marks:

▶ Ask questions, then more questions.

Editing a story about a fund that paid child care costs for mothers in school, Marks wondered why a businesswoman was donating the money. Marks sent the reporter back to ask. The reporter learned that the businesswoman had struggled through a similar situation in her own life, a fact that made for a more compelling story.

"You can't be afraid of asking a question, or asking that follow-up question," Marks says. "A lot of young reporters don't understand that's the deal with the job."

▶ Make the hard calls.

When a city administrator was charged with drunken driving, Marks had him called to get his side. "He had no comment, but we were the only people who called," she says. "He thanked me. When you're fair and balanced, even if they don't like what's going on, they appreciate it if you call."

What your audience wants and needs is an understanding of how the actions of government affect them. Will the new city ordinance on liquor licenses quiet the noisy bar down the street? Does the town council's budget for the highway department include money to repair the giant pothole on Elm Street? Will the planning commission approve the variance allowing a four-story apartment building to be built next to the park? These questions matter to people. They rely on reporters for answers.

Your audience also relies on you to hold public official accountable. Bureaucrats and politicians at any level could be tempted to cut ethical corners if they think no one is watching. The zoning board might bend the rules to accommodate a friend of a friend. The county commission might bury key facts about the environmental impact of a controversial new shopping mall. The state legislature might decide to vote itself a pay raise during a midnight session.

This chapter introduces the personalities and issues you'll encounter covering local government. Hopefully, it will also show you the excitement and challenge of a beat that is a critical training ground for young reporters. If you can learn to cover the officials and agencies that make a city or town function, you'll have the basics you need to cover your state capital — or Congress. You may even decide that you love local government reporting, with its instant feedback and the chance to make a difference. Whether you stay at the local level or move on to bigger leagues, your work will matter.

Although the chapter talks about politicians and how to cover them, it doesn't delve into the mechanics of politics — the elections and daily gamesmanship of Republicans versus Democrats and conservatives versus liberals. Politics is certainly part of the big picture — too large, in fact, for this little book. Instead, we'll focus on covering how the actions and decisions of government affect your audience. The intrigues and vagaries of politics can be a detour from that mission.

GOVERNMENT BEAT ▶ PEOPLE

Developing solid relationships with the people you cover is crucial on every beat. It is even more important in government reporting. You can't be everywhere and know everything — even in a small town. Establishing contacts in the offices and departments of government and on the streets of your community will help you track the issues your readers want to know about.

Government offices deal with reporters in different ways. Some allow employees to speak freely. Others limit contact to official spokespeople, known in the trade as flaks. You obviously need to know everyone who can help you in your reporting. That's a constant challenge

DeWayne Lehman
Press Secretary

One weekend when DeWayne Lehman was a deputy press secretary for the mayor of Boston, he got a call at home from a reporter seeking comment. Lehman wasn't on duty. The reporter was supposed to go through the office. Still, Lehman answered the question. Then the next day he read the column, in which he was quoted as saying only one thing: "How did you get this number?"

That was the last time Lehman spoke with that reporter. "The quote conveyed that the press shouldn't be bothering the mayor's press people," he says. "It was simply a 'gotcha' move."

Lehman has perspective on the tricky relationship between reporters and government media people. He was a reporter and an editor for small-community papers before he crossed over to government public relations. He now heads the news office at the University of Massachusetts-Boston.

"I like reporters," he says. But not all reporters. "I avoid the ones I feel I can't work with — the ones I can't trust. A few reporters are out for the gotcha — the line taken out of context."

Lehman appreciates fair reporters, such as the one who called him about allegations that Lehman's boss was giving raises to staff members who supported a particular candidate.

"A couple of people did get raises and he could have connected the dots in a way that would have supported a sensational story," he says. Instead, the reporter gave Lehman time to collect records showing that the raises had started long before the election campaign.

"He waited on the story and saw we weren't hiding anything," he said. "It was one of those moments where one or the other person takes the first step to understanding."

Lehman offers these tips on dealing with flaks:

▶ **Show up.**

Get out and meet with public relations people regularly. "A lot of times PR people only hear from a reporter when they want something today," he says. "Grab a lunch. Get to know them so when you do need something, there will be a relationship."

▶ **Be understanding.**

What seems like stalling is simply standard procedure. Collecting information can take time. Responses have to be cleared through the government hierarchy. "Being respectful and understanding that the PR person has a job to do gets you further than treating them as an obstacle," he says.

because contacts change. The spokeswoman for the mayor who proved so useful may be replaced by a less cooperative person. You have to learn to adjust to each new personality.

Reporters and government officials often have dueling agendas. Reporters are usually in a rush to get responses for stories that may be less than flattering to their subjects. Those in government, especially the public relations people, want to present their bosses or departments in the best light. They want to take more time to craft what they say, or they may simply hope you'll give up and go away. This is yet another reason why you need to develop connections. It's harder to blow off someone you know.

Speaking directly to the source you need for a story is always best. That can be easier to do in a smaller municipality. Many local governments don't have public relations people. You can walk into the mayor's or town manager's office and start a conversation. Bigger municipalities and state government departments have official spokespersons you must deal with. These people can be protective of their bosses and try to shield them from tough questions. Don't assume that this protectiveness has been dictated by their superiors. The people whose comments you need may be more open to questions than their underlings think they are. It's always worth asking. Responses to your questions will be quicker and less filtered when you talk to them rather than through an intermediary.

Directors of Communications

Top federal, state and big-city officials usually have someone who handles media questions for all aspects of the administration's operations. This system makes sense if you look at it from a politician's or bureaucrat's point of view. They want to control the message. They would face problems of credibility and accuracy if different people provided different and inconsistent policy statements.

The best way to work within this framework is to develop relationships up and down the organizational ladder. Meet with the director of communications on a regular basis; discuss issues both on and off the record to keep informed and develop trust. The director will be more willing to give you background if he or she is confident that what is said off the record stays off the record. This trust trickles down to other PR people. If they know their boss trusts you, they will be more helpful.

Departmental Flaks

Larger governmental divisions, such as public health, environmental agencies and transportation departments, often have their own public relations people who handle specific questions rather than larger issues involving policy. They can tell you how many buses are being repaired or how long the sewer work will take. Many have been in their jobs for years; they are not subject to political appointment. So they should be quicker to respond when they know who you are.

Mayors and Managers

The title and duties of a city or town's head official vary among jurisdictions. The mayor is usually a city's top elected official. Mayors' responsibilities can differ. Some cities have strong mayor systems where the mayor has the power to set policy, agendas and budgets. Weak mayor systems give the final say to the elected board of aldermen, councilors or supervisors. Some mayor positions are more ceremonial; day-to-day operations are handled by an appointed city manager answerable to the board or council. These managers are

▶ ▶ ▶ **BEAT BACKGROUNDER** ◀ ◀ ◀

MUNICIPALITIES

Municipal is an all-encompassing word for cities, towns, townships and villages — the basic unit of local government. These terms are not interchangeable; the correct one depends on the community's governing structure. Cities generally have a mayor and city council or board of aldermen. Towns place more power with the legislative body — the town council or board of selectmen. These definitions can shift from state to state, so do your research on local terminology. Don't be misled by population numbers. Some towns in your state may be larger than some of the cities.

Whatever kind of municipality you cover, its government has more day-to-day impact on the lives of your audience than the state legislature or Congress. Municipal officials are usually responsible for the condition of streets; they oversee the paving and plowing necessary to keep traffic flowing. They also determine the speed you can travel on the roads and where the stop signs and traffic lights are placed.

Local government determines how and when your trash is picked up. It sets the rules for where you can build a house or rent an apartment. It decides where businesses can locate, what hours your favorite bar can operate, whether the new restaurant down the street can serve alcohol and whether you can smoke a cigarette there.

Most municipalities pay for all this with property taxes determined by the assessed value of residential and commercial buildings. That makes property taxes big news to city or town residents. Municipalities also receive money from fees for business licenses, auto excise taxes, parking and traffic tickets. When you start covering a municipal beat, one of the first things you'll need to study is where the money comes from and where it goes.

common in towns and villages. The government of smaller municipalities may be overseen by the chair of the selectmen or other elected board. These are usually part-time, volunteer positions held by people who work full-time jobs elsewhere.

Whatever his or her title, the office of your municipality's top person is where information about your city or town converges. Citizen concerns and management issues flow into the office; policy decisions and managerial edicts flow out. This individual generally knows what is going on in the different municipal departments and can comment on the issues you are covering.

Elected Representatives

City and town voters elect a group of citizens to write ordinances and make policy and budget decisions. In cities, that group may be called the board of aldermen, the city council, or the board of supervisors. In towns, the elected representatives may sit on a town council, board of selectmen or a body with some other name.

Some towns in Michigan, Minnesota and the New England states hold open town meetings where all residents get to debate and vote on issues of budget and policy. These are truly democratic events where everyone's voice and vote carry equal importance. Unfortunately, over the years, some of these towns have grown so large that an open meeting of all the residents becomes impossible to stage and town meeting has been replaced with representative government.

The boards and councils hold regularly scheduled open meetings that take up issues ranging from municipal budgets and tax rates to appeals of decisions made by other bodies, including the zoning and parking departments. These councils may also take up questions about liquor licenses (your town may have a separate liquor licensing board). These can often generate great articles based on the tawdry stories you'll hear at these hearings.

Most of these boards and councils have a secretary or director you'll need to check in with for agendas of upcoming meetings and information about issues brewing in the background. Although you can probably get meeting agendas from the municipal website, you'll still want to talk with someone. Without a real conversation you might miss the interesting issues hiding behind those printed words.

Speak with the members of these elected boards on a regular basis. They can brief you on policy questions, gossip about how people will vote on upcoming issues and give you a heads up when a new concern develops. If they're not accustomed to your presence and your interest, they're not likely to think of you when something big is going on.

The Bureaucracy

Much of your time covering municipal government will be spent navigating its offices and agencies. The word for this — *bureaucracy* — has come to carry a negative

LEGISLATIVE AND EXECUTIVE

ALL JURISDICTIONS OF GOVERNMENT, including municipalities, counties, states and the federal government, are divided into two main branches — the executive and the legislative. The third branch, the court system, is discussed in a separate chapter. Simply put, the legislative branch (Congress, the state legislature, county commissions and municipal boards of aldermen, councilors, supervisors) establishes rules and laws and sets the budget for government. These legislators are chosen by the citizenry. U.S. senators are elected by the entire state, and county commissioners are elected by the entire county. Most other legislators, including congressional representatives, state representatives and senators, members of city councils and boards of selectmen, represent voters within a district whose boundaries are set by population. Congressional districts are drawn to include no more than 700,000 residents. State legislative districts also are set by population. However, in some cities and towns voters choose from a list of candidates who represent the whole city or town. These are called at-large candidates.

Legislative bodies are required to conduct business in public with some specific exceptions, usually called executive sessions. Most state press associations have a pocket summary of your state's open meetings law. (You can find the full law online or link to it through a site such as sunshinereview.org.) Be sure you are clear on the provisions for executive sessions, which allows boards and committees to meet in private to discuss personnel matters, including hiring, firing and disciplinary actions. But the move can often be abused. When elected officials declare they are going into executive session, ask for the board's reason and check the law to make sure it's valid. State laws also require that decisions reached in executive session be made public within a certain time period. This is the public's right to know, not just journalists'. You're helping everyone when you make sure elected officials follow the law.

The executive branch — headed by the president at the federal level, the governor at the state level and mayors and managers at the local level — implements and enforces the laws and budget directions passed by the legislative branch and is responsible for the day-to-day operations of government. The president oversees a vast federal bureaucracy of departments, secretariats, agencies, offices and bureaus, from the Department of State to the Department of Interior. Governors have similar responsibilities over state operations. Mayors have the final say on the administration of the police, fire departments, highway departments, health offices, building inspectors and other municipal functions.

State voters elect other executive officers who operate independently from the governor, such as the state attorney general, state treasurer and secretary of state. Municipalities may have elected officials who don't answer directly to either the executive or legislative branch. For instance, some cities and towns elect an independent assessor to determine the value of real estate. Establishing separate elective offices makes these officials directly responsible to the voters.

connotation. But it is an accurate description of the working part of government that is run by unelected administrators, supervisors and directors. In most cases they are appointed with the approval of the mayor or managers and the elected board or council. These employees face fewer political constraints because they generally have held their jobs for years and enjoy some autonomy. Much of your day-to-day information will come from these people. Here's a look at some of those you're likely to deal with.

City or Town Clerk The clerk is responsible for all the records, documents and paperwork that flow through municipal offices, from the filings of proposed ordinances to the applications for marriage licenses. Most municipal clerks serve for years. They have valuable institutional memories that can prove useful to a new reporter. Tapping into this knowledge as part of a general conversation will help you fit together the jigsaw pieces of government.

Treasurer Most municipalities have a treasurer who handles money matters. This office oversees the collection of property taxes, excise taxes, licensing fees, fines and other monies. Some treasurer offices provide a list of tax delinquents — the homeowners and businesses that owe money to the city or town. The treasurer is responsible for depositing and investing the money. Smaller municipalities sometimes combine these duties with the clerk and assessor's office.

Assessor The assessor has the powerful job of establishing (assessing) the value of residential and commercial properties. Cities and larger towns have staff people to do assessing; smaller towns contract the work out. The value the assessor assigns to a property determines how much property tax the owner will pay. These taxes provide most of the municipality's revenues. The city or town establishes a certain mill rate for property taxes, which is then multiplied by the assessed value of the home in order to determine the tax bill. The mill rate may be divided into a tax for general revenue and another for schools. For example, a home is assessed at $300,000 and the mill rate is $5 per $1,000 of valuation. Multiplying 5 by 300 gives you a tax bill of $1,500. As you can see, a shift in the value the assessor assigns a property can mean an increase of thousands of dollars in individual property taxes.

It's no surprise that the assessor's work can be the focus of many angry challenges, which are usually heard by citizens who have been appointed to a review board. The assessor's office is also an important resource to track property values in the different neighborhoods of your city or town.

COUNTY, STATE AND FEDERAL GOVERNMENT

COUNTY

Nearly all the states are divided into counties. But the power of county governments varies widely. In some states, counties administer schools, jails, nursing homes, highways, fire protection and law enforcement, paying for them with a mix of property, income and sales taxes and direct fees for services. In other states, counties have few duties; over time they have surrendered jurisdiction to municipal and state governments.

STATE

State government determines whom you can marry and where you can be buried. Bureaucrats and lawmakers decide how much you will pay for your health and auto insurance, what children must be taught in school, when those children can be tried as adults in court and how the elderly will be cared for in nursing homes.

Local reporters must keep up with what is happening in the state capital. Decisions made there have a direct impact on cities and towns. State government mandates many of the tasks of local government and provides some funding to pay for it. State governments get their monies from various taxes and fees. All but nine levy their own income taxes on state residents. All but five have sales taxes.

FEDERAL

The U.S. Constitution establishes the federal government's authority over foreign policy, trade, national defense, interstate commerce and programs concerning the health and welfare of the entire nation. The federal government administers vast networks of public land, highways, railroad lines, airports and utilities. It oversees the nation's agriculture, lumber and fishing industries. The list goes on and on. According to the U.S. Office of Personnel Management, the federal government employs 2.7 million people — not counting security agencies such as the CIA.

The federal government's multitrillion-dollar budget is supported by income taxes on its citizens. Other money comes in from inheritance taxes, custom duties, the licensing of natural resources, fees and fines. Some 39 percent of the federal budget is spent on social entitlement programs such as Social Security, Medicare and Medicaid. An additional 1 percent goes to mandatory programs, including aid to state and local government for education, transportation, housing and health care.

Federal programs and federal money will have an impact on your community and will figure into your duties as a local reporter. You'll need to follow initiatives in Washington, D.C., and explain how new laws, regulations and executive orders will affect your audience.

Highway Department (Traffic and Parking) The repair and maintenance of a municipality's roads is overseen by a road commissioner, an administrator or a supervisor. This person's duties are of great interest to the citizens, but highway departments offer little public oversight. Some will announce plans for repair and construction jobs on town roads; others won't. You shouldn't count on official announcement; that's why regular visits to the department are important.

These administrators also may be in charge of parking enforcement and traffic management, two volatile issues for citizens. The placement of a stop sign or the timing of a red light can generate hot debate. You'll be surprised how riled residents can get over cars speeding through their neighborhoods or changes in the way residents and nonresidents are allowed to park their cars. Some of the angriest meetings you will witness will deal with changes in parking regulations.

Public Works Your municipality may have a separate public works administrator who oversees everything from garbage pickup to sewer and water system repair. These services are important to your audience. Any changes in the department's routine are big stories; even a switch from Tuesday to Thursday garbage pickup can bring a storm of comments.

You'll have to dig for stories here. Water flows, toilets work, garbage is removed. Nothing to report. Then something goes wrong — a pipe breaks and floods a street, or sewers back up with unpleasant consequences. When the unusual does happen, it may be hard to speak with officials if they haven't already gotten to know you during the quiet times.

Planning and Zoning Administrators If your municipality has a planning officer, he or she will be responsible for the big picture of how the town will grow. Can the farm down the street be subdivided into a hundred house lots? Does the proposal for a new big-box store in town have enough parking? Should the company pay for road improvements? The planner administers the process of answering those questions, usually by working with a board of appointed or elected citizens who make the final decision. Whoever heads the office will be able to tell you about any new projects or policies.

Zoning administrators oversee the rules about the size, placement and purpose of residential, commercial and industrial properties. Zoning ordinances also dictate where various types of businesses can locate and the number of people who can reside in homes or apartment buildings. People are always seeking exceptions, known as variances, to these rules. Those exceptions are decided by citizens appointed or elected to a zoning board.

The issues may seem mundane, but they can be very important to neighbors. Should the board grant a variance to someone who wants to extend an addition to his house beyond the 25-foot setback from his neighbor's property? Should the board consider the objections of a homeowner opposed to her neighbor's plan to build a house 4 feet taller than zoning rules permit? These turf wars over property rights and development help determine the look and feel of your town and are closely followed by many members of your audience. That makes the head of zoning an important person to check in with regularly.

Inspectors Most municipalities have inspectors who check to see that buildings are built properly, that restaurants are clean and that food stores comply with consumer and health regulations. This is a department that seems to get coverage only when something goes wrong. Someone falls ill, the victim of a badly prepared cheeseburger. A shoddily constructed wall collapses in an apartment building.

This department has reams of data: What landlords have the most building violations? Where are the foreclosed properties? Who hasn't shoveled their walk? Which restaurants regularly receive high marks for cleanliness, and which don't? Much of the information about these regular inspections is tucked away in the department's paperwork. They are public records; you are entitled to review what the inspectors have filed. But it will be much easier if you develop a relationship with the department. Spend the morning with an inspector on his or her rounds. You'll learn some things about your town that will pay off later.

Parks and Recreation Directors The parks superintendent and recreation directors get little attention until things go wrong. It isn't much of a story if basketball courts and ball fields are well maintained, but these officials will be in the spotlight if children get poison ivy after running through a wooded park or if the town pool is closed because of a high bacteria count.

Appointed officials such as a parks director thrive on good publicity. They will appreciate your interest and the occasional feature on a recreational program or park repair.

Rank and File Government employees populate all strata of daily life — highway and sanitation workers, clerks, secretaries, social workers, fish and game wardens, and health inspectors. In addition to knowing their job and what's happening in their department, all have wisdom and information that could help you piece together a fuller picture of government.

You will interview some of these workers for a specific story: a recreation director who runs a successful program; the highway workers who work long hours clearing snow-covered roads. Each one might be a useful contact in the future. Take the time to talk with them. Get their phone numbers and e-mail addresses, and collect that information on a contact sheet categorized by departments.

Don't stop there. If you see a government worker on the job and have the time, stop and strike up a conversation. Ask the highway department engineer and a maintenance worker about their jobs. How long have they worked for the city? How have their jobs changed? How do they like the work? Let them talk. Identify yourself as a reporter and explain that your curiosity is a natural affliction. You don't have to write anything down. You don't even have to ask their names. Just tap them for some bit of knowledge that expands your understanding of local government. Give them a business card. You may never hear from them, but there's always a chance that sometime, when they're angry or troubled about something going on in their department, these people might remember that reporter they spoke with and reach out to you. The more ears and eyes you have out there, the better.

Citizens In the rush to get official pronouncements and reactions, it's easy to forget that regular people are the ones affected by the laws and regulations, the taxes and the policy decisions you write about. Nothing helps readers understand these issues more than seeing how changes affect their neighbors. Hearing their stories illustrates the bigger points of government. Some complicated change in property tax rules is best explained by homeowners affected by the change. Describing their situation will bring more people into the story — the goal of any reporter.

Also get to know the people outside government who are involved in your community. Members of civic groups and associations are important contacts. Some groups focus on specific issues, such as Friends of the Oak Street Library or the Better Parks Association. Find the community development corporations, community health centers and business alliances. Seek out the pastors of the local churches — they know about all kinds of activity and social issues in the community.

Sign up for local mailing lists and search the Web for neighborhood blogs and newsletters. Read what's being covered there, and be sure to read the audience comments about your stories. Use Google Alerts to track groups and issues that interest you. You can set up an alert that will let you know when anyone on the Internet mentions a particular town committee or neighborhood. These alerts can serve as a sentinel for the meetings you'll want to attend.

When you go to meetings, introduce yourself to the leaders and give them your card. A handful of people may be particularly outspoken at these meetings. Even if you don't quote them for a story, get their contact information and give them yours.

Find the people in the neighborhoods who keep track of things. Introduce yourself to the barber, the insurance agent, the superintendent of the large apartment building. These are people who know everybody's business.

The website of a neighborhood association in Boston's Dorchester neighborhood

Source: www.columbiasavinhillcivic.org

GOVERNMENT BEAT ▶ Places

The day-to-day routines of government take place in offices and cubicles far from the public eye. In a perfect world you would make the rounds of all these places each day; bureaucrats can be valuable sources about what is going on in the warrens of government.

Your first assignment on a new beat is to find all the offices associated with government and introduce yourself to the people you'll be covering. It helps if someone, perhaps the reporter who had the beat before you, takes you around for your initial meet-and-greets. But don't confine yourself to visiting government offices — go everywhere; attend everything. Go to chamber of commerce meetings and zoning board hearings. Sit in on tax abatement sessions. Haunt community events such as street fairs and outdoor concerts, anywhere you can get a feel for the area and the people who live there.

navigating local government checklist

- ☐ **Learn the community's geography**
- ☐ **Physical boundaries**
- ☐ **Political districts**
- ☐ **Government offices**
- ☐ **Social hangouts**
- ☐ **Make the rounds of introductions**
- ☐ **Attend political and social meetings**
- ☐ **Find community websites**

Navigating Your Community

You can map a city or town in many ways.

A municipality has a physical geography. What are the municipal boundaries? What are the neighborhood names? Do the business districts carry special designations? Where do people live and work? You can find some of this on the U.S. Census website. The finer details can be found on official city maps that delineate neighborhoods and zoning districts.

Municipalities have a political geography. They're divided into wards, precincts and districts, the way the nation is divided into states. These boundaries are the municipality's legislative districts, represented by councilors or aldermen. Get familiar with the system so you know who represents each district.

Cities are also divided by state and congressional legislative districts. Who represents your area in the state legislature and in the U.S. Congress? Larger municipalities may contain more than one of these districts.

Locate the government offices. Who works in the town or city hall besides the mayor, manager and clerk? Do the treasurer and town attorney maintain offices there? Other bureaucrats work elsewhere; the highway superintendent may be based at the town garage. You'll need to know everyone's location to make your regular rounds.

Finally, explore the social geography — the places where bureaucrats and regular citizens hang out and swap stories. Find the coffee shops, luncheonettes and bars frequented by municipal officials and workers. Figure out the informal meeting places for your community, whether they're high school sports events or the dump on Saturdays. Start hanging out in these places yourself. This is where you get to know people and where people get to know you.

Making the Rounds

community rounds checklist

- ☐ Mayor or manager's office
- ☐ Clerk's office
- ☐ Treasurer's office
- ☐ Council/aldermen/selectmen
- ☐ Highway department (traffic and parking)

- ☐ Public works
- ☐ Planning and zoning commissions
- ☐ Inspectional services
- ☐ Parks and recreation

The duties of a government reporter depend on the size of his or her municipality and news organization. In a small town you may cover every level of government, from zoning board hearings to school committee meetings. You may even be assigned to cover these different parts of government in multiple towns. In larger cities, reporters specialize; some news organizations have separate City Hall, education, and public safety beats. Whatever your duties, you will need the same set of reporter's tools: commitment, consistency and curiosity.

Maintaining a regular presence at City or Town Hall will show government officials you are committed to the job. Producing a consistent stream of stories that look at both the successes and missteps of government will earn you the trust of your sources and audience. People may not like everything you write, but they will come to respect you. Most of all, you'll need a healthy curiosity and enthusiasm about the issues and personalities on your beat. If you take the time to find out what's interesting about a topic, you're far more likely to produce a story that's interesting to your audience.

The most common — and powerful — question you can ask on your rounds of the mayor's office, the highway department, the inspection agency and the planning commission is *"What's new?"* Of course, you'll also have specific questions on pending topics and new issues your reporting has uncovered. If you've received information about a street in disrepair, ask what is being done. If you've been tipped that neighbors plan to petition the council about a noisy bar in a residential area, ask for comment. It's easier to get a response during your regular stops than to wait for a callback when you're facing deadline.

Don't be afraid to *keep* asking the same questions. If maintenance problems at the city pool remain unresolved, ask about the issue at every visit, even if you are told each time nothing is new. At some point there will be a resolution, and if you don't ask, they might not tell.

Depending on your duties, your rounds will generally include checks with the various elected officials and bureaucrats detailed in "Government Beat: People" in this chapter. Here are things you'll be looking for as you make your way door-to-door:

▶ Ask about any upcoming meetings of the various commissions or boards. Get the agendas for these meetings and review them. Zoning hearings can become contentious screaming matches. But don't wait for the meeting agenda. Stop at the zoning office to see what applications have been filed for variances and waivers.

▶ Check with the clerk's office for any filings that have come in or for notices and postings that have gone out about the city's or town's business. Stop at the inspector's offices to see if any health or safety violations have been filed.

▶ Monitor the parks, highways and public works departments for any planned construction or repair programs. Are any recreational programs about to launch? Encourage these departments to use your organization as a way to promote their activities.

▶ Stop at the treasurer's office to see how tax collections are going. Check how the budget estimates compare with the real numbers of revenues and expenses. You don't have to write about every person who is behind in his or her payment, but you can look for trends or prominent people who may be behind in their taxes.

▶ Larger cities have cushy offices for city councilors and their staffs. Town councilors or selectmen in smaller communities often have no office in Town Hall. They are often volunteers who work full-time at something else. You'll probably contact them at home or at their day jobs.

GOVERNMENT BEAT ▶ Documents

Here's a reason bureaucracy is not such a bad thing: It keeps lots of records.

Birth certificates, death certificates, wedding licenses and divorce filings. Businesses have to register with the state; so do convicted sex offenders. Municipalities track property values and home sales. Your dog has a paper trail from its license and rabies inoculation. Your car's records show how much it cost and who else has owned it. Parking tickets and automated toll pass records show where it's been.

Many records are a keystroke away on your computer; others may require a bit more digging or perhaps filing a request under your state public records law or the federal and states' Freedom of Information Act (FOIA). The information available online offers all sorts of possibilities limited only by your imagination. Part of your routine should include a check of government records to verify a hunch, illustrate a point or do some digging for a story idea.

Census, labor, and public health records offer insight into population trends. How many people live in your area compared with 10 years ago? Is the unemployment rate getting better or worse? What kinds of jobs are being created; what kinds are being lost? How is the marriage rate or divorce rate trending? Are drunken driving accidents increasing or decreasing? Is the number of suicides up or down?

Records let you track the personal and professional lives of the people you write about. The data show where they have lived, what they paid for their homes and how much they sold them for. You can search for the professional certifications or licenses they have held and any disciplinary action taken against them. You can find arrest records and bankruptcy filings. You can check for campaign contributions. Social networking allows you to find their friends and business associates.

With records you can follow the money of publicly traded companies, public officials and tax-exempt charitable organizations. What is the financial health of the new business that wants to open in your town? Can you find any dealings between that company and the city councilor pushing to get it a tax break? How does the charity making a big fundraising drive spend the money it receives? If your beat includes a small town without computer resources, you may have to resort to an old-fashioned paper chase. But it's all there, tucked away in the records.

Where to Find the Records

Nearly every transaction monitored by government is recorded somewhere. Finding, sorting and interpreting the data get easier with the launch of each search engine and every expanded public digital initiative.

Federal Databases A starting point for every reporter new to a beat should be the U.S. Census website. You can click your way to a collection of useful background data about your community, including population, housing, median income and local employment details. The site also offers maps and multimedia content that illustrate the data. The Census' *T*opologically *I*ntegrated *G*eographic *E*ncoding and *R*eferencing (TIGER) system will overlay data such as residents' ages and income onto detailed maps of your region, town or even neighborhood. Try it out to get a feel for its potential.

The Federal Election Commission's website allows you to follow the cash raised and spent by candidates for federal office and the donors and public action committees that support them. Even if your beat is local politics, it's useful to see who is making contributions to whom. Most states have similar sites to track local candidates.

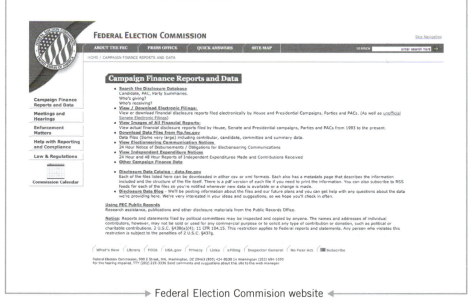

→ U.S. Census website ←

Source: www.census.gov

→ Federal Election Commision website ←

Source: www.fec.gov/disclosure.shtml

National Archives website

Source: www.archives.gov/research/tools/checklist.html

The National Archives offers databases on government contracts and grants, along with information on military service, business filings, labor unions and the stock market. Again, this is a fun site to play around with in your spare time.

State Databases Some states have archive divisions, such as Utah's Division of Archives and Records Services. These sites provide one-stop shopping for historical data on births, deaths, business dealings and legislative actions.

Other states categorize data by subject and jurisdiction. The New Jersey Department of Banking and Insurance website can search for people holding licenses in professions, from home repair salesperson to pawn broker. All you do is fill in the name.

Secretary of state websites offer a range of useful information. Businesses are required to file information with the state, including the names of their officers, incorporation details and tax information. Tax-exempt charities must file detailed information, called 990 Forms, on salaries and other expenses. Secretary of state offices also collect state and local elections data and details about each municipality and

Utah Archives website

Source: www.archives.state.ut.us/index.html

New Jersey Department of Banking and Insurance website

Source: https://www6.state.nj.us/DOBI _Lic
Search/Jsp/bnkSearch.jsp

county such as, the page on the city of Louisville from the Kentucky secretary of state's website.

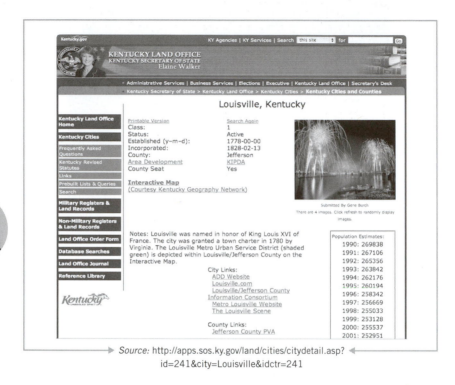

Source: http://apps.sos.ky.gov/land/cities/citydetail.asp?
id=241&city=Louisville&idctr=241

State public health departments collect data on births and deaths. They analyze out-breaks of flu and other diseases. Many keep birth and marriage certificates and divorce decrees. The following page from Georgia's Department of Community Health analyzes violent deaths by cause and location.

Municipal Databases Various municipal departments also keep online records. You can check property values on homes and businesses in the assessor's office or see delinquent tax lists in the treasurer's office. Inspectional services often maintain websites listing unsafe buildings and commercial establishments that have been cited for health and safety violations.

Commercial Databases Public record searches can be done through commercial sites that — for a fee — gather data about individuals or businesses across the range of state departments and divisions. Most offer standard fees for basic searches of names,

2009 Georgia Data Summary
VIOLENT DEATH REPORTING SYSTEM

Types of violent death included: Suicide, homicide, unintentional firearm injury, legal intervention, and deaths of undetermined intent.

DESCRIPTION

- The Georgia Violent Death Reporting System (GVDRS) is part of the National Violent Death Reporting System (NVDRS)

- Funded by the Centers for Disease Control and Prevention, National Center for Injury Prevention and Control (CDC/NCIPC)

- Population-based system which is able to report on multi-victim incidents as well as on individual persons (victims and suspects)

MULTIPLE SOURCES OF DATA

GVDRS combines data from several sources which include:

- Death certificates
- Medical examiner and/or coroner records
- Law enforcement records
- Supplemental homicide reports
- Crime laboratory records

CURRENT STATES PARTICIPATING IN NVDRS

NVDRS GOALS

- Inform decision makers and program planners about the magnitude, trends and characteristics of violent death

- Evaluate state-based violence prevention programs and strategies

NUMBER OF GEORGIA RESIDENT VICTIMS BY TYPE, 2006

Type of Violent Death	2006 #	2006 %
Suicide	904	51
Homicide	616	35
Undetermined intent	200	11
Unintentional firearm	13	1
Legal intervention	38	2
Total	1771	100

SUICIDE AND HOMICIDE
BY GEORGIA PUBLIC HEALTH DISTRICT, 2006

Public Health District	Suicide #	Suicide Rate	Homicide #	Homicide Rate
1-1 Northwest (Rome)	58	11.3	14	2.7
1-2 North Georgia (Dalton)	40	12.2	6	1.8
2 North (Gainesville)	33	7.2	11	2.4
3-1 Cobb-Douglas	66	9.4	22	3.1
3-2 Fulton	70	8.6	101	12.4
3-3 Clayton County (Morrow)	12	5.1	39	16.5
3-4 East Metro (Lawrenceville)	80	11.1	46	6.4
3-5 DeKalb	49	7.4	98	14.7
4 LaGrange	56	9.1	28	4.6
5-1 South Central (Dublin)	12	8.9	13	9.6
5-2 North Central (Macon)	36	7.6	22	4.6
6 East Central (Augusta)	43	10.1	29	6.8
7 West Central (Columbus)	14	4.0	24	6.8
8-1 South (Valdosta)	17	7.5	10	4.4
8-2 Southwest (Albany)	22	6.2	19	5.4
9-1 Coastal (Savannah)	56	11.5	45	9.2
9-2 Southeast (Waycross)	24	7.5	26	8.1
10 Northeast (Athens)	42	11.5	20	5.5
Unknown GA county of Residence	174	---	43	---
Total	904	11.0	616	7.5

Note: Rates are per 100,000 population. These are crude rates, rather than age-adjusted rates.

Georgia Department of Community Health, Division of Public Health – 2 Peachtree Street, NW – Atlanta, GA 30303 – (404) 657-2585 – GA-GVDRS@dhr.state.ga.us – http://health.state.ga.us
Date updated: September 2009
Publication Number

Source: http://health.state.ga.us/pdfs/epi/cdiee/CDIEE%20
Data%20Summaries%202009/GVDRS%202009%20Data%20
Summary%20Sheet%20082809%20v5.1.pdf

addresses, telephone numbers and e-mail addresses, arrest and bankruptcy filings, property ownership and address changes. It's best to learn to do this kind of research yourself, but it can be helpful to use commercial search sites to improve your skills.

The Phone Book Once a main tool for reporters, this old school reference material still offers up good information. If someone owns a business and isn't picking up the phone at that address, you can get her home address through the assessor's records and her phone number in the white pages. The phone book is also a great way to find political candidates if their campaign offices are closed or to check the spelling of a resident's

FILING A FOIA REQUEST

S OMETIMES WHEN PUBLIC OFFICIALS are not forthcoming, you'll have to make a formal request for information not readily available in databases. The Freedom of Information Act, passed by Congress in 1966, establishes the rights of citizens to get nearly all records, from internal policy papers to e-mails between officials. In addition, each

---

Date request mailed

Agency Head or Keeper of the Records
 Name of Agency
 Address of Agency
 City, State, Zip Code
 Re: Massachusetts Public Records Request

Dear _____:

This is a request under the Massachusetts Public Records Law (M. G. L. Chapter 66, Section 10).

I am requesting that I be provided a copy of the following records:

[Please include a detailed description of the information you are seeking.]

[Optional: I recognize that you may charge reasonable costs for copies, as well as for personnel time needed to comply with this request. If you expect costs to exceed $10.00, please provide a detailed fee estimate.]

As you may be aware, the Public Records Law requires you to provide me with a written response within 10 calendar days. If you cannot comply with my request, you are statutorily required to provide an explanation in writing.

Sincerely,

Your Name
Your Address
City, State, Zip Code
Telephone Number [Optional]

▶ *Figure 8.1* FOIA Request Template ◀

state has its own law, with names such as open records or sunshine laws. These laws establish procedures on how to request information and set guidelines government must follow in handling such requests.

Federal agencies, from the Department of Justice to the Agency on Aging, provide information on their websites on how to file FOIA requests. Many have a form letter you can copy and send. Most states have similar sites. The form letter on the previous page appears on the Public Records Division section of the Massachusetts secretary of state's website:

A FIOA request is fairly straightforward. The trick is to be very clear about what you want. If you are vague, the agency can deny or delay your request. Use specific language about subject matter, names and dates. File a more detailed request if your first FIOA attempt comes back without the information you wanted.

Government sites also include information on how to appeal a FOIA rejection or slow action on a request. That can include filing a lawsuit against an uncooperative agency. Many states allow petitioners to reclaim their legal costs from the government agency, another powerful way to encourage compliance. The threat of a lawsuit can be all it takes to pry loose information to break a big story.

name. Of course you don't have to store a complete set of phone books. Most are accessible online, along with reverse directories, which can tell you who lives at an address or the name attached to a telephone number. This, unfortunately, won't help if the phone number is unlisted.

How to Use the Documents

Public records can be used in different ways. Demographics, business filings and historical archives put individual stories into a broader context. A piece about demand at your town's food kitchens has more meaning if you can show that unemployment is up. A bad car crash involving a teen driver has greater significance if data show a rise in these kinds of accidents. A story about declining property values offers more insight if the sales numbers are compared with those of other times of boom and bust.

The use of campaign records is a staple of governmental reporting. Although you'll find few revelations, a careful assessment of the numbers keeps politicians honest. Who gave what to whose campaign? How was it spent? Did the contributor own a business that benefited from action initiated by the politician?

Jeff Gottlieb

Ruben Vives

Ruben Vives and Jeff Gottlieb
The Los Angeles Times

When Los Angeles Times reporter Ruben Vives was assigned to cover communities in southeastern Los Angeles County, he did what a reporter new to a beat should do: He spent time in the communities, talked with local activists and government officials, and attended city council meetings.

Some of those municipalities faced economic troubles. One of them, Maywood, was planning to disband its police department because it couldn't insure its police officers and other employees. In fact, at a council meeting Vives learned that Maywood was about to lay off all workers and contract with the neighboring city of Bell to cover city services. The plan caught Vives' attention, and, with senior Times reporter Jeff Gottlieb, he began to dig.

They decided to check on Bell, a city of nearly 37,000 and one of the poorest in Los Angeles County. A routine call to the district attorney to see if the city was the subject of an investigation found that the DA was looking into why part-time council members in Bell were making $100,000 a year. Gottlieb and Vives went to Bell City Hall to speak with the city administrator. When he refused to meet with them, the reporters asked to see his contract.

Under the California Public Records Act, public officials are required to provide access to municipal records, including contracts, expense accounts and public meetings minutes that would show city council votes on salaries and other spending issues.

But the city clerk wouldn't provide the administrator's contract or other public records.

"They made us fill out a public records request and charged us a buck for the Xerox copy," Gottlieb recalls. "That set off an alarm."

The two reporters learned that local citizens had tried to get the same information to check on rumors the administrator was making between $300,000 and $400,000. Those requests were denied on technicalities.

"They were told they didn't fill out the forms correctly and were too vague," Gottlieb says. "Citizens ask questions like: 'How much does the city administrator make?' but don't request a document that has the information. We tried to be specific with dates and documents. We asked for minutes, contracts of the city manager, the assistant city manager and the police chief. We asked to see the expense [for travel and other costs] paid to city council members."

Gottlieb and Vives not only knew how to ask for documents but also had another advantage: the legal resources of a major metropolitan newspaper. If Bell officials failed to comply with their request in 10 days, the Times would file suit to get the records and ask the judge to charge the officials the legal costs.

behind the beat

"You have to put the money up front to pay these lawyers. People can't afford it, but the officials knew that we could," Gottlieb says.

After nine days of daily calls to the clerk, the reporters were told that the Bell city manager wanted to meet with them at a small city park. Gottlieb and Vives arrived at a small room used for Boy Scout meetings where they were met by the city manager, the assistant city manager, the police chief, some city council members, including one from Maywood, and two attorneys. The records and files sat on a nearby table.

Knowing the reporters could now find the answers, the officials began answering questions. The Bell city manager named his salary: $700,000 a year — the highest public official's salary in Los Angeles County. The police chief was getting $457,000 — double what he had made in a larger city.

The records showed the city councilors were getting $100,000 a year for their part-time job. And although they claimed they had to pay their expenses out of those salaries, the records showed the city had been billed for those costs.

The revelations led to a series of stories by Gottlieb and Vives that finally showed local residents what their officials were up to and resulted in the resignation of the city manager and other officials, who were indicted on criminal charges. The pair went on to investigate the financial dealing in other Los Angeles County municipalities. They were awarded the 2011 Pulitzer Prize for Public Service.

Vives is modest about their accomplishments. "It's basic reporting," he says. "If anyone was covering the city the way they should, they would have uncovered what we did."

You can find the data to answer these and other questions. Property records, business records, even articles in obscure publications provide facts and details. When combined and put into context, these different lines help to connect the dots.

GOVERNMENT BEAT ▶ Stories

Government reporters face all possibilities of stories on their beat. They must track a variety of scheduled meetings. The town council or board of aldermen holds regular weekly or monthly sessions. Zoning boards and licensing commissions do as well. Traffic and parking commissions, historic site panels and community health organizations also hold public meetings. Check the websites for meetings; keep a planning calendar.

Sometimes you can't attend everything at once. If that's the case, call the major players before a meeting and do a preview or advance story. If your community-access cable channel runs videos of government meetings, you can check up on what happened without having to attend. Those videos tend to replay frequently or may be available on the town website. You can even link your readers to that site.

Money is an ever-present story. At this writing, the rising costs of government workers' health care policies and pensions are a growing problem across the country. Stories on how government is coping in times of tight budgets are important to citizens who pay for, and rely on, government services. A story about budget cuts to a program for disabled students can look like a dry recitation of numbers. A story about a family trying to cope with loss of services for their child makes the issue real to your audience.

Stories that offer insight into day-to-day life are always well-read pieces. Check on the traffic volume or fluctuations in parking tickets and parking meter revenues. Has the amount or type of garbage the public works department collects changed? If your municipality has a recycling system, these ups and downs can affect revenues and taxes. Keep track of water usage, especially during summer months, when drought can affect water supplies. Some news organizations monitor water consumption as a metric for the ebb and flow of population and business trends. A spike in usage bears investigation.

Hearings and Meetings

The mainstay of government reporting is the constant stream of public meetings that officials are required to hold on a regular basis. The town or city council may meet on a weekly, semiweekly or monthly schedule. So too do the zoning and planning boards and fire and police commissions. County governments have similar schedules. Various state commissions also hold regular meetings. State legislatures hold hearings to gather public comment on proposed bills.

All these meetings and hearings can seem tedious. The drone of planning commission discussions about the diameter of new sewage pipes or a city council debate on lighting regulations can lull the best of us to sleep. Therein lies the challenge for the reporter: how to make the seemingly mundane interesting to an audience you are trying to inform. This is where creativity, thought and legwork make a difference. Remember, boring stories are the product of boring reporters. Don't cover these stories as if you were a stenographer, simply noting who said what. The meeting is a small part of the reporting you should be doing. Your readers need to know what happens at these meetings, but more importantly, they need to know what it means to them. You must be prepared to explain the impact of the vote a committee or council took on a specific issue.

Before the Meeting

premeeting checklist

- ☐ Get the agenda
- ☐ Research the items
  - ☐ Learn the history
  - ☐ Understand the impact of the proposals
- ☐ Identify and contact the proponents/ proponents
- ☐ Find people affected by the issue

Boring reporters come to a meeting unprepared and then try to write something out of lackluster dialogue. That approach is unlikely to produce anything interesting. Better stories lurk behind a debated issue. Look for those stories before the meeting begins by interviewing people in the know, and then follow up after the meeting ends.

Research Most government agencies are required to give advance notice of meetings and provide an agenda. If an agenda is not available, get it from the staff.

Research the topics. Look for background in previous stories. Find out who has proposed the bill or regulation. Who supports the issue? Who is against it? Who are the citizens or citizen groups on either side? Reach out to those people to get background. Find people affected by the issues. They may not plan to attend the session, but their perspective is an important way of explaining the issue to your audience.

This advance work will help you understand the larger issues behind the meeting. You will have a scorecard of the opponents and proponents; you won't have to scramble for names and titles during the meeting. You'll have contact numbers for sources you can call after everyone has fled.

This footwork also allows you to write part of the story before the meeting starts. You can sketch out the sections of the story that explain background, history and the importance of the subject. Some media organizations call this below-the-dash material. If you're on a deadline, having this material ready to go can be a great comfort.

Write an Advance You can use some of this new knowledge to write an advance story about the upcoming meeting. Advances perform an important function for your audience, allowing them to learn about issues while there's still time to attend a meeting and make their views known.

The Meeting

meeting checklist

☐ **Arrive early**
　☐ Scout the area.
　☐ Set up your equipment.
　☐ Find the key people.

☐ **Take complete notes; annotate as you go**
☐ **Follow up with those who testify; get phone numbers**

Once you've done your preparation, you're ready to attend the meeting. But remember, it isn't a simple matter of showing up, taking notes and dashing off a story. Here are some things to remember.

Arrive Early Getting there before the event begins gives you time to check out the venue, find a good vantage point and set up your microphone or video camera if you're going to provide multimedia coverage. Use the time to find the key players and to introduce yourself, ask questions and get contact information. Arrange for follow-up interviews after the session ends.

Get Good Voices, Not All Voices Some hearings will include the testimony of many people who repeat the same themes. You don't want to quote or record them all. Make choices. Quote those who best state the issues. Listen for personal stories, emotional statements or other factors that can add drama and insight to your story. Chances are you'll get less and less new material with each speaker. Still, don't get lulled by the repetition; you could miss a key element of the public commentary.

Don't Be a Slave to Proceedings You may want to follow up on a statement made by someone who leaves after saying his or her piece. Don't hesitate to follow that person out of the hearing room to ask questions. You probably won't miss anything important, but if other reporters are there, ask them to keep track of what is said while you're gone. Reporters are good about covering for each other. We're desperate people who understand we may have to make a similar request.

When you do follow that person out of the room, explain who you are and get the person's cell phone number. You can call this individual when you have more time, rather than trying to ask all your questions in a rush. You'll also have another contact for the future.

Blogging Blogging is the most immediate way to report what's happening at the hearing or meeting. But the form presents some challenges. You might not be allowed to clack away at your laptop during an official proceeding. If you can, you'll be trying to do several things at once, which means you won't do any of them well. Chances are that your audience isn't waiting with bated breath for a minute-by-minute recounting of a zoning board meeting. You don't have to present testimony in real time. If something significant happens, you can file the first few hundred words of the major points that will be in your print or online story. What action was taken? Who spoke? What was the general mood of the meeting and the speakers?

on the web

Patch.com New Jersey

When an election looms or a civic issue faces a vote, the residents of Westfield, N.J., track the debate from their computers and smartphones by linking to the frequent updates John Celock posts on the Westfield Patch.com site.

Celock even turned the potentially leaden subject of school budget cuts into an up-to-the-minute breaking news story.

"A lot of the reporting was instantaneous," he says.

Celock has won over an audience of citizens and town officials with his ability to report more stories and more details than the weekly newspapers or suburban sections of the metro daily, which provided less-than-complete coverage of the upscale community 20 miles outside of New York City.

"I don't have to put all the issues into one 1,000-word story," he says. "I can break them out in separate stories."

Patch is part of a hyperlocal movement that, at this writing, is reinvigorating community-based reporting in hundreds of sites around the country. Metro dailies have also joined the movement, adding coverage of suburban towns and city neighborhoods as separate pages on their websites. Formerly sleepy community weeklies have gone online to compete.

Thanks to the Web, hyperlocal reporting isn't subject to the old journalistic constraints of time and space. There are no once-a-day deadlines; breaking stories are filed immediately. There are no limitations on the number or size of articles; a hyperlocal website is an infinite newspaper.

Celock says some town officials were surprised at first with the speed his stories are published and read.

"It was very new for everyone in town government," he says.

Now people get impatient if they don't see a story they pitched the day before.

"I tell them I have to check that out," he says. "If you explain to people why you are holding something — and doing that with everyone — they appreciate the fact you are doing a thorough job."

Celock, a Columbia School of Journalism graduate, finds the job more gratifying than his earlier work, which included covering New York City and state politics.

"It is very satisfying to talk to people and really see the impact these issues of local governance have on the everyday lives of people," he says.

Unless the city council president takes a swing at the mayor, it shouldn't be necessary to rush out raw video. An edited video of an event is much more viewable than minute after minute of drone. If you have audio from the meeting, you can grab sound snippets to go along with your written story. If you do produce a video, remember the rules of storytelling. Capture some of the meeting along with quick interviews from officials and the public who attended the hearing. Let them help to tell the story.

Writing the Story

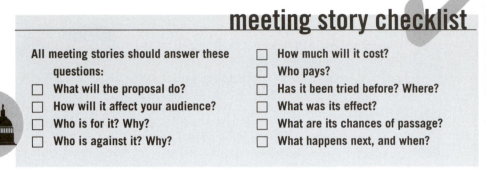

meeting story checklist

All meeting stories should answer these questions:
- ☐ What will the proposal do?
- ☐ How will it affect your audience?
- ☐ Who is for it? Why?
- ☐ Who is against it? Why?

- ☐ How much will it cost?
- ☐ Who pays?
- ☐ Has it been tried before? Where?
- ☐ What was its effect?
- ☐ What are its chances of passage?
- ☐ What happens next, and when?

The meeting or hearing has ended. Your notebook and recorder are loaded with material. The below-the-dash material awaits. What do you do with all this stuff? Your task is to tell your audience not only what happened but, more importantly, what it means to them. And you have to do this in a way that's interesting and accessible.

Journalists should report impact, not process. It's up to you to decide what's most important to your audience and how much space to give each point. Sometimes a meeting will spend hours debating a small matter that merits a single sentence in your story. Or it could take just minutes to pass a measure that has a much greater effect on your readers.

Here's some advice on how to put it all together:

What Is the Significant Information? Here's a lede you should vow never to write:

> *The board of aldermen met Thursday night at City Hall to discuss a variety of issues related to Shelbyville's annual budget.*

Interesting? No. Does it make you want to read further? Not a chance. The lede hits all the traditional Five Ws (*Who, What, When, Where* and *Why*), but these are matters of process, not impact. It explains nothing about the substance of the meeting and will most likely drive your audience away. An important test of any lede is to ask yourself *Did I have to be there to write this?* If it reads like an agenda list, try again.

All stories need action, impact and context — especially meeting and hearing stories. For the citizens of Shelbyville that means *which* details of the annual budget were discussed at the meeting. Will the town's schools get more or less money? What about the cops and firefighters? How will the budget affect property taxes? And how will a change in property taxes affect the citizenry? Any one of those items would draw readers into the story.

Compare our bland lede to this one:

> *The proposed annual budget for Shelbyville will mean $2 million more for the town's schools, $500,000 less for the police department and a "modest" increase in town property tax rates.*
>
> *"We're hoping to keep any increase to 3 percent," Mayor Abraham Simpson told the board of aldermen at its regular City Hall meeting on Thursday night. "We think that's pretty modest considering our financial problems."*

More interesting? Our hypothetical lede has three significant details (more money for schools, less money for cops and some increase in taxes) that should give readers a reason to read on. Some of those Five Ws about process have been demoted to secondary details in the second paragraph. The quote from Mayor Simpson helps illustrate one of the key points in the lede, further engaging the readers.

Stories can be more compelling if you show how the issue affects an individual. If, for example, you did your homework and found the city council was contemplating a 3 percent property tax increase, you might go out ahead of the meeting and find an example of what it would mean to one vulnerable homeowner:

> *Some months Lenny Franklin has to decide which household bill will have to wait until his next Social Security check. Now the 71-year-old retired power plant worker says he doesn't know how he can afford a bigger property tax bill.*
>
> *"They say only 3 percent," he says while raking his immaculate front lawn on Chestnut Street. "That's another $150 to me. That's not an 'only.'"*

Last night Mayor Abraham Simpson told the board of aldermen the city was contemplating a "modest" 3 percent hike in the city's property tax. Although it will be the first increase in three years, it was still bad news to Franklin and other homeowners on fixed incomes.

It's the same story but with a personal hook that brings the consequences of the aldermen's vote home to readers. People grasp issues better when they are illustrated through someone's life. By finding out the details of the upcoming meeting, then walking down the street and spotting Mr. Franklin raking his leaves, you have the elements of a more compelling story.

Put the Details in Context This is where all that legwork pays off. If the meeting is about the town budget and you know the background about the line items from your reporting, you can speak with authority about what those details mean. How does the proposed budget compare with last year's? Is it more or less than the rate of inflation? How will it affect you audience's pocketbooks? How does it compare with the budgets of neighboring towns?

Avoid "Tennis Volley" Organization You risk giving your audience a kind of virtual whiplash if your story shifts back and forth between debate points, giving the pro argument, followed by the con argument, followed by the pro argument . . . You get the idea. Present one side's argument in detail before going on to the rebuttal. Your lede should summarize the various sides.

Don't Quote Everyone Some new reporters feel they should honor all voices by quoting as many speakers as possible. But doing so clutters the story with repetition and keeps you from exercising judgment. Your job is to choose the best statements, testimony and debating points to illustrate the issues. Use quotes from those who made the most clear and compelling points, and skip the rest. If you want to convey the general attitude at a meeting, you can give a general tally of those for and those against.

Explain What's Next If a proposal passes, explain when the regulation or law takes effect and what it will mean. If action on the issue is delayed, tell your readers when it will be taken up again. If it fails, detail what chances it has of being brought up again.

Follow Up Reporters sometimes let stories fade away. A big issue — a proposal to raise property taxes or lower speed limits — generates high interest, then drops off the public radar. When a plan is sent out for more study or a board takes it under advisement, the hot-button issue can grow cold in the rush of newer news. Letting that happen is a disservice to readers who care about the outcome.

If the council votes to set up a study committee, make a note to check the progress. If the committee goes silent on an issue after a hearing, push the lawmakers to say whether this issue is dead or moving in another direction. Keeping track of these issues raises your odds of getting an update on the story before anyone else.

But be aware that some proposals are perpetual topics. For instance, a single town councilor will make a career of campaigning for some recycling plan that is strongly opposed by the majority. Note in your story that this issue has been brought up for the past X number of years and has no support even if it has been sent out for further study.

STORY SCAN: A MEETING STORY

This story from the Newark, N.J., Star-Ledger was filed to a website within hours after a city council meeting. Though it's short and factual, the reporter uses good background and details that take the story beyond a simple piece about a property tax increase.

Newark City Council Floats 16 Percent Tax Hike

NEWARK - The Newark City Council adopted a series of amendments to the city budget today that would increase property taxes by 16 percent, representing an increase of $780 for the average homeowner.

The lede combines the council's action with an explanation of its impact on the individual homeowner. This story was filed to the newspaper's website immediately after the meeting, so there is no time reference other than "today."

*Another graf filled
with good details and
background that help
put the tax increase in
context of other issues
facing the city.*

*More context to show
how the different
budget pieces fit
together.*

The tax hike, combined with roughly 850 layoffs, is the city's response to one of the worst budget crises in decades, but the hit to taxpayers is far less than budget officials had previously warned, thanks largely to a plan put forward by the council to sell a spate of city buildings and lease them back.

After weeks of grueling negotiations between the state, county and city, the sale/leaseback plan is expected to infuse $40 million into the 2010 budget. With a series of other one-time revenues as well as some last minute cuts, the city has filled an $83 million deficit created after the failure of Mayor Cory Booker's plan to create a municipal utilities authority.

*Now we get into
council reaction
with some more
background about the
proposal.*

"I don't love the idea of a sale/leaseback. I don't think any of us do. It's not sustainable," said West Ward Councilman Ronald Rice at a special meeting of the council today. Rice proposed the idea months ago as an alternative to the MUA. But with less than three months left in the budget year, the other option would have been a steep tax hike to Newark property owners.

"With the failure of the MUA, if we had not explored this possibility we would be talking about a 40 percent tax increase," said At-Large Councilman Carlos Gonzalez, who chairs the council's budget committee.

*Additional information
about the impact of
the council's decision.
A number showing the
average dollar increase
would help further
illustrate what all these
numbers mean.*

Taxpayers saw their bills go up by 7 percent in the third quarter. Fourth quarter bills will tack on the remaining 9 percent.

*A quick description of
what happens next.*

The council still has one week to make further cuts before adopting the budget. The council plans to meet on either Oct. 13 or Oct. 14.

Resources

Links

Facts and Figures
▶ U.S. Census, www.census.gov
▶ Federal Election Commission, www.fec.gov/disclosure.shtml
▶ The National Archives, www.archives.gov/research/tools/checklist.html

Government Groups
▶ National Association of Secretaries of State, www.nass.org
▶ National Association of Towns, www.natat.org
▶ National Conference of State Legislators, www.ncsl.org
▶ National Governor's Association, www.nga.org
▶ The National League of Cities, www.nlc.org
▶ The United States Conference of Mayors, www.usmayors.org
(*Note:* Most states have their own association of towns and cities.)

Terms and Procedures
▶ IRC Politics, www.ircpolitics.org/glossary.html
▶ Robert's Rules of Order, www.robertsrules.com
▶ Your Dictionary, www.yourdictionary.com/dictionary-articles/american-government-definitions.html

Assignment Desk

Develop profile story ideas for three aspects of your local government. Each story should involve some issue, personality or recent event and provide you a chance to learn more about a department or person within your beat. Not all the ideas have to focus on an individual, but they should include the voices and insights of the people affected by the issue. These story ideas can be the topic for a classroom discussion.

Extra Credit Turn one of these ideas into a story. Research the details, history and personalities before you interview officials. Talk with people affected by the issue. After you've produced your piece, make a list of all the things you learned and all the people you talked with. See if the local newspaper or community website would be interested in using the product of your hard work.

CHAPTER 9

EDUCATION

Who would want the education beat? Isn't chasing cops-and-robbers stories more exciting than getting the scoop on the school superintendent's resignation? Wouldn't chronicling the life-and-death exploits of firefighters be more thrilling than interviewing the school librarian about a new computer system? How can blogging murder trial testimony from the courtroom compare to tweeting about a heated school board debate over extending the school day?

So it would seem. But in reality, covering your community's schools will keep you busier, offer bigger challenges, and provide a larger, more engaged audience than those other beats. The financial stakes are higher; schools take a greater percentage of municipal budgets than do police and fire departments combined. The opportunity for in-depth reporting is greater; schools produce an endless flow of data offering insight into the ways students and their teachers succeed or fail. The social themes are more numerous; schools are barometers of a huge array of issues, from racial inequality and immigration to creation theory and sex education, from bullying and drug use to subsidized lunches and union negotiations.

Education is central to everyone's history. We all spent years in school; we all have memories of teachers, classmates and seminal classroom experiences. Far fewer of us have had that same continuing experience with the police and fire departments. What most of us know about courts comes from Hollywood exaggerations or a few days of jury duty. But we all know about schools. Census data show that one American in five is a student; one in four of us — including faculty, staff and volunteers — spends some part of the day in a school.

Parents care deeply about education and its impact on their children's lives and futures. Taxpayers and homeowners, whether parents or childless, also care. Education takes a bigger gulp of our tax dollars than any other single item. We all care about the consequences of the education system. We follow test scores and rankings. We fret when the data show our community's children lagging behind students in other states or nations. We claim bragging rights when our schools rank at the top.

Schools are essential to our sense of community. Friday night high school football games, school plays and dances are major social events in many places. Parents form friendships and political alliances around the issues involving their children's education. Emotions rise and tempers flare at meetings about simple changes in curriculum. You'll understand how seriously a community takes education when you cover a school board meeting where teacher layoffs are discussed.

Schools are not just a local beat. Issues from testing standards to federal aid formulas play out on the national stage. Columbia University's National Access Network identifies 45 states where lawsuits have been filed challenging formulas used to fund public education. Federal funding of education has increased over the decade, raising the debate about how much influence Washington should have over local schools. Federal laws, most notably the No Child Left Behind Act of 2001, have raised awareness of educational strengths and weaknesses around the country through standardized testing. Local districts and states must provide other details on enrollments and teacher effectiveness that allow comparison between school districts and states.

"Education reporting has changed to a significant degree," says Linda Perlstein, the public editor at the Education Writers Association's website. "You used to be able to be a local reporter and not pay that much attention to Washington. That's really changed over the last three to five years. The conversations that people are having now are on the national wonky level. That's where the impact is happening."

Your stories will be part of those conversations. Parents, teachers, students and school officials will reach out to you as you report about changes in school populations, test scores and other education outcomes.

That's not to say it will be easy. Principals and superintendents may try to limit your access to schools and students. Teachers may not want to speak with you, even about non-controversial issues, for fear of losing their jobs. All who are involved in education will monitor your reporting. They have strong, divergent opinions, and they won't be shy about criticizing your work.

Jaime Sarrio,
The Atlanta Journal-Constitution

Jaime Sarrio understands the importance of education from a very personal perspective.

"I see why the stakes are so high because of the benefits education has had on my life," she says. "It allowed me to achieve things that other members of my family haven't been able to achieve."

Sarrio's education has continued over the seven years she's worked the school beat, in Gwinnet, Ga., the Nashville Tennessean and now the Journal-Constitution. Along the way, she has learned the nuances of the beat and some things about her own personality.

"I had to get over this desire for people to like me," she says. "Now I've gotten more skeptical and aggressive."

Sarrio gets assertive when principals and superintendents try to deny her access to schools or records. She has no hesitation about challenging them. "I ask them to show me where it says I can't come into their schools," she says.

She uses her softer side to develop contacts with the school districts' staff, including secretaries and counselors. If she needs a student perspective, she will stake out the school parking lot or go to the local Starbucks where high schoolers gather after class. She got to know the auditors at one district while reviewing credit card records.

"By the time I left, the auditors were saying, 'You have to check this person,'" she says. "You find people in the districts who are frustrated and are willing to talk."

Sarrio has these tips for new education writers:

▶ **Know the data.**

Spend time with someone from the state department of education who can show you how to use the volumes of federally mandated reports. "Learn how to access data for trends and patterns," she says.

▶ **Know your state's open records laws.**

Bureaucrats and department secretaries often think they can refuse reporters access to a school because children are involved. In fact, many states have laws that allow reporters to visit. Sarrio challenges officials even when a visit or document she is seeking isn't critical to her story.

▶ **"Everything is worth fighting for" she says.**

"You have to train them that you have the right to the information. You have to say, 'You're not allowed to deny me.'"

SCHOOL BEAT ▶ People

It can be said without much exaggeration that nearly everyone in your community figures into the education beat. There are many more stakeholders than the administrators, teachers, students and staff. Parents and relatives of the students have a role to play. Community residents weigh in when they think schools aren't teaching children to be effective citizens. Taxpayers want to know that their money is being spent wisely. Getting to know the different players can take time and patience. As always, getting out and meeting people will work much better than relying on the phone or e-mail.

State Education Commissioner, State Education Department

Although the state education offices may be hundreds of miles from your beat, it's important to reach out to the commissioner and the commissioner's staff. These officials set many requirements and goals for public schools; they also oversee the distribution of state funding to local districts. These are the people you will need to check with about pending regulations, legislation and recently passed state laws.

The commissioner and the staff have an important perspective on what is happening around the state. Much of the education data you will use is on the state education department's website. It would serve you well to get an orientation from commission staff on the various online databases.

Check for organizations that include education commissioners and commissions from neighboring states, such as the Southern Regional Education Board. These groups have an overview of education trends within your region.

School Board (School Committee; Board of Education)

In most cases members of the school board or school committee are elected by the public. (In rare instances, local school boards may be appointed by the governor, mayor or town and city councils.) These are usually nonsalaried positions, and candidates are not required to have a background in education. Employees of the school district are not allowed to run.

School board elections can be contentious contests over issues of money or curriculum. Some candidates are motivated by politics; school boards are sometimes the first rung in a politician's ascent to higher office. Other candidates are driven by social issues; sometimes groups will put up candidates who share their views on the teaching of evolution, sex education, or a particular interpretation of history. Because school board elections often draw fewer voters, candidates representing a narrow view on one issue can be elected. If their positions are seen as too extreme, more voters will turn out for the next election to choose another candidate.

In most cases the board has a say in all hiring, from the superintendent on down. It approves curriculum and rules for students and employees, sets the annual budget submitted by the superintendent and votes on supplementary spending requests. School board members have little to do with the day-to-day operation of the schools, but they are important people to know. Some boards will want you to speak only to the chairman or chairwoman. That shouldn't stop you from talking with the other members. Board members are often briefed on school issues not discussed in public. Developing good relationships with several members can get you an earful about what's happening below the surface in your district that you might not get from the superintendent or other administrators.

Superintendents

School districts are led by superintendents (called directors in some places), who are usually appointed by the school board after a long search process. The superintendent, in partnership with the school board, has the power to hire and fire, establish policies and spend money. He or she oversees the day-to-day operation of all the schools in a district. It is a powerful, high-paying job but also a demanding one that's vulnerable to public opinion. If students aren't doing well, if the faculty are unhappy and especially if the budget is running dry, the superintendent's days may be numbered.

So it's no surprise that some superintendents are wary of the media. Many superintendents, especially those in bigger districts, have one or more press secretaries to deal with reporters. Some superintendents will want any official comment to be cleared by their office. As with other beats, it is important to get around the wall of flaks and spend time with superintendents. If you have a good relationship with the superintendent, it is easier to get those at every level to speak with you.

Principals

Most schools are led by a principal answerable to the district superintendent. Principals oversee the conduct of teachers and students in the classroom and the care and maintenance of the school building. Even if you were never sent to the principal's office for punishment, the threat of that journey still lingers with many of us. But, in fact, principals are more than Grand Inquisitors handing out punishments. They serve as mentors to young teachers, counselors to students and advisers to parents.

Being a principal has always been a tough job; in recent years new federal and state accountability requirements have made it tougher still. The U.S. Labor Department estimates that 40 percent of the nation's principals are nearing retirement age. Although a pool of qualified candidates exists for many principal positions, fewer people are applying, especially

from the source

Jesse Register
Director of Metropolitan Nashville Public Schools

Dr. Jesse Register has earned a figurative degree in media relations during the three decades he has served as a school superintendent in North Carolina and Tennessee.

"I've gotten better at it as I've gotten more experienced," says Register, who heads the 80,000-student Metropolitan Nashville Public Schools. "I've learned it's hard to keep secrets or shy away from responding to reporters. That just backfires."

Register's school district is in the news nearly every day. He does a monthly call-in show on one of the local television channels. His communications department has three people to deal with the media and several other employees who maintain the district's Facebook and Twitter accounts. That's important for a district where more than 20 percent of students grew up speaking Spanish, Kurdish, Arabic, Somali, or one of nearly 90 other languages.

If Register has any frustration related to communication, it's the task of educating reporters. At times the major newspaper in town doesn't have a reporter dedicated to full-time coverage of the schools beat. The TV news departments send whoever is available when news needs covering.

Reporters come to him with a story-of-the-day mentality. If one state makes national news for cutting back on teachers' bargaining rights, the local reporters will call Register for comment. He'd rather see reporters focus on the issues that face Nashville schools. "You really don't see people who do in-depth work or get below the surface on the hot topic of the week," he says of reporters.

Register has one main piece of advice for reporters: Build contacts with your subjects by being a constant, trustworthy presence. "Take the time to establish relationships with your key people and try to be straightforward with them," he says. "Let them know what you're reporting. If you lose their confidence, you won't have a good working relationship."

for jobs in rural areas and inner-city schools. Some places, such as Washington state, are looking outside the traditional education disciplines for candidates with managerial skills.

Principals are valuable contacts; they have one ear to the events within their schools and another to policy and budget issues before the town council and school board. They can offer insight into how well a new initiative is working in the classrooms or foresee problems that may show up later. Principals are also your entrée into their schools — most districts require visitors to make a first stop at the principal's office. This requirement offers you the chance to have regular conversations with the principal about his or her school and the bigger issues at the district level. Some of these conversations will be off the record. That's OK. It's important to nurture sources and let them see that they can trust you.

Teachers

Teachers can be your most important sources. As the frontline troops of education, they know what's happening in their classrooms and can offer insight about what's happening in their schools and districts. They have important views on how local, state and national policies are playing out in their lesson plans and students' education.

You'll want to make contacts with teachers at all levels. New hires can offer a fresh perspective on their jobs. Experienced teachers provide an institutional memory that may run deeper than that of their principal or superintendent. Award-winning teachers are subjects for interesting feature pieces, but they also can be valuable, continuing sources of information. Specialists in math and science can help you understand changes in curriculum.

You can find teachers in a variety of ways. The best approach is to visit the schools, introduce yourself and hand out business cards — lots of business cards. Each time you do a story involving a teacher, make sure to get his or her cell phone number and e-mail address. You can also look up teachers on Facebook, and find Facebook pages for various teachers' groups, from specialty associations to individual school pages. If you blog, use it to trawl for contacts. Note that you've heard about some new policy or development and ask teachers for their opinions.

Many state education departments provide a database of all certified teachers with their names, specialties, years of experience and salary levels. Look for specialty groups, such as the Delaware Math Teachers Association or the Idaho Association of Art Teachers. Members of these organizations can be helpful when you are writing about their area of expertise.

Finding teachers willing to talk can be another matter. Those who belong to unions may feel somewhat protected to speak out; nonunion teachers may be concerned about losing their jobs. Their openness can also be set by the culture of their school and their superintendent. The unwillingness of a district superintendent to talk with the media can trickle down to the faculty. The general rules of good reporting apply here: Spending time in schools and showing that you are fair, trustworthy and interested in education can help gather a good set of teacher contacts.

Unions

Teachers in your school system may belong to a national union or a local professional association. Slightly more than half the nation's public school teachers are members of unions with collective bargaining rights. Other teachers belong to teaching associations.

The National Education Association is the largest union, with 3.2 million members, including public school teachers, other school staff members and college faculty. The American Federation of Teachers has 1.5 million members in 3,000 local affiliates. Other teacher's unions include independent education associations (IEAs) at the local, state and national levels and local-only teacher unions (LOTUs).

Teachers have become the focal point of debate over national education reform measures that tie teachers' salaries and tenure to the success of their students. Critics say unions impede education reform by protecting bad teachers. Union advocates say teachers are a key component of education reform and, with administrators and parents, share the responsibility for students' performance. Tighter state and local budgets in recent years have put pressure on teacher unions to retreat on wages and benefits. Several states have sought to end their collective bargaining rights.

Make contact with whatever organization represents the teachers in your district. These unions or professional associations often offer views that individual teachers may be cautious about stating. Officials in these groups can provide insights about issues affecting the whole district or individual schools and may give you a heads-up on demands and grievances before they are made public. But don't assume the union or association speaks for all teachers. Some members may disagree with their organizations; in some jurisdictions not all teachers will be members. In either case it may be hard to tease out opposition views to labor's positions. Teachers may be afraid to come out against what their colleagues favor. You should still try — perhaps in off-the-record conversations — to gauge the support the labor organization has with its membership.

Other Staff

You can find sources other than teachers and administrators. Librarians, school nurses, secretaries, teacher aides — even lunchroom and custodial staff have specific insights into daily operations and unusual events. But all must be nurtured in advance. That's why you should visit the schools in your area on a regular basis. Try to meet all levels of employees. Come up with stories that require you to interview the building superintendent and the cafeteria workers. With each contact, you broaden your grasp of what's happening.

Librarians do more than arrange books on shelves. At many schools they are the information technology leaders. Computers now supplement — and in some school libraries, have replaced — reference books. Librarians procure access to online databases. They wrestle with the tricky question of limiting access to sites some parents consider inappropriate for students. Librarians may also monitor what students are looking at on the Web to get insight into student interests in both popular culture and academic pursuits. And, of course, they still deal with books. Librarians keep up on the latest fiction being read by children and young adults. They follow trends in textbooks and other classroom materials. All this can help you understand the educational currents in your schools.

Librarians can be at the center of controversy. Parents may challenge the selection of books available to their children. Others may jump in to defend those books. *Catcher in the Rye* was once a touchstone in the debate over appropriate language and subject matter for students. It has been supplanted by new books that take on contemporary themes of sex, drug use and gender identity. Librarians can be active voices in budget debates; spending on books and other library materials are often the first to face the budget ax.

School nurses are also part of the budget debate. Because it's expensive to have nurses at each school, many schools are cutting back at the same time that more students need

medical services. A rising percentage of students are on medication for diabetes, hyperactivity and other conditions. Most schools require nurses or other personnel to administer the medications students must take during the day. The rise in food and other allergies also has become a medical issue in schools.

Nurses cannot provide you with information about specific students, but they can talk about medical trends at their schools. If you develop a good relationship, they might give you off-the-record details about an emergency or other incident.

Teacher's aides are another set of eyes in the classroom. If they trust you, they may talk about issues or incidents that trouble them. Aides are often closer to students in age and temperament; they may have insight into the social structures and cultures within the student body. They may be less cautious about speaking with reporters, but again, only if you make the effort to get to know them and develop a relationship of trust.

Secretaries and administrative assistants are the people who produce and monitor the flow of paperwork and the daily schedules and agendas of their bosses. They're the first people you speak with on the phone and the ones who check you in for a school visit. A good relationship with the staff speeds access to both faculty and administration. They can provide a heads-up on planned events and offer insight into issues such as attendance and disciplinary problems. They can also be another off-the-record source for breaking news.

Parents

Few things stir people's emotions more than the welfare of their children. That's why schools can be such an important and anxiety-ridden subject for parents. They see the quality of education as one of the most important factors in their children's futures. That makes parents an important source for school reporters.

Parents have strong opinions on everything: the quality of teachers, the effectiveness of curricula, the responsiveness of the administration, the actions and behaviors of their child's classmates. If their children do poorly on standardized test, you'll hear criticism about the way they were taught. If their children are having a hard time socially, parents may call to complain about an atmosphere that allows bullying. You can't write a story off each grievance — there will be too many, and most will be too personal. But listen and take note. Tell the parents you'll look into the issue. Ask if they know anyone else who feels as they do. Over time some of these complaints will form a pattern that will merit a story. Even if they don't, the dialogue you've begun with parents may lead to other stories.

You can meet parents at school board meetings and parent-teacher association gatherings, where people with concerns will make themselves known. Take the time to introduce yourself and hand out business cards. Get their contact information, including e-mail and Facebook pages. Invite them to contact you.

When you visit a school, look for parent volunteers. The fact that they are donating their time shows they are interested and involved. Go through the same routine of trading contact information. That parent you've spoken with may spread your name and contact information to many friends.

Students

Ultimately, education is about students. What happens to them during their days, weeks and months in school? What's the outcome of their lessons, homework and tests? Are they being prepared to live productive, useful lives? Are they getting the social experience and skills necessary to become responsible adults? These are important, complicated questions that every education writer needs to ask.

Too often the answers come back in the form of numbers. How many students scored at competent or advance levels in their standardized tests? How many failed? How many students advanced to the next grade? How many graduated? Of that number, how many went to college? How many students speak English as a second language? How many qualify for school breakfast and lunch? You could write story after story citing these figures without ever speaking with a student. That's not a good idea.

Reporters may write these easier, one-dimensional stories because they are uncertain about approaching or identifying students under 18 without a parent's approval. Besides, how useful is it to quote a 7-year-old who says he hates school because it's dumb?

But students have valid viewpoints. You can ask them how they like a new course or a new school. You can recount what an excited third grader has to say about her science fair project (it would be best to have her parent's permission). If you write about a classroom lesson, populate your story with the students in the class. If you write about an

Students and Privacy

Writing about students raises tricky questions. What rights do children and their parents have to privacy? What rights do reporters have to use their names? Although answers seem to exist in court precedence, school officials often believe they can limit reporters' access to their students.

The Family Education Rights and Privacy Act of 1974, better known as FERPA or the Buckley Amendment, sets rules over who can see a student's educational records. Parents have the ultimate say until the child turns 18. Then students take over responsibility; they must even give permission for their parents to see the records or be notified about disciplinary problems.

FERPA is often misinterpreted over the issue of speaking with students. The Student Press Law Center, a nonprofit organization for student journalists, says FERPA "has become a roadblock for student and professional journalists covering education," noting the law's "vague definitions and broad — sometimes conflicting — interpretations have led schools to apply the law in ways its sponsor never intended."

The question of using a student's name or picture would seem to have been answered by the 1979 Supreme Court case of Smith v. Daily Mail, where the court ruled that the First Amendment protects reporters who use the names of minors if the information is obtained legally and "truthfully" reported.

But parents and school officials are understandably nervous about having their children's names and pictures spread by the media. And the children's feelings must be considered. It's fine for a sportswriter to describe a professional athlete's game-losing foul or error in great detail. It's another matter with a 12-year-old basketball player. Even if the Supreme Court gives you the legal right, is it right to print the name of a student who's complaining about cyber bullying?

The decision to use a child's name or picture should be made on a case-by-case basis. The best practice is to go to the parents. Many schools have directories that list student names with their age, address and telephone number. These directories are considered public record. You can use them to find a specific child. Call the parents, identify yourself and explain what you're doing and why you'd like their child to participate in the story. It's not wise to call a student without his or her parents' knowledge. They have good reason to be nervous about strangers contacting their child.

awards assembly, list the honorees and provide a sense of who they are and what they've accomplished. If the school is evacuated because of smoke or fire, you would want to talk to some of the students to help readers see what happened through the eyes of the children.

Some schools ease the way for reporters to quote students by having parents fill out a form at the beginning of the year, giving permission for their child to be interviewed or photographed. If you're going to a school for a specific story, let the administration know what types of students you want to speak with. They can go through these release forms to make sure the parents have cleared the child who will be part of your story.

More possibilities exist when you're writing about high school students. You can talk to students outside the school building, in the parking lot or at coffee shops or fast-food restaurants where they hang out. Make it clear to the students that you're a reporter. Wearing your media identification will help them see you're on the job and not some creepy adult stalking teenagers. Hand out business cards. If you have a blog, make sure the link is on the card.

Asking for a student's personal information — e-mail address and cell phone number — can be problematic. You don't want any of your actions called into question. Parents, school officials and students all have a heightened awareness of predators. You don't want to be mistaken for one. If you've established relationships with high schoolers, be mindful of the way this generation communicates. Forget about leaving messages on voice mail or e-mail. Text or tweet them.

SCHOOL BEAT ▶ Places

Every beat reporter will tell you the most important thing you can do is to step away from the computer, get off the phone, leave the newsroom and spend time in the places you cover. As an education reporter, regular trips to the schools and district offices will provide you a better understanding of the beat, nourish your list of story ideas, and help develop contacts. When news breaks, those visits and those contacts will help you gain access and response.

Look for other, less obvious places to visit. Go to the high school's athletic fields and talk with the players and coaches. Go to the assemblies, concerts, fairs and plays, whether they take place at school, a community center or a city park. Keep an eye out for community service projects sponsored by student groups, from car washes to volunteering at the local senior citizen center. Check out any adult literacy, adult education programs or other off-hour activities at your schools. All can make for good stories and good contacts.

Navigating Your Districts

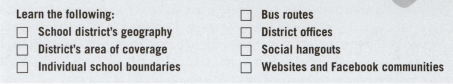

navigating schools checklist

Learn the following:
- [ ] School district's geography
- [ ] District's area of coverage
- [ ] Individual school boundaries

- [ ] Bus routes
- [ ] District offices
- [ ] Social hangouts
- [ ] Websites and Facebook communities

You will need several maps to understand your beat. Study the boundaries of the school district or districts you cover. Which towns and which neighborhoods are included? Are there provisions to allow students who live outside the district to attend its schools? Districts are generally divided into geographic areas that feed specific schools. Some school districts bus students across town or between towns to achieve racial balance and, in rarer cases, economic diversity. Find out how that is determined. Get maps that show the school bus routes. All this will help you to understand where students from the different towns and neighborhoods go to school. Having all this information in your computer or accessible on your smartphone will come in handy when you need to locate an incident or illustrate a story with a locator map.

Find the locations of the school district's administrative offices. Depending on the size and shape of the district, those offices may be part of a larger school campus or housed separately. Check to see if the district has other facilities such as maintenance buildings, school bus depots or off-campus auditoriums, gymnasiums and playing fields.

Making the Rounds

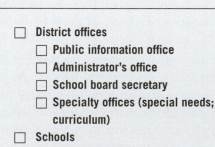

rounds checklist

- [ ] District offices
  - [ ] Public information office
  - [ ] Administrator's office
  - [ ] School board secretary
  - [ ] Specialty offices (special needs; curriculum)
- [ ] Schools
  - [ ] Principal's office

- [ ] Art studios
- [ ] Science labs
- [ ] Teacher's rooms
- [ ] Virtual stops
  - [ ] Facebook pages
  - [ ] Blogs
  - [ ] Parent/teacher websites

Try to get out to the schools in your beat on a weekly or monthly schedule. Schools begin their day early, usually hours before reporters are expected in the newsroom. Early-morning visits — perhaps just before the start of classes — are a great time to schmooze with the faculty, staff and students waiting to start the day.

▶ ▶ ▶ BEAT BACKGROUNDER ◀ ◀ ◀

SCHOOL DISTRICTS

THE NATION'S 14,000-PLUS SCHOOL DISTRICTS have a variety of sizes, categories and missions.

Most fall under the heading of independent districts, autonomous government units with the power to raise taxes and spend the revenue. Independent district boundaries usually, but not always, follow municipal or county lines.

Dependent school districts are run by state or municipal governments, with some variations. Virginia schools have no authority to levy taxes. Maryland school systems are run by county governments. New York has both independent school districts and others run by their cities. In Hawaii, the state Department of Education runs one statewide school district.

School districts are defined in other ways:

▶ A *unified district* comprises all grade levels, including elementary and secondary schools.

▶ A *central district* is run by a single administration.

▶ A *regional school* district educates students from multiple towns.

▶ The words *union* or *consolidated* indicate the district is made up of a number of formerly separate independent school districts.

▶ The word *joint* in a district's name indicates that it includes territory from more than one county.

Some districts are formed around vocational or technical high schools that teach trades such as plumbing and carpentry as well as academics. These schools draw a specialized population from a wider geographic area than one school district.

Other districts are formed around special instructional needs. Called by various names, such as *intermediate school districts* or *regional education service districts* (RESD), these units focus on specific issues such as bilingual education or programs for the deaf and blind.

District Headquarters Try to make regular weekly stops at the district offices. Visit the public information office to say hello. If you're working a story, have your questions ready for the media person or other contacts who can help. But don't stop by only when you have a story to discuss. A friendly chat has great value in establishing relationships.

The same goes for the superintendent: If you don't have a specific story to talk about, a quick hello and a bit of socializing will do. If access to the superintendent is difficult, see if you can create a standing appointment with him or her each week. It would be a terrific way to develop your relationship and handle multiple issues and questions in one sitting.

Try to hit the other offices. Are there assistant superintendents with specific jobs, such as special needs, buildings and grounds, teacher development, enrollment and retention? Try to anticipate the stories you'll be working on for the next couple of days and start your reporting process with these people. Ask the reporter's favorite question, "What's new?"

— but try to ask it at the end of your conversation rather than the beginning. Starting with "What's new?" can put people on the spot and cause them to draw a blank. Asking the question at the end of a conversation is more likely to spark a thought about other interesting things.

Schools Emily Alpert, an education writer with voiceofsandiego.org, whom you'll meet later in the chapter, considers regular school visits the education reporter's equivalent of police ride-alongs. "It's a reality check on what you're hearing in the school district offices," she says.

State laws differ on journalists' right to enter schools. California gives reporters free rein unless the administration can prove the visit would be disruptive. Other states have more caveats for reporters' visits. You should be clear about your rights. But even if you're not required to ask permission or register at the front desk, it's not a bad idea to make the stop anyway and make a courtesy call to the principal to chat about story ideas you're considering.

Each school has its own character. Some places are welcoming; the staff will be happy to see you and have plenty to say. You may find people at other schools more standoffish. They may have less to say and measure their words carefully. That difference often depends on the attitude of the principal, another reason you want to develop a good relationship with him or her. Teachers and other school employees will be more forthcoming if they see the principal is comfortable with you.

Watch for special events at your schools. The relaxed atmosphere of school fairs, assemblies and graduations can make it easier to mingle; you'll make good contacts while showing you're part of the community.

School Board Except in a few big-city school systems, school board members don't maintain offices at the school department. The board may have a few full-time staff members to handle paperwork and do research, but for the most part you'll have to seek out board members at their homes or businesses.

Because most board members are elected, they tend to be available to reporters. They have positions or causes they want to publicize, and re-election to consider. Arrange to meet individual board members for a cup of coffee every few weeks — more often if some large issue is brewing. Each board member can offer a perspective that may not be a story in itself but may become part of some future story or contribute to your understanding of the beat.

Virtual Rounds Monitor what's being said about the schools you cover in the blogosphere and other places on the Web. Schools maintain websites. Parent groups gather around their own blogs. Teachers blog about their classroom experience. Some district superintendents offer their personal perspective on the Web. Citizen and professional journalists post to a variety of hyperlocal news sites and draw comments from readers. Facebook, Twitter and other social networking sites are alive with student commentary on their schools, teachers and courses. Student media such as school newspapers, websites and even newscasts on local cable access offer insight to what's on students' minds.

Visit the established sites and do regular searches for new ones. You can set up Google Alerts to let you know what's being said about your schools. The commentary and observations you'll turn up will broaden your understanding of what's happening on your beat. The information you find online is only a start. It's your job to sort out facts from gossip, to dig deeper and to find what you need to produce solid, factual stories.

Many news organization's websites include blogs devoted to education (for example, the Houston Chronicle's School Zone: http://blogs.chron.com/schoolzone). If you don't have an education blog, see if you can start one. You'll also want to monitor the other blogs on the subject.

Education encompasses a range of volatile issues that many individuals and groups feel are not covered well by traditional media, making it fertile territory for blogging. The voices you'll find in blogs can be great resources for stories in your area and for ideas on what's happening in education around the nation. Here are some places to check and categories to think about:

Education organizations offer a nationwide perspective. Former Washington Post reporter Linda Perlstein blogs as the public editor for the Education Writers Association, at www.educatedreporter.com, with the goal of improving schools coverage. Hechinger report.org, based at Columbia University, lists its mission as "informing the public about education through quality journalism."

Emily Alpert, voiceofsandiego.org

Emily Alpert gets lots of help when she covers a San Diego Unified school board meeting.

The education writer for voiceofsandiego.org sends out tweets every few minutes to her 2,300 Twitter followers, giving them a sense of the action and what people are saying. While she tweets from her laptop or smartphone, followers tweet back with questions, comments and information.

"The immediacy is just so cool," she says. "It's a great way to communicate with people in the community. If something is unclear, questions come in and tune me into that. A lot of these people help me ask better questions."

A nonprofit news site, voiceofsandiego aims to investigate issues uncovered by other local media. Alpert says the questions asked by her audience help with that mission. The back-and-forth improves her stories and helps her see which issues to focus on for the finished story that reaches a much larger audience than social networking alone. "A lot of people aren't into Twitter," she says. "I'd be missing a lot of communities and voices without the other stories."

Alpert and her site take full advantage of the Web for both reporting and presentation. When San Diego schools faced a $120 million budget deficit in 2011, voiceofsandiego.org created an interactive map that allowed its audience members to click on an area to see how many teachers in each school had received layoff notices and what percentage of the school's staff that number represented. Another map showed how much each school spent to educate each student. It allowed readers a quick way of seeing how their schools measured up.

In addition to a stream of substantial stories about California's second-largest school district, Alpert sets a goal of filing two blog posts each day asking readers for input. She hands out cards with her Twitter handle and looks through Facebook for alumni of schools she covers.

"I search for people who went to specific schools, and once I find some, I go through their friends list," she says. Alpert will then reach out to these alumni for stories. They answer back, often bringing in other friends to add to her knowledge.

But the 27-year-old reporter doesn't rely only on the Web. She tries to visit at least one of the many schools in the district each week. "I'll call the principal and say, 'I'm coming by, can you show me what your campus looks like?'" she says. "The principal will take time to show off, and some of those things I see turn into really good stories."

Regional blogs offer insight into what is happening in a particular area. Some examples: Educatedguess.org is part of Thoughts on Public Education, a nonprofit forum on education policies in California. EdNewsColorado.org is a blog on Rocky Mountain states issues written by a former Denver Post reporter. Gothamschools.org is a nonprofit news source on New York City public schools.

School officials have also taken up blogging and tweeting. A San Francisco school board member posts a blog on the San Francisco Chronicle site (www.sfgate.com/cgi-bin/

blogs/rnorton/detail?entry_id=58724). The National School Boards Association maintains a blog (http://boardbuzz.nsba.org), as do groups such as the National Association of Secondary School Principals (www.nassp.org) and the National Association of Elementary School Principals (www.naesp.org).

EDUCATION BEAT ▶ Documents

Although every beat produces lots of data and documents, education reporters have access to information that offers more opportunities for analysis. You can track teachers' level of education, salaries, experience and their success as determined by their students' comprehensive test scores. Student data includes information about age, grades, test scores, dropout rates, family income levels, race, ethnicity, frequency of discipline and developmental or educational issues. These and other federally mandated records allow you to compare schools and school systems on categories such as spending, teacher compensation and student outcomes. The data are readily available at the local, state and national levels. Much of the data can be imported from the Web and put into databases and spreadsheets.

The schools beat also provides documents that track administrative actions, policy statements and personnel records, including superintendent contracts. As on all beats, e-mails are considered part of the public record. So are school board minutes — even those from executive sessions — and meetings of official parent-teacher groups.

All this information makes it easy to take the beat beyond school board meeting stories and features on classes and programs at your schools. Your audience's interest in education demands that you go further. But, as always, remember that raw numbers are just a starting point to direct your reporting.

Where to Find the Documents

Thanks to federal reporting mandates, education data are easily accessible on the Web. School districts must report to the state department of education such information as standardized test results and demographic data on students and teachers. The state departments compile the data and send it to the U.S. Department of Education, which also compiles and interprets the numbers. All these data are available to the public.

State rules vary on what data must be submitted by school districts and how that information is processed. You can find individual school "report cards" or rawer data to interpret. It is a good idea to get a briefing on the information from someone at the state level before you start trying to analyze it.

Holly Hacker and Josh Benton
Dallas Morning News

The Wilmer-Hutchins Independent School District in Dallas County, Texas, was known for its high dropout rates and history of official malfeasance more than for any kind of academic excellence. So when it was announced that third-graders at one district elementary school had scored at the top in statewide standardized testing, Dallas Morning News reporters Joshua Benton and Holly Hacker wondered what was going on.

At the time, the state rated schools largely on the percentage of students who passed standardized tests. Benton and Hacker decided to dig deeper and downloaded those scores from a state website. What they found in the raw data made them even more curious.

"Nearly all the kids had passed the test with perfect scores," says Benton, who now serves as director of Harvard's Nieman Journalism Lab. "They were far ahead of the gifted and talented schools in Houston. We looked at the special ed classes and found they also outscored the gifted and talented kids."

Interviews with teachers and students in the district uncovered several incidents of cheating. Benton was told of teachers who walked up and down the rows of test-taking students, giving advice on how to answer the questions. There were also accounts of brighter students being asked to change the answers on their classmates' test sheets.

The two reporters produced a series of stories about Wilmer-Hutchins that resulted in a state investigation. The district was eventually dissolved, and its schools were incorporated into the Dallas district. But Hacker and Benton weren't finished yet: They wondered whether similar stories were lurking in the data from other districts. "Just because you've written your big story, you shouldn't put it away and expect things to change," Hacker says.

Hacker and Benton began doing what statisticians call "regression analysis," a process that looks for deviations in standardized test score results. They learned that if third graders did well on the state's math test, they usually did well on reading tests. Were there any districts where this wasn't the case? Usually, students in fourth grade should score close to how they did in third grade. Did a large number of fourth-graders make miraculous improvements? Did districts with poor numbers in other areas of scholarship do remarkably well on the standardized tests?

Hacker said this statistical reality check is "the laser that points you in the right direction." By running the numbers through computer analysis, the pair found that 400 out of the state's 7,000 schools stood out as outliers from the expected results.

State officials downplayed the reporters' findings and hired a private firm to analyze the testing data. Instead of repudiating the reporters' questions about those 400 schools, the company

behind the beat

found nearly 700 where the test scores seemed off. Benton wrote about that study and the state's weak response. Officials simply sent out letters asking superintendents whether any cheating had occurred in their districts. The lack of state interest in addressing the problems whetted the pair's appetite for more.

"When you look at all of the stuff the schools are doing that are based on test scores — hiring, firing, raises and graduation — wouldn't you expect investigations to see what it means?" Hacker asks.

Buoyed by the rewards of statistical analysis, Benton and Hacker had another go at the numbers, working with Canadian researchers who had developed a method of finding patterns in the way students answer questions on standardized tests. The system helped sort out cases where several students had the same wrong answer for numerous questions. It found where groups of students answered wrong questions in a suspiciously similar way. After more reporting, Hacker and Benton wrote a third series of articles detailing how answer patterns at many high schools and charter schools around the state showed strong evidence of systematic cheating on the state graduation test.

Hacker and Benton's work earned them several state awards Investigative Reporters & Editors honors, recognizing the series as the best social science journalism, and the Education Writers Association prize for top investigative project. The experience also taught the pair the importance of digging into the numbers.

"You can't be afraid of data," Benton says. "The education beat is as data rich as any beat can be. To be a good education reporter, you need to be comfortable with the numbers."

Local Sites You can find a multitude of data from different online sites. Some school systems, such as Des Moines, Iowa, provide comprehensive reports on school-by-school data in a number of categories, including yearly enrollments, Advanced Placement (AP) testing, college achievement tests and much more.

Media organizations often access data from local or state records and provide searchable databases for their audiences. One example is this webpage (shown on the following page) from the Springfield, Mo., News-Leader that gives viewers a searchable database for 32 pages of school security incidents for one school year. The site also has similar databases for teacher pay, test scores and other demographic information.

Private groups also gather raw data and crunch it for specific audiences. Catalyst Chicago, an independent newsmagazine that reports on Chicago public schools, offers a range of data on students, teachers, test scores and schools. Here is an image of one site (page 219) that compares yearly Chicago schools attendance with average state attendance. You can see the wide assortment of other data groups on the page.

News-Leader website database

Source: http://php.news-leader.com/DBTools/ Search.php?PageID=477

State Sites State education departments are the wholesalers of education data. They collect information from the local school districts, distill it, place it into database form and send it on to the federal education agencies. As a result, state sites may be more comprehensive than local or national venues.

Most states offer websites through their education departments or agencies. New Jersey's site provides both a macro and micro view of schools, allowing people to look at various metrics for individual schools. For example, see on page 220 the site's report on the Brookside School in the Allendale, N.J., school district: http://education.state.nj.us/rc/nclb09/reports/03/0040/03-0040-010.html.

The data may be offered at other state sites. See on page 221 the list of school data on the Minnesota Legislature's library website. It offers access to test scores, teacher licensure, school district data and individual school report cards.

Other states make it easier for the public to understand all those numbers. Idaho has a searchable database that allows the public to look at No Child Left Behind data as well as

Catalyst CHICAGO
INDEPENDENT REPORTING ON URBAN EDUCATION SINCE 1990

Our Network: Catalyst Chicago | Gotham Schools | EdNews Colorado | Philadelphia Notebook

SEARCH: FIND
BROWSE PRINT ISSUES   ADVANCED SEARCH

CATALYST GUIDES: CHICAGO PUBLIC SCHOOLS   GRANTS   RESOURCES   REFORM HISTORY

RSS FEEDS
FREE EMAIL ALERTS

HOME
CATALYST NOTEBOOK
OPINIONS
CATALYST CAUCUS
COMMUNITY CALENDAR
AUDIO ARCHIVE
ABOUT US
MEMBERSHIP

AdChoices

Oak Creek Ranch School
College Prep Boarding School. 38yrs Proven Success. ADD/ADHD Teens.
OCRS.com/Arizona-B...

K12 Online High School
Your Child Deserves an Outstanding Education Discover K12 Today!
www.K12.com

Data Central: Student Attendance Rate

Students
Attendance
Chronic Truancy
Annual dropout rate
Graduation Rate
Limited English-Proficiency
Low-Income
Mobility
Racial/Ethnic Background
Enrollment

Test Scores
Elementary:
ISAT Overall
ISAT Reading
ISAT Math
NAEP rankings
NAEP scale scores
High schools:
ACT Composite
Prairie State: Reading, Math, Writing
Prairie State: Overall

Teachers
Gender
Racial/Ethnic Background
With Master's and Above
Experience
Classes not Taught by Highly Qualified Teachers

A perfect attendance rate (100%) means that all students attended school every day.

	Chicago	Illinois
2009	90.5%	93.7%
2008	89.9%	93.3%
2007	91.3%	93.7%
2006	92.2%	94.0%
2005	92.%	93.9%
2004	92.3%	94.2%
2003	92.2%	94.0%
2002	92.1%	94.0%
2001	91.5%	93.7%
2000	91.6%	93.9%
1999	90.9%	93.6%
1998	91.5%	93.9%
1997	91.1%	93.8%
1996	17.1%	21.2%
1995	89.2%	93.4%
1994	88.7%	93.2%
1993	89.1%	93.4%
1992	89.8%	93.6%

→ *Catalyst Chicago Website* ←

Source: www.catalyst-chicago.org/ stat/?item=17&cat=0

information on teacher quality, graduation rates, and proficiency rates for reading, math and other subjects. The data for the Bear Lake County school district are on page 221.

National Sites National data sites allow you to do one-stop shopping by comparing your local numbers against national averages. Your first stop should be the National Center for Education Statistics (NCES), http://nces.ed.gov, which compiles various categories of education data, including separate sites for urban and rural schools. For example, if you're writing about student-teacher ratios for schools in Palm Beach County, Fla., you can find the past few years of data for the county as well as the state and the nation, giving you an instant context for what the local numbers mean.

The NCES also provides National Assessment of Educational Progress (NAEP), the largest continuing assessment of American students' knowledge and skills in various subjects. Assessments are conducted regularly using standardized testing in mathematics, reading, science, writing, the arts, civics, economics, geography and U.S. history. NAEP information includes data on large groups of students (all fourth-graders, for instance)

New Jersey Education Department website

Source: http://education.state.nj.us/rc/ nclb09/reports/03/0040/03-0040-010.html

and groups within those populations, (girls, boys, ethnic backgrounds).On page 222 you can see the "Nation's Report Card" page on math proficiency for 12th-graders.

Other federal agencies also have school data. On page 223 is the page from the U.S. Bureau of Labor Statistics website that tracks college enrollment for high school graduates from 1959 to 2009.

You can find commercial websites that also track education information. For example on page 224 is a webpage on Tulsa schools from eSchoolprofile.com, a company that collects information directly from individual schools and school districts.

How to Use the Documents

These rich deposits of data can be mined in different ways. If you're doing a story about a local issue, such as attendance rates or dropout percentages, you can find the specific numbers for your schools on either the local or state website. To put those numbers in context, you can compare them with state and national numbers, showing how your schools stack up against neighboring districts or districts across the country.

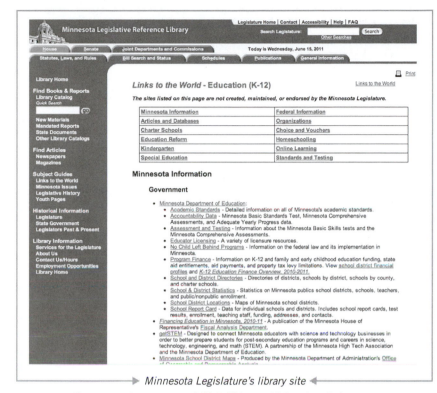

Minnesota Legislature's library site

Source: www.leg.state.mn.us/lrl/links/ links.aspx?links=educat#minnesota

Bear Lake County Idaho school report card

Source: www.sde.idaho.gov/reportcard/Index/2009/033

ies NATIONAL CENTER FOR EDUCATION STATISTICS

U.S. Department of Education
Institute of Education Sciences

NewsFlash Staff Contact Site Index Help KIDS

Search all of NCES

SEARCH

Publications & Products | Surveys & Programs | Data Tools | Tables & Figures | Fast Facts | School, College, & Library Search | Annual Reports | What's New | About Us

ElSi *quickFacts*

? Help/Tutorial   (i) About the Data   ElSi Options ▼

Select a Level ▼

State
District
Public School
Private School

→ *NCES data on student teacher ratio for Palm Beach County, Fla* ←

Source: http://nces.ed.gov/ccd/elsi/quickFacts.aspx

The Nation's Report Card

Home | About The Nation's Report Card | Help

Search

...the official site for results from the National Assessment of Educational Progress

Mathematics

Grade 4 National Results
Grade 4 State Results
Grade 4 District Results
Grade 8 National Results
Grade 8 State Results
Grade 8 District Results
Grade 12 National Results
Grade 12 State Results
Sample Questions
Classroom Context
About the Assessment

Information for...

◉ Educators
◉ Media
◉ Parents
◉ Policymakers
◉ Researchers
◉ Students

Resources

◉ About the Nation's Report Card
◉ Data Tools
◉ FAQ
◉ Glossary
◉ Contacts

Summary of Major Findings

Twelfth-graders' performance in mathematics improves since 2005

Nationally representative samples of more than 49,000 twelfth-graders participated in the 2009 National Assessment of Educational Progress (NAEP) in mathematics. On the national level, results are reported for students attending public and private schools across the nation.

⊙ The average mathematics score in 2009 was three points higher in 2009 than in 2005.
⊙ Average mathematics scores were higher overall in 2009 than in 2005 for all racial/ethnic groups and for male and female students.
⊙ The percentages of students at or above *Proficient* (26 percent) and at or above *Basic* (64 percent) were higher in 2009 than in 2005.

See all the grade 12 national results.

Information For... so reported for twelfth-grade public school students in the 11 states that participated in the first twelfth-grade state pilot program in 2009. The states that participated are Arkansas, Connecticut, Florida, Idaho, Illinois, Iowa, Massachusetts, New Hampshire, New Jersey, South Dakota, and West Virginia.

⊙ Compared to the nation, average mathematics scores at grade 12 were higher in the following states: Connecticut, Iowa, Massachusetts, New Hampshire, New Jersey, and South Dakota.
⊙ Compared to the nation, average mathematics scores were lower in the following states: Arkansas, Florida, and West Virginia.
⊙ Compared to the nation, average mathematics scores were not significantly different in Idaho and Illinois.

See all the results for the 11 states that participated.

Students responded to questions designed to measure their knowledge and abilities across four content areas: number properties and operations; measurement and geometry; data analysis, statistics, and probability; and algebra. Find out more about what the mathematics assessment measures.

For more information, browse the report online or download a copy of the report.

Six states score higher than national average in mathematics

Compared to the nation, average mathematics scores were

□ higher in Connecticut, Iowa, Massachusetts, New Hampshire, New Jersey and South Dakota;
□ lower in Arkansas, Florida, and West Virginia; and
□ not significantly different in Idaho and Illinois.

□ State did not participate.

→ *National Report Card on Math* ←

Source: http://nationsreportcard.gov/math_2009/summary_g12.asp

U.S. Bureau of Labor Statistics

Source: www.bls.gov/opub/ted/2010/ted_20100428.htm

Look for corollaries and anomalies. Does the school with the highest disciplinary rate produce higher- or lower-than-average test scores? Does the economic health of the students, as determined by the percentage receiving subsidized breakfasts and lunches, affect disciplinary rates? Do schools with the highest grade point averages (GPAs) have the highest SAT scores? If not, grade inflation may be a problem. You might expect schools from more affluent neighborhoods to have higher attendance rates. But if a school with a high percentage of immigrant children comes in higher, you may want to find out why. Looking over all these numbers is a starting point you can use to start asking questions.

You can also cross-check names in various lists. One easy step that many news organizations take is to compare the employment lists of school bus drivers, custodians or substitute teachers with databases for registered sex offenders or people convicted of drunken driving. The Detroit News compared the database of school employees in Michigan with the state police criminal history database and discovered that about 2,500 people employed by Michigan schools in 2005 had been convicted of crimes, including homicide, sexual assault and kidnapping.

eSchoolprofile
Largest national school database online.

Tulsa Schools

This special eschoolprofile is an overview of school options in **Tulsa**. Click on the links to view lists. All Tulsa area schools are included. You are currently viewing the **Tulsa elementary Schools**. When you want a comprehensive 12 page free report on a few selected local **Tulsa schools**. Click here for a Tulsa public Schools Report or here for a Tulsa private Schools Report. Choose any three schools in **Tulsa** county Oklahoma. Compare Tulsa city schools. For schools in other counties not listed go to bottom of this page and click on Home.

* * * Scroll down to view lists * * *

Tulsa Public Schools

97 Public Schools	51806	Students
11 High Schools	11361	Students
17 Middle Schools	11138	Students
69 Elementary Schools	29307	Students
3 Districts		
$4630 - $6295 Dollars per student		
20 - 23 Ave Class Size Grade 1		
25 - 30 Ave Class Size Grade 8		

Tulsa Private Schools

12 Private Schools	8076	Students
5 High Schools	5176	Students
0 Middle Schools		Students
7 Elementary Schools	2900	Students
$2150 - $7799 Tuition		
12 - 30 Ave Class Size Elementary		
17 - 30 Ave Class Size Middle		
14 - 25 Ave Class Size Upper		

AdChoices ▷ ◁ ▷

Academy Central Elementary School
1789 West Seminole Street
Tulsa, OK 74127

Addams Elementary School
5323 South 65th West Avenue
Tulsa, OK 74107

Alcott Elementary School
525 East 46th Street North
Tulsa, OK 74126

Anderson Elementary School
1921 East 29th Street North
Tulsa, OK 74110

Barnard Elementary School
2324 East 17th Street
Tulsa, OK 74104

Bell Elementary School
6304 East Admiral Boulevard
Tulsa, OK 74115

Berryhill Elementary School-North
3128 South 63RD West Avenue
Tulsa, OK 74107

Berryhill Elementary School-South
3128 South 63RD West Avenue
Tulsa, OK 74107

Boevers Elementary School
3433 S. 133rd E. Ave.
Tulsa, OK 74134

Briarglen Elementary School

Everest Career College
Career-Focused Training Programs.
Contact Everest Now For More Info!
www.Everest.edu

→ *Tulsa school data* ←

Source: www.eschoolprofile.com/city/tulsa.asp?list=elementaryschools

▶ ▶ ▶ **BEAT BACKGROUNDER** ◀ ◀ ◀

NO CHILD LEFT BEHIND

THE NO CHILD LEFT BEHIND ACT (NCLB) has been a game changer in national education policy. Signed into law by President George W. Bush in January 2002, the bill expanded the federal role in education by establishing mandates in testing and student achievement for every public school in the nation. The law was intended to improve education by making states and schools more accountable for students' progress.

The most controversial aspect is its requirement for the annual math and reading testing of students in grades 3 through 8. Standardized science tests were added later. The tests measure whether all students meet state academic standards. A sample group of fourth- and eighth-graders in each state must also participate in the NEAP testing program in reading and math every other year. This reliance on testing has brought complaints that students spend too much time learning how to take the test and not enough time learning how to think.

The law requires that students reach a "proficient" level on state tests by the 2013–2014 school years. Individual schools must meet state-defined targets for "adequate yearly progress"; states must furnish annual "report cards" that show how students are doing in various categories. Districts must provide report cards showing school-by-school data.

Schools that fail to meet these targets two years in a row must get help from the state and offer students a choice to attend other public schools. Students in schools that fail three years in a row must be offered supplemental educational services, including private tutoring. Continued failure could lead to a takeover of the school district by the state.

Another major area of controversy is teacher standards. All public school teachers specializing in core curriculum must be classified as "highly qualified" (certified and "demonstrably proficient") in each subject they teach. Some states and school districts link teachers' salary and advancement to how well their students do on their standardized tests.

The law continues to be debated. Some educators believe NCLB hurts public schools, especially those with high populations of underprivileged students. They complain school districts haven't been given the money needed to meet federal mandates. Political conservatives argue the federal government shouldn't set education rules for the states. But other education experts say the law is necessary to improve outcomes at many public school districts. Federal officials point to increases in Washington's funding of education as evidence of the government's financial commitment to the law.

SCHOOL BEAT ▶ Stories

The subject of schools and education crosses many lines of society, all of which can make for fascinating stories.

Schools are hotbeds of social issues. The bullying of one student by others has become a big story in recent years. The horrors of school bullying and the debate on who holds responsibility touch on nearly everyone's school experiences. Gay rights for students is a related subject; as more students come out about gender issues, they face dangerous social currents in the halls of their schools. Immigrant populations, both legal and illegal, are growing in many school systems, raising questions about these students' assimilation into American life. The issues of racial and economic diversity in student populations remain an important story.

Education stories can mirror political debate. Your community may be divided over the question of language: Should the schools offer bilingual classes or require English-only instruction? The school budget, which is usually tied to property taxes, is a volatile issue for a municipality's voters. Charter schools are a hot-button issue. Proponents say publically financed selective schools give students from the lower economic rungs the same opportunities as affluent students. Others argue such schools undermine the idea of public education. Textbooks, sex education and other curriculum issues can also become volatile political flashpoints during school board elections.

Schools have become a nexus of labor issues with the move to more public accountability of teachers. As school budgets get tighter, the public has become more vigilant about the cost of teacher salaries, pensions and health care. Teacher unions and school officials may clash over the question of tenure for under-performing teachers. The general community may debate the use of student test results to determine teacher pay and advancement.

And, finally, of course, there are a multitude of education issues. Teachers and parents have strong feelings about the time students spend preparing for standardized tests. Interpreting those test results can be a full-time job. Curriculum changes need to be analyzed. The movement to longer school days and school years is a hotly debated topic. So are reports about student-teacher ratios. You will never lack for new issues to report.

▶ ▶ ▶ **BEAT BACKGROUNDER** ◀ ◀ ◀

REPORTING BUDGETS

THE ANNUAL SCHOOL DISTRICT BUDGET is one of the most common and challenging assignments for any education reporter. The budget affects the entire community. It determines the kind of education each student will receive. How much will be spent on books, supplies and activities? How much money will be available for art and music classes, school plays and team sports? The budget sets the salaries for hundreds — perhaps thousands — of teachers and school personnel. Most important for the whole community, the budget determines a significant part of the property tax rate, a figure that affects businesses, homeowners and even renters, who may pay more to cover their landlord's higher tax bill.

Reporting budget stories starts with numbers. The reporter's task is to determine which numbers are important to the community and how to explain their impact. If you say the school board plans to cut after-school programs by $50,000, you haven't told your audience much; that's like reporting just one team's score from a ballgame. Numbers have meaning only when put in context. What is the total budget for after-school programs? If it's

$1 million, the $50,000 cut represents 5 percent; if the total is $100,000, the program has been cut by 50 percent.

Don't confine comparisons of numbers to the district's past and present budgets. Look at how other districts budget. Do they spend more or less per student? Are their teacher salaries higher or lower? These comparisons help your audience judge what it's getting for its tax dollars.

Here are some line items you will find in a budget document, their significance and how to present them.

Enrollment includes all students in the district. The budget document should break enrollment down to individual school populations with separate entries for students with special needs and disabilities. All of these numbers should be compared with last year's to show trends. If the enrollment is up, a cut in total spending takes on greater significance.

Operating funds are the total amount budgeted for the day-to-day expenses of the district, including salaries, materials, maintenance and energy costs. How much does the superintendent get in pay and benefits? What are teachers paid? Individual salaries may not be in the main budget documents, but they are public record. Examine those figures; they hold more than a little interest for your audience.

Per-pupil cost provides a quick look at how your district's spending compared with that of other districts around the state. This number doesn't include all spending, just expenditures common to all districts. Some items, such as transportation and debt service, are not part of this formula.

Capital funds show what the district plans to spend on larger equipment and improvements, including construction or repairs on school buildings, school buses and computer systems. In some cases the school board may ask voters to approve a bond for a major construction project. The vote on that request is handled separately from the rest of the budget.

Debt load shows how much money the district owes on bonds and other borrowing it has done through the years. This is a significant number because repaying debt reduces the amount of money the district has available to spend on students.

Revenues show where the money comes from to pay all of the above. School districts have revenue sources besides property taxes. The state provides each district with some amount of funding determined by a formula set by the state legislature. The district may receive other state aid for specific programs such as special education or transportation. It also receives federal money under various programs and special grants. These figures must be put into the context of previous years' funding.

Reserves are money set aside for such anticipated items as legal settlements and expenses from unanticipated events, such as a major roof leak or storm damage.

Tax rate. Once the budget is set, it is used to determine the property tax rate. Property tax bills usually include two rates: one for schools, one for the municipality's general fund. A total tax rate of $10 per $1,000 would mean the owner of a $200,000 house would pay $2,000 in taxes.

STORY SCAN: Grading the Teachers

The advantage of the schools beat is there are few routine stories. You will cover the setting of the yearly budget and attend the school board meetings. But for the most part, you will be free to explore the many issues of education. The chapter on the government beat discusses how to cover meetings, so let's take a look at the kind of story an education reporter can aspire to write.

In its 2010 series, Grading the Teachers, the Los Angeles Times analyzed seven years of data on math and English achievement tests to gauge the effectiveness of individual teachers. Times reporters visited more than 50 classrooms and interviewed teachers, administrators and parents. The Times posted all the data online, garnering more than 200,000 hits from Los Angeles residents within a few hours.

The ambitious project shows what reporters can do by first looking at the data, then going out to observe and interview the subjects of those data.

The writer begins with an evocative classroom scene that gives the reader a sense of being there. This technique helps draw interest and humanize the coming subject matter that will deal with numbers and other data.

It's a Wednesday morning, and Zenaida Tan is warming her students up with a little exercise in "Monster Math."

That's Tan's name for math problems with monstrously big numbers. While most third-graders are learning to multiply two digits by two digits, Tan makes her class practice with 10 digits by two — just to show them it's not so different. On this spring day, her students pick apart the problem on the board — 7,850,437,826 x 56 — with the enthusiasm of game show contestants, shouting out answers before Tan can ask a question. When she accidentally blocks their view, several stand up with their notebooks and walk across the room to get a better look.

The answer comes minutes later in a singsong unison: "Four hundred and thirty-nine billion, six hundred and twenty-four million. . . ."

The writer adds more classroom details along with a reference to a popular movie to help his audience relate to the more complicated issues they are about to read.

Congratulations, Tan tells them, for solving it con ganas. That's Spanish for "with gusto," a phrase she picked up from watching "Stand and Deliver," a favorite film of hers about the late Jaime Escalante, the remarkably successful math teacher at Garfield High School in East Los Angeles.

The Los Angeles Unified School District has hundreds of Jaime Escalantes — teachers who preside over remarkable successes, year after year, often against incredible odds, according to a Times analysis. But nobody is making a film about them.

Most are like Zenaida Tan, working in obscurity. No one asks them their secrets. Most of the time, no one even says, "Good job." Often even their own colleagues and principals don't know who they are.

As part of an effort to shed light on the work of L.A. teachers, The Times on Sunday is releasing a database of roughly 6,000 third- through fifth-grade teachers, ranked by their effectiveness in raising students' scores on standardized tests of math and English over a seven-year period.

Diane Hollenbach, who recently retired from Broadous Elementary School in Pacoima, was the most effective elementary school teacher of the roughly 6,000 analyzed by The Times.

"The ones that love their students and love their job do well," she said. "You can't bottle that, and you can't teach it." Others had wide-ranging advice for their fellow teachers.

The writer transitions from the classroom scene into a sequence of paragraphs that explain what the story is about.

This is followed by a series of paragraphs that explain the paper's process in identifying the 100 most effective teachers, noting there is no pattern about who these teachers are or where they teach. By using statistical analysis, the project's reporters found what the teachers had in common were their results. Their students' English test scores increased by an average of 12 percentage points and 17 percentage points on their math exams.

Then the story transitions to the central subject — the individual teachers

The writer wisely goes from the wonky details of the data analysis to quick conversations with the real people who represent those numbers.

Jilla Sardashti, who taught last year at Parmelee Avenue Elementary School in the Florence-Firestone neighborhood, said she teaches critical thinking skills from the first day of school.

"These kids are as smart as any other kids in the district," said Sardashti, whose students are mostly poor and Latino and often still learning English. "I'm really good at figuring out what they need, and I provide them with experience to know about the world around them."

Hollie Bloch, who retired in July from Balboa Gifted Magnet in Northridge after teaching in the district 39 years, said that challenging students — especially high-achieving ones — was essential.

"I teach Shakespeare to children," she said. "If the teacher's expectations are high, and you have control of the classroom, those kids should do well."

Said Aldo Pinto, a 32-year-old teacher at Gridley Street Elementary School in San Fernando: "The biggest challenge is getting them to buy into the fact that school is important."

He does that by telling students his own story as the son of Mexican immigrants.

Pinto, like most other teachers interviewed, said his good results had not been recognized.

"No one is ever really singled out, neither good nor bad," said Pinto. "The culture of the union is: Everyone is the same. You can't single out anyone for doing badly. So as a result, we don't point out the good either."

"When I worked at a bank, I was employee of the month," he added. "For LAUSD, for some reason, it's not a good thing to do."

Note the use of details: the age and experience of the individual teachers, where they teach and their specific tricks. Details and specifics are the best way to hold interest.

The writer then moves from the specifics to another general theme — the fact that the school system does little to acknowledge or draw from individual excellence.

RESOURCES

Links

As detailed in the "Education Beat: Documents" section, you can find numerous websites at the local, state and national level that track education issues. The list below is intended as a good start. But don't rely on this alone. Researching the Web will uncover scores of other sites, and each one on this list will link to many more.

Education Blogs
▶ www.onlineuniversities.com/blog/2010/02/50-best-blogs-for-education-leaders

Family Education Rights and Privacy Act
▶ www2.ed.gov/policy/gen/guid/fpco/ferpa/lea-officials.html

Government Sites
▶ National Center for Education Statistics, http://nces.ed.gov
▶ U.S Department of Education, www.ed.gov

Journalism Sites
▶ Education Writers Association, www.ewa.org
▶ Journalist's Toolbox, www.journaliststoolbox.org/archive/education

News Sites
▶ ASCD Smartbrief, www.smartbrief.com/news/ascd
▶ Education News, www.educationnews.org
▶ The National Access Network, www.schoolfunding.info

No Child Left Behind
▶ Defining the law, http://www2.ed.gov/nclb/landing.jhtml
▶ Data, www.eddataexpress.ed.gov

Unions
▶ American Federation of Teachers, www.aft.org
▶ National Education Association, www.nea.org

Assignment Desk

Drawing data from federal and state education department "report cards" compare your school district's test scores to regional, state and national averages over the past five years. Find a few school districts with similar student populations and demographics to use as baselines. Chart how your district did in various tests over the years in comparison with these districts. Also draw comparative numbers from total state and national figures. While you are at it, look for any demographic changes that may add to an understanding of the scores. How did your school district's population change over those five years? Did the number of students increase or decrease? Were there changes in minority and immigrant populations? Look for similar changes in those comparative districts.

Sidebar Write a story that uses this comparative data. Speak with teachers and administrators from your district to get their perspective on what those scores mean to them. Interview education experts to put those local numbers in perspective. Look for recommendations from all sources on how your district could improve its numbers.

APPENDICES

APPENDIX 1: POLICE CODES

Law enforcement agencies have traditionally used variations on the 10 Code for communications between dispatchers and officers in the field. We are all familiar with the phrase 10-4 ("I understand"). The rest are below, courtesy of the Association of Public Communications Officers (APCO).

Codes may vary from department to department, so always check. Some departments have gone to a new code base that dispenses with the 10 prefix.

10 Codes

- ▶ 10-0   Caution
- ▶ 10-1   Unable to copy — change location
- ▶ 10-2   Signal good
- ▶ 10-3   Stop transmitting
- ▶ 10-4   Acknowledgement (OK)
- ▶ 10-5   Relay
- ▶ 10-6   Busy — stand by unless urgent
- ▶ 10-7   Out of service
- ▶ 10-8   In service
- ▶ 10-9   Repeat
- ▶ 10-10 Fight in progress
- ▶ 10-11 Dog case
- ▶ 10-12 Stand by (stop)
- ▶ 10-13 Weather — road report
- ▶ 10-14 Prowler report
- ▶ 10-15 Civil disturbance
- ▶ 10-16 Domestic disturbance
- ▶ 10-17 Meet complainant
- ▶ 10-18 Quickly
- ▶ 10-19 Return to . . .
- ▶ 10-20 Location
- ▶ 10-21 Call . . . by telephone

- ▶ 10-22 Disregard
- ▶ 10-23 Arrived at scene
- ▶ 10-24 Assignment completed
- ▶ 10-25 Report in person (meet) . . .
- ▶ 10-26 Detaining subject, expedite
- ▶ 10-27 Drivers license information
- ▶ 10-28 Vehicle registration information
- ▶ 10-29 Check for wanted
- ▶ 10-30 Unnecessary use of radio
- ▶ 10-31 Crime in progress
- ▶ 10-32 Man with gun
- ▶ 10-33 Emergency
- ▶ 10-34 Riot
- ▶ 10-35 Major crime alert
- ▶ 10-36 Correct time
- ▶ 10-37 (Investigate) suspicious vehicle
- ▶ 10-38 Stopping suspicious vehicle
- ▶ 10-39 Urgent — use light, siren
- ▶ 10-40 Silent run — no light, siren
- ▶ 10-41 Beginning tour of duty
- ▶ 10-42 Ending tour of duty
- ▶ 10-43 Information

- ▶ 10-44 Permission to leave . . . for . . .
- ▶ 10-45 Animal carcass at . . .
- ▶ 10-46 Assist motorist
- ▶ 10-47 Emergency road repairs at . . .
- ▶ 10-48 Traffic standard repair at . . .
- ▶ 10-49 Traffic light out at . . .
- ▶ 10-50 Accident (fatal, personal injury, property damage)
- ▶ 10-51 Wrecker needed
- ▶ 10-52 Ambulance needed
- ▶ 10-53 Road blocked at . . .
- ▶ 10-54 Livestock on highway
- ▶ 10-55 Suspected DUI
- ▶ 10-56 Intoxicated pedestrian
- ▶ 10-57 Hit and run (fatal, personal injury, property damage)
- ▶ 10-58 Direct traffic
- ▶ 10-59 Convoy or escort
- ▶ 10-60 Squad in vicinity
- ▶ 10-61 Isolate self for message
- ▶ 10-62 Reply to message
- ▶ 10-63 Prepare to make written copy
- ▶ 10-64 Message for local delivery
- ▶ 10-65 Net message assignment
- ▶ 10-66 Message cancellation
- ▶ 10-67 Clear for net message
- ▶ 10-68 Dispatch information
- ▶ 10-69 Message received
- ▶ 10-70 Fire

- ▶ 10-71 Advise nature of fire
- ▶ 10-72 Report progress on fire
- ▶ 10-73 Smoke report
- ▶ 10-74 Negative
- ▶ 10-75 In contact with . . .
- ▶ 10-76 En route . . .
- ▶ 10-77 ETA (estimated time of arrival)
- ▶ 10-78 Need assistance
- ▶ 10-79 Notify coroner
- ▶ 10-80 Chase in progress
- ▶ 10-81 Breathalyzer
- ▶ 10-82 Reserve lodging
- ▶ 10-83 Work school crossing at . . .
- ▶ 10-84 If meeting . . . advise ETA
- ▶ 10-85 Delayed due to . . .
- ▶ 10-86 Officer/operator on duty
- ▶ 10-87 Pick up/distribute checks
- ▶ 10-88 Present telephone number of . . .
- ▶ 10-89 Bomb threat
- ▶ 10-90 Bank alarm at . . .
- ▶ 10-91 Pick up prisoner/subject
- ▶ 10-92 Improperly parked vehicle
- ▶ 10-93 Blockade
- ▶ 10-94 Drag racing
- ▶ 10-95 Prisoner/subject in custody
- ▶ 10-96 Mental subject
- ▶ 10-97 Check (test) signal
- ▶ 10-98 Prison/jail break
- ▶ 10-99 Wanted/stolen indicated

Police Codes

Code 1	Answer on radio	Code 6	Out of car to investigate
Code 2	Proceed immediately w/o siren	Code 6A	Out of car to investigate, assistance may be needed
Code 3	Proceed w/ siren and red lights	Code 6C	Suspect is wanted and may be dangerous
Code 4	No further assistance necessary	Code 7	Out for lunch
Code 4A	No further assistance necessary, but suspect is not in custody	Code 8	Fire alarm
		Code 9	Jail break
Code 5	Uniformed officers stay away	Code 10	Request clear frequency
		Code 12	False alarm

Code 13	Major disaster activation	586	Illegal parking
Code 14	Resume normal operations	586E	Vehicle blocking driveway
Code 20	Notify news media to respond	594	Malicious mischief
Code 30	Burglar alarm ringing	595	Runaway car
Code 33	Emergency! All units stand by	647	Lewd conduct
Code 99	Emergency!	901	Ambulance call/accident, injuries unknown
Code 100	In position to intercept		
187	Homicide	901H	Ambulance call — dead body
207	Kidnapping	901K	Ambulance has been dispatched
207A	Kidnapping attempt		
211	Armed robbery	901L	Ambulance call — narcotics overdose
217	Assault with intent to murder		
220	Attempted rape	901N	Ambulance requested
240	Assault	901S	Ambulance call — shooting
242	Battery	901T	Ambulance call — traffic accident
245	Assault with a deadly weapon		
261	Rape	901Y	Request ambulance if needed
261A	Attempted rape	902	Accident
288	Lewd conduct	902H	Enroute to hospital
311	Indecent exposure	902M	Medical aid requested
314	Indecent exposure	902T	Traffic accident — non-injury
390	Drunk	903	Aircraft crash
390D	Drunk unconscious	903L	Low flying aircraft
415	Disturbance	904A	Fire alarm
415C	Disturbance, children involved	904B	Brush fire or boat fire
415E	Disturbance, loud music or party	904C	Car fire
		904F	Forest fire
415F	Disturbance, family	904G	Grass fire
415G	Disturbance, gang	904I	Illegal burning
417	Person with a gun	904S	Structure fire
459	Burglary	905B	Animal bite
459A	Burglar alarm ringing	905N	Noisy animal
470	Forgery	905S	Stray animal
480	Hit-and-run (Felony)	905V	Vicious animal
481	Hit-and-run (Misdemeanor)	906K	Rescue dispatched
484	Petty theft	906N	Rescue requested
484PS	Purse snatch	907	Minor disturbance
487	Grand theft	907A	Loud radio or TV
488	Petty theft	907B	Ball game in street
502	Drunk driving	907K	Paramedics dispatched
503	Auto theft	907N	Paramedics requested
504	Tampering with a vehicle	907Y	Are paramedics needed?
505	Reckless driving	908	Begging
507	Public nuisance	909	Traffic congestion

909B	Road blockade	927D	Investigate possible dead body
909F	Flares needed		
909T	Traffic hazard	928	Found property
910	Can you handle?	929	Investigate person down
911	Advise party	930	See man regarding a complaint
911B	Contact informant/Contact officer		
		931	See woman regarding a complaint
912	Are we clear?		
913	You are clear	932	Woman or child abuse or open door
914	Request detectives		
914A	Attempted suicide	933	Open window
914C	Request coroner	949	Gasoline spill
914D	Request doctor	950	Burning permit
914F	Request fire dept.	951	Request fire investigator
914H	Heart attack	952	Report conditions
914N	Concerned party notified	953	Check smoke report
914S	Suicide	954	Arrived at scene
915	Dumping rubbish	955	Fire under control
916	Holding suspect	956	Available for assignment
917A	Abandoned vehicle	957	Fire under control
917P	Hold vehicle for fingerprints	960X	Car stop — dangerous suspects
918A	Escaped mental patient	961	Take a report or car stop
918V	Violent mental patient	962	Subject is armed and dangerous
919	Keep the peace		
920	Missing adult	966	Sniper
920A	Found adult/Missing adult	967	Outlaw motorcyclists
920C	Missing child	975	Can your suspect hear your radio?
920F	Found child		
920J	Missing juvenile	981	Frequency is clear or need radiological
921	Prowler		
921P	Peeping Tom	982	Are we being received or bomb threat
922	Illegal peddling		
924	Station detail	983	Explosion
925	Suspicious person	995	Labor trouble
926	Request tow truck	996	Explosion
926A	Tow truck dispatched	996A	Unexploded bomb
927	Investigate unknown trouble	998	Officer involved in shooting
927A	Person pulled from telephone	999	Officer needs help — urgent!

Here is some of the basic fire equipment you are likely to encounter. While you don't need to list the types of engines used at a fire, familiarity with the equipment will help you understand what you're watching. And it's nifty to be able to use the jargon with sources and friends.

Pumpers

Pumpers, also called "rescue pumpers," are the workhorses of many departments. They carry their own water supply and draw water from hydrants or rivers and lakes. The trucks carry a variety of equipment, including ladders, hoses, poles, axes and ventilating machines. You are likely to see at least one pumper at every fire scene.

Quints and Quads

These trucks are hybrids of an aerial truck and a pumper. They come in a range of configurations. Quints and Quads can pump water or use water tanks, and they carry snorkel hoses and aerial and ground ladders. The name comes from the number of functions the trucks can perform. Quints are growing in popularity among departments of all sizes, especially smaller departments looking for an all-in-one fire truck.

Tractor-Drawn Aerials

Also known as a tiller truck, these long, tapered vehicles are often deployed in older cities with narrow streets. Its rear wheels are steered by an operator sitting at the back of the truck, allowing for more maneuverability.

Tower Ladders

A variation on the turntable ladder truck, tower ladders have buckets mounted at the top of the ladder that provide safe platforms for firefighters to operate snorkel hoses or evacuate people from the higher stories of a burning building. These trucks are more common in big city and airport fire departments.

Heavy Rescue Vehicle

Also called a rescue squad or heavy rescue, these trucks are rolling toolboxes carrying equipment, such as the "jaws of life," ropes and winches to extricate victims in car crashes, building collapses and other rescue calls. These trucks are often dispatched to accident scenes.

GLOSSARY

CHAPTER 5 ▶ Cops and Crime

Law enforcement officers have a specialized language that ranges from legalese (*perpetrator*) to slang (*skell*). Police calls and crimes are expressed in numeric shorthand (a 10-10 report over the police radio means "fight in progress" [see Appendix 1]). You can find detailed law enforcement dictionaries online. But keep in mind that cop talk can differ from jurisdiction to jurisdiction. So, as always, ask for the meaning of a word you don't understand.

Some acronyms, such as SWAT, are widely used in conversation, while others remain incomprehensible to the uninitiated (see "Acronyms"). The following glossary is only a start. Translating all the law enforcement words, terms, abbreviations and numbers could fill a book.

Acronyms ▶ commonly used police acronyms

ADW ▶ assault w/ a deadly weapon

BT ▶ bomb threat ("Bravo Tango")

CP ▶ complaining party

DB ▶ dead body

DMV ▶ vehicle registration

DOA ▶ dead on arrival

ETA ▶ estimated time of arrival

GOA ▶ gone on arrival

GTA ▶ grand theft, auto

HBD ▶ has been drinking

J ▶ juvenile

PC ▶ person complaining or penal code

PR ▶ person reporting

QT ▶ secrecy of location required

SWAT ▶ special weapons and tactics

UTL ▶ unable to locate

VIN ▶ vehicle identification number

Terms

AMBER ALERT ▶ A coordinated, statewide emergency alert sent out when a child is reported missing or in danger. Officially, *AMBER* stands for America's Missing: Broadcasting Emergency Response. The name originally refers to Amber Hagerman, a 9-year-old child who was abducted and murdered in Arlington, Texas, in 1996. AMBER alerts are sent to the public through the news media.

ARREST ▸ The action by law enforcement officials of taking a suspect into custody. An arrest may be authorized by a court-issued warrant or based on a law officer's assessment that there is probable cause a crime was committed.

ARREST WARRANT ▸ An order from the court giving law enforcement permission to arrest a specific person. This person will be then formally charged with a crime.

AUTHORIZED STRENGTH ▸ The maximum number of sworn officers a law enforcement agency is authorized by local or state regulation to employ.

BROKEN WINDOW THEORY ▸ The idea, based on criminology studies, that abandoned cars, broken windows and other signs of disorder are subtle cues to residents that crime and anti-social behavior will be tolerated in a particular neighborhood. The theory has given rise to policing activities, such as zero tolerance policies, that encourage monitoring and maintenance of urban areas to prevent vandalism from escalating into more serious crime. The theory and its resulting policies have been credited with lowering crime rates in cities such as New York and Boston beginning in the late 1990s.

CAD (COMPUTER AIDED DISPATCHING) ▸ A wireless laptop computer system that allows police in patrol cars to receive and send information without relying on voice communication. CAD allows officers on patrol to access information about a car they have stopped or a suspect they are seeking.

COMMUNITY POLICING ▸ A system that emphasizes contact between police and residents of the community they patrol. In the community-policing model, officers who patrol the streets take a greater role in their neighborhood, attending community meetings, setting up local offices in shopping areas and reaching out to community leaders. It is thought these actions integrate police better into their communities and encourage citizens to take a more active role in helping the police.

COUNTY POLICE ▸ Sworn police with a county jurisdiction. County police do not take on all the duties of county sheriffs, such as court duties. County police represent about 1 percent of the nation's local departments.

DEADLY FORCE ▸ The legal right of police officers to use force with the intent to kill. The standards for the use of deadly force may vary between departments, but it is usually authorized in situations where the life or safety of a police officer or a citizen is in danger. This is called a *defense-of-life* situation.

DISORDERLY CONDUCT ▸ A common, catchall charge that police use to control disruptive behavior. Disorderly conduct includes such actions as public drunkenness, brawls, disturbing the peace or loitering. A disorderly conduct charge is typically used in situations where the disruptive actions are not a serious public threat. The charge usually carries a misdemeanor punishment.

DOMESTIC DISTURBANCE ▸ A common incident in policing in which officers are called to a home where a dispute between residents has become loud or threatening. Officers receive extensive training in defusing such volatile situations. They also have the authority to arrest someone they suspect of domestic violence — the assaultive behavior of one individual against another.

DRIVING WHILE INTOXICATED (DWI) ▸ Also known as *driving under the influence (DUI)*. A major enforcement issue for police making traffic stops. Police must scrutinize all drivers they stop for signs of impairment due to the use of alcohol or drugs and can conduct field sobriety tests that evaluate a driver's motor and cognitive skills. Drivers can be asked to take a Breathalyzer test, breathing into an instrument that measures blood alcohol content (driving with a reading of 0.08 is a chargeable offense in most jurisdictions). Drivers do not have to submit to such tests on Fourth Amendment protections of self-incrimination.

ENTRAPMENT ▶ A boundary line and gray area for police. Entrapment occurs when the authorities, often acting undercover, encourage someone to commit a crime that the person might not otherwise have committed. An example would be if an undercover detective poses as an arms dealer to persuade someone to purchase an illegal weapon. A court will usually look to whether the idea for the illegal act originated with the defendant or with law enforcement.

FALSE ARREST ▶ When the police take someone into custody on charges they know won't hold, such as someone speaking loudly who is arrested for disturbing the peace. Most often the charges are dropped and the person is released. Citizens can sue police for false arrest, but they rarely succeed because of various protections against liability.

FIELD TRAINING ▶ A supplement to classroom training for new police officers that gives them practical experience in patrolling a beat under the supervision of a field training officer.

FRESH PURSUIT ▶ An ongoing police attempt to catch a fleeing suspect. This can include a high-speed pursuit, where police vehicles and helicopters chase a suspect car. These chases — often a favorite for real-time coverage by television news channels — are controversial, especially when they end with the deaths or injuries of bystanders.

LETS ▶ (Law Enforcement Telecommunications System): A Web-based system that compiles data about a suspect from various databases. The system, known by other acronyms, allows police to search for information based on name, phone number, vehicle and crime event. The system uses geographic information system (GIS) technology to help police quickly locate a suspect's address and the location of previous police calls.

LINEUP ▶ A procedure for identifying a crime suspect. The process is familiar to anyone who watches police procedural dramas. Suspects, along with volunteers, are placed in a room and viewed by a crime victim or witness through one-way glass. Police also use a photo lineup, providing the witness with pictures of suspects to see if he or she can identify a suspect.

MIRANDA WARNING ▶ A statement police must give suspects informing them they can decline to answer questions and have an attorney present when they are interviewed by police. The name refers to a Supreme Court case (Miranda v. Arizona) that found statements given by Ernesto Miranda were not admissible in court because he had not been informed of his constitutional rights, nor had he waived those rights to answer questions without legal counsel. Any statements made by a suspect who has not been *Mirandized* cannot be used against him or her in court.

NATIONAL CRIME INFORMATION CENTER (NCIC) ▶ A nationwide database established by the FBI to help local law enforcement agencies locate and capture fugitives and find missing persons and stolen property. The center compiles information from across the nation to help local agencies see connections of criminal actions across state lines, including bank robberies and serial murders.

ORDINANCE ▶ A local statute passed by a city or town council that is enforced by the police. Most ordinances address less serious issues such as the noise level of a car or the closing times of bars.

POLICE-TO-POPULATION RATIO ▶ A standard measure for the level of police protection in a community, usually expressed as the number of sworn officers per thousand population. This is a useful tool in comparing the police departments of cities with widely different general populations.

POLYGRAPH ▶ Better known as the "lie detector." A device used in the interrogation of an individual to measure physical responses such as breathing, heart rate and skin conductivity (sweat). Because of controversy about the accuracy of measuring someone's honesty, polygraphs are not allowed as evidence in court. But law enforcement officers and prosecutors can use the device, with the permission of the individual, to determine whether to pursue a case.

PRELIMINARY INVESTIGATION ▶ The first stage in the investigation of a crime that usually includes five steps: identifying and arresting any suspects, providing aid to any victims in need of medical attention, securing the crime scene to prevent loss of evidence, collecting all relevant physical evidence, and preparing a preliminary report.

PROBABLE CAUSE ▶ A requirement for police to show they had good reason to stop citizens, search them or go into their homes or cars uninvited. Probable cause can be invoked if police believe a crime is being committed or has just taken place.

PROTECTIVE CUSTODY ▶ The act by law enforcement of providing for the safety of a crime victim, a witness to a crime, or someone they think may be in danger. Police sometimes will use protective custody as a pretense to hold a person they want to keep off the streets – either for the individual's own safety or to keep him or her from speaking with others.

RACIAL PROFILING ▶ The controversial police practice of stopping individuals based on their race or ethnicity rather than any suspicion of criminal activity. African-American legal rights activists refer to such questionable traffic stops as *DWB (driving while black)*. Racial profiling can also include people of Middle Eastern (terrorism) or Hispanic (immigration) origin. Although official policy prohibits such actions, police motives are scrutinized in every high-profile incident involving the stopping or questioning of minorities. Many jurisdictions require police to include the race of the person involved in every stop they make. These reports are part of the public record.

RESISTING ARREST ▶ An additional criminal charge used as a threat by police when they attempt to take a person into custody. You can be charged with resisting arrest if you don't comply with an officer. The charge of resisting arrest can remain even if the other charges are dropped. Reporters should understand this and comply with police orders.

RESPONSE TIME ▶ The elapsed time between a report of a crime and the arrival of police on the scene. Response time is usually noted on police reports and can be used to analyze police effectiveness. Response times also can be studied to see if police react differently to the reports of crime in various neighborhoods.

RIDE-ALONG ▶ A practice in many departments where a civilian, often a reporter, goes on patrol with regular officers. A ride-along is recommended for anyone trying to understand the day-to-day dimensions of policing.

STOP AND FRISK ▶ The lawful search for a concealed weapon of a person suspected of a crime. Police can "pat down" a person they take into custody or even someone they are questioning. The objective is to protect the officer from concealed weapons. The law limits these searches to frisking. Any other search for evidence requires a warrant or sufficient probable cause.

STOP STICKS (SPIKES) ▶ Nails or other sharp devices that are placed in the path of a car fleeing police. Stop sticks are designed to cause a slow leak in the tires of the vehicle rather than a sudden blowout that could result in a serious accident.

STRONG ARM ROBBERY ▶ A robbery in which the assailant uses threats and physical force rather than a weapon to steal private property.

SWORN OFFICER ▶ A police officer who has been trained, certified and authorized to arrest a citizen. In many jurisdictions only sworn officers are authorized to carry guns at all times. A nonsworn officer does not have to be state certified and has no powers of arrest. These officers have such duties as writing parking tickets and citations.

THREE STRIKES ▶ A law in many states that mandates a life sentence for a defendant convicted of his or her third felony offense. An impending third conviction gives police and prosecutors a powerful tool to win the cooperation of a suspect in a crime investigation.

VANDALISM ▶ The willful or malicious destruction of public or private property.

WATCH ▶ A term used in many departments for a police work shift. Although watch times can vary, the police workday is divided into three watches. The day watch can typically begin at 7 a.m., the afternoon watch at 3 p.m. and the night watch at 11 p.m. The officer with overall responsibility for a watch period is often referred to as the watch commander.

ZERO TOLERANCE POLICING ▶ A policing policy used by some departments that deploys aggressive enforcement of minor crime or the appearance of crime. The philosophy of such a policy is that vigorous enforcement of criminal and civil laws will help restore order to communities and encourage residents to take an active role in maintaining order.

CHAPTER 6 ▶ Fires and Emergencies

You have to know the jargon if you're going to speak with emergency responders. Here are some common terms to help you understand the basics. *A Reporters Guide to Fire Equipment* (Appendix 2) will familiarize you with different fire vehicles. The National Fire Protection Association provides a dictionary of terms and codes adopted by fire departments around the country. You can access it through the association's website at www.nfpa.org.

ALARM ▶ A call for a fire company to respond to a fire. Most departments have a central dispatch office that receives reports of fires and sends the closest, most appropriate unit to the scene. Often, other units are sent, creating a multiple alarm response.

BACKDRAFT ▶ An explosive condition when an air-starved fire suddenly receives oxygen, causing super-heated gases to ignite. Anyone caught in a backdraft could be seriously injured or killed.

BOOSTER LINE ▶ Also known as a *red line*. A hose, usually one inch in diameter, used for small fires. The hose is supplied from a fire truck's booster tank.

COMPANY ▶ The crew and equipment assigned to an individual fire vehicle.

DECK GUN ▶ A large, fixed water nozzle attached to a fire engine. Deck guns deliver a higher volume of water than handheld hoses but are less maneuverable.

DRAFTING ▶ The use of water from a source other than a hydrant. In these cases, pumper trucks draw water from cisterns, lakes, ponds and swimming pools. This is a common practice for rural areas without hydrant systems.

ENGINE or **PUMPER ▶** A fire truck capable of pumping water from its own tanks or water sources other than hydrants. Pumpers carry tanks holding between 500 and 1,000 gallons and hand lines to fight the fire.

EXPOSURES ▶ Buildings near a burning structure that are at risk of catching fire themselves. A primary focus of firefighters is to protect other exposures to keep the fire from spreading.

FAST ATTACK ▶ When the first engine company on the scene begins its efforts by using water carried in the booster tank. Typically the next company on the scene is assigned to secure a water supply.

FLASHOVER ▶ The sudden ignition of all flammable material in a room or structure. This happens if the heat created by the fire reaches a temperature high enough to ignite everything in the space at once. Firefighters have less than two seconds to evacuate a room reaching flashover.

FOAM ▶ A concentrate mixed with water or air that is applied to material that could catch fire. The foam creates a barrier between the material and the heat, preventing ignition. Foam is used on flammable liquid fires (gas or oil) and on some automobile and structure fires.

FORCIBLE ENTRY ▶ When firefighters must break down locked doors and barred windows to enter a burning structure. A variety of hand and power tools can be used.

FORWARD LAY ▶ When hose is laid from the hydrant to the fire. A reverse lay runs the hose from the fire back to the water source.

HAND LINE ▶ A small-diameter hose (1.5 to 1.75 inches) used to apply water directly to the fire.

INCIDENT COMMANDER ▶ The officer in charge of an emergency operation. Higher-ranking officials may be at the fire, but this officer, often the first on the scene, remains the one in charge. The term for this officer varies among departments.

JAWS ▶ A rescue tool that cuts and pulls metal. Better known as Jaws of Life, a copyright name for one of many similar products

KELLY TOOL ▶ A forcible entry tool.

MASTER STREAM ▶ A large and fixed stream of water projected from hoses attached to aerial ladders and pumper trucks.

MUTUAL AID ▶ Fire crews from other cities and towns who are often called on to help with a fire or move into the affected city to provide backup should another fire break out.

OVERHAUL ▶ The securing of a structure following a fire. Firefighters check for hidden "hot spots."

RAPID INTERVENTION TEAM (RIT) ▶ A truck or rescue company on call in case a firefighter is injured or trapped in a burning building.

RESCUE COMPANY ▶ A fire unit equipped and trained to perform search and rescue, treat the injured and extricate victims in motor vehicle accidents. The duties of a rescue company can vary in different parts of the country.

STICK ▶ The long maneuverable ladder on a ladder truck. Sticks vary in length from 65 feet to 100 feet depending on the needs of the department.

TILLER ▶ A type of ladder truck with a rear cab from which a firefighter steers the back wheels. Because tiller trucks can steer in the front and the back, they are able to make turns that other ladder trucks cannot.

VENTILATION ▶ The venting of smoke from a building. In positive *pressure ventilation (PPV)* a powerful fan is placed at the front door of a structure and blows air inside, creating pressure inside the building to force the smoke out. In *negative pressure ventilation (NPV),* the process is reversed.

CHAPTER 7 ▶ Courts

There are a lot of words to learn when you start out on the court beat. If you're covering the courts regularly, a copy of *Black's Law Dictionary* would be a good investment. You should keep a couple of Web links, such as www.uscourts.gov/Common/Glossary.aspx or http://dictionary.law.com, in your computer, or phone Web browser for quick reference. In the meantime, here's a list of the terms to get you started. Keep in mind as you read that many of these definitions can vary from state to state.

ADMISSIBLE ▶ A determination by the court that evidence or testimony is allowable in a trial. A judge allows the use of such information if he or she finds it is relevant to the case and does not violate rules of evidence.

AFFIDAVIT ▶ A sworn statement by an individual about an issue before the court. Affidavits are generally filed in advance of trials or other court action. The statement is signed by the individual affirming the statement is true.

AMICUS CURIAE ▶ Latin for "friend of the court." Refers to legal briefs filed by a person or an organization interested, but not directly involved, in a case.

APPEAL ▶ A request by the losing side in a case asking a higher court to review the decision for errors in procedure or law. If the appellant is successful, the lower court's decision will be overturned. The other side in such a case is the "appellee."

ARBITRATION ▶ Also known as *ALTERNATIVE DISPUTE RESOLUTION*.): A quasi-legal alternative to long, costly court trials. Instead of a judge or jury, arbitration is usually conducted by an arbitrator, who makes a ruling after listening to presentations from both sides. The opposing parties usually agree to accept the arbitrator's decision before they present their arguments. Many states require some form of nonbinding arbitration in the hope that the proceedings will show the opposing sides the risks they face in a jury trial.

ARRAIGNMENT ▸ The first court hearing for a person charged with a crime. Arraignment hearings are heard by judges or magistrates and feature a recitation of the charges against the defendant, who then enters a plea of guilty or not guilty. The judge then decides whether the defendant will remain in custody or be able to post bail.

ASSAULT ▸ An often misunderstood term. In many states, assault is simply a threat of harm, not the actual use of force, which is called *battery*. Check for the specific definitions of these two terms in your state law codes.

BAIL ▸ Money, either cash or a bond, given to a court as assurance a defendant won't run if released from jail before trial. Bail for minor crimes is usually set by a fixed fee schedule. Bail for serious charges is set by the judge at the defendant's first court appearance. A defendant can be released on personal recognizance without bail. A court may set a high bail or deny bail altogether in cases involving severe crimes or where there is concern the defendant will flee. Since many defendants can't afford the full cost of bail, bail bondsmen front the money for a fee paid by the defendant. Because they could lose the bond if the defendant does not appear for trial, bondsmen have broad powers to pursue the defendant.

BAILIFF ▸ A uniformed officer who maintains order in the court and provides for the security of the jury.

BENCH ▸ A word with literal and figurative meanings. The judge sits on the bench, a raised platform from where he or she officiates. *Bench* is also a general term for the judiciary.

BURDEN OF PROOF ▸ The requirement to prove disputed facts. In criminal cases, it is the prosecution's "burden" to prove the defendant committed the crime; it is not the defendant's burden to prove his or her innocence.

CHANGE OF VENUE ▸ A request made to the court — usually by the defense in a high-profile case — to move the trial away from where the crime or action occurred. An argument for a change of venue usually involves claims that the media attention given to the case could affect a jury's impartiality. Moving the trial to another location would draw jurors less tainted by pre-trial publicity.

CLASS ACTION ▸ A lawsuit brought on behalf of a large group of plaintiffs with a common legal claim. Cases often involve consumers suing large companies, such as drug companies or car manufacturers, or workers bringing action against an employer. Class action suits can take years, but they are an option for those who cannot afford legal costs. The biggest winners are often lawyers, who claim a healthy percentage of the settlements.

CONCURRENT SENTENCE ▸ Prison terms for two or more offenses served at the same time. Two 10-year sentences served concurrently means a maximum of 10 years behind bars. In a *consecutive sentence*, the convicted would face 20 years in prison.

CONTEMPT OF COURT ▸ A citation issued by a trial judge to control behavior within a courtroom or activities outside the courtroom. Someone can be found in contempt if he or she causes a disturbance or fails to heed warnings about being disrespectful to the judge or others in the courtroom. Contempt citations are also issued if someone willfully fails to obey a court order, such as a request to produce information. Contempt citations can carry a fine and/or jail time. Journalists have been ruled in contempt of court for speaking with a juror before the case is deliberated. On rare occasions contempt citations have been issued against reporters who refuse to say where they obtained information relevant to the trial.

CONTINUANCE ▶ The postponement of a trial, hearing or other court activity until a later date. Continuances are granted at the request of one or both sides to allow more time to prepare for trial or to react to a development in the courtroom. Some states require fees from those seeking continuance to discourage too many delays.

DAMAGES ▶ Money awarded to the winning plaintiff in a civil lawsuit. *Special damages* are determined as all the costs connected to an injury, including medical bills, lost wages, repairs to or replacement of damaged property or the losses from a contract. A plaintiff may also seek *general damages* that result from the other party's actions but have a less specific price tag. These damages include pain and suffering, loss of physical or mental abilities, loss of reputation, loss of business and other long-term harm. The *punitive* or *exemplary damages* are accessed as punishment for a defendant's actions. On occasion punitive damages can be greater than the actual damages.

DELIBERATION ▶ The process in which a jury or judge determines the outcome of a case. Jury deliberations are done in isolation as members weigh the facts they heard during trial.

DEPOSITION ▶ Testimony given under oath and recorded for use in court at a later date. This is usually done in a lawyer's office without a judge present.

DISCOVERY ▶ The pretrial phase in which each party can demand documents, items of evidence and depositions from the other party. Defense and prosecution (in a civil trial, the plaintiff) can demand such material, but criminal defendants have the constitutional right to avoid incriminating themselves.

DOCKET ▶ A calendar listing cases awaiting court action. *Docket* is also used as a verb to describe the placing of a case on the list or to note action taken in court regarding the case.

DOUBLE JEOPARDY ▶ Bringing charges against someone who has already been acquitted on those charges. The Fifth Amendment of the Constitution prohibits this action, which was possible during colonial times. The amendment states: "nor shall any person be subject for the same offence to be twice put in jeopardy of life or limb . . . " However, defendants found not guilty in a criminal trial can be sued in civil court for the same alleged actions.

EXCLUSIONARY RULE ▶ A Constitution-based doctrine that prohibits the use of evidence obtained in violation of a defendant's rights. An example would be evidence taken from someone's home without a proper search warrant.

EXCULPATORY ▶ Evidence or testimony that clears a defendant of guilt or blame. Such evidence may show the actions of the accused were justifiable and were taken with no criminal intent.

EXTORTION ▶ The use of threat, intimidation or false claim to obtain money or property. Extortion can include *blackmail*, which is a threat to expose embarrassing, damaging information about the intended victim.

FELONY ▶ A serious crime usually punishable by at least one year in prison. A felony is more severe than misdemeanor crimes, such as petty theft, disturbing the peace and public nuisances, which carry lesser punishments.

GAG ORDER ▶ An order issued by a judge prohibiting attorneys and other parties to a pending lawsuit or criminal prosecution from making public statements about the case. Gag orders are generally issued to limit pretrial publicity, which could influence potential jurors. The First Amendment prevents judges from restricting what the media can report, so restrictions apply only to participants under the court's control.

GRAND JURY ▶ A group of citizens (traditionally 23) selected in a county or federal court district to hear evidence of criminal accusations in felony cases or in cases of potential public wrong-doing by city and county officials. Grand jury members usually serve a year and are selected from a list of nominees drawn from voting records in the county or district. Grand jurors hear evidence presented by the prosecutor and then decide whether the accused should be indicted. Grand juries operate in secret to protect the integrity of the investigation and the privacy of a suspect.

HABEAS CORPUS ▶ Latin for "You have the body." Most often, a writ of habeas corpus is a judicial order requiring authorities to justify why they are holding someone in custody.

HEARSAY ▶ Testimony based on secondhand information rather than the personal knowledge of the witness providing the information. You'll hear opposing attorneys objecting to such testimony in court by rising to say, "Hearsay." The judge will then rule whether the testimony is based on the direct knowledge of the witness.

IN CAMERA ▶ Simple translation: In private. A discussion by both sides in the judge's chambers, away from the jury and the public. Sometimes the judge and opposing lawyers will hold discussions at the side of the judge's bench, out of the hearing of the jury and courtroom audience. These chats are called *sidebars*. Not to be confused with the journalism term for secondary stories that accompanies a main story.

INDICTMENT ▶ A formal accusation handed down by a court or grand jury against someone charged with a criminal offense.

INJUNCTION ▶ A court order preventing someone from taking a specific action. *Preliminary injunctions* and *temporary restraining orders (TROs)* are issued while a judge determines whether a permanent injunction is needed.

MAGISTRATE ▶ Anyone performing a judge's functions. Judges are magistrates, but not all magistrates are judges. In some states, magistrates are officers of the court who hear small-claims lawsuits and minor criminal charges or conduct preliminary hearings to determine if there is enough evidence to hold a defendant for trial. Magistrates in federal courts conduct routine hearings.

MANSLAUGHTER ▶ One kind of unintentional death. There are degrees of manslaughter, from voluntary (such as a deadly fistfight) to involuntary (a fatal car accident). The exact terms for manslaughter can vary from state to state.

MISTRIAL ▶ A trial that is ended because of an error in procedure that might compromise the verdict. A mistrial also is declared if jurors fail to agree on a verdict, a situation called a *hung jury*. The case can then be retried before a new jury.

MOTION ▶ A document asking the court to take a specific action related to the case (for example, a motion to dismiss).

NOLO CONTENDERE ▶ A plea, simply translated as no-contest, which sidesteps the word *guilty*. A defendant who pleads nolo contendere ("nolo," for short) is not contesting the charges but is not admitting guilt. The legal effect is the same as a guilty plea except it can't be used as an admission of guilt in related civil cases.

PLEA ▶ A defendant's response to the charge that he or she committed a certain crime. Defendants give their plea at an arraignment. Pleas are most often given as "*guilty*" or "*not guilty*," but can also be "*no contest*" (nolo contendere) or more rarely "*not guilty by reason of insanity*," which means the defendant will attempt to show he or she was not sane when the crime was committed.

PROBABLE CAUSE ▶ The requirement necessary for the arrest, search and other law enforcement actions. Probable cause is also determined by a court before it issues an indictment. Police must have probable cause to make an arrest or search a home without a court warrant. Probable cause can be such things as finding a weapon or illicit drugs in plain sight or the sight of someone running from a crime scene. A judge or grand jury must determine there is probable cause to issue a criminal indictment.

PRO BONO ▶ The full term — *pro bono publico*, or "for the public good" — describes legal work donated by a lawyer for clients who can't afford an attorney.

REASONABLE DOUBT ▶ Jurors in a criminal trial are told by the judge that they can find a defendant guilty only if they are certain "beyond a reasonable doubt." Sometimes they may hear the phrase "to a moral certainty." This element of criminal law can cause great debate when some jurors and spectators feel there is no doubt, while others are not so certain. Reasonable doubt is a stricter standard than *preponderance of the evidence,* the guideline set for jurors in a civil case.

RECUSE ▶ An action taken by a judge who determines he or she shouldn't hear a case because of a conflict of interest. Judges recuse themselves if they know one of the parties in a case or have a financial interest that could be affected by their ruling.

REMAND ▶ To send back. This can refer to a defendant who is returned to jail or prison, or to a case that an appeals court sends back to the lower court with instructions to fix issues raised in an appeal of the original verdict.

SEQUESTER ▶ To set apart. Juries in high-profile cases are often sequestered in a hotel during a trial or for final deliberations to limit jury members' access to news reports or family and friends who may discuss the case. The action is taken to ensure a juror's impartiality. Witnesses can be sequestered in another part of the courthouse to keep them from hearing other testimony that might influence what they say. This action is sometimes referred to as *exclusion*.

SMALL-CLAIMS COURT ▶ A small, informal court that hears claims over small amounts of money. The various reality court shows on television are a good representation of small-claims court, where two sides present their case to a judge who makes a quick ruling. The size of the claim is limited — different states have different ceilings — there are no filing fees and lawyers are not permitted to represent clients.

STANDARD OF PROOF ▶ The requirement that prosecutors must prove someone's guilt beyond a reasonable doubt in criminal cases. Plaintiffs in civil cases are generally required to prove their claims by a "preponderance of evidence."

SUBPOENA ▶ A written command by the court that requires a person to appear before the court or to provide requested information.

SUMMARY JUDGMENT ▶ A decision by a judge that the prosecutor or plaintiff has failed to prove his or her case or that a civil defendant has no defense. Such a decision means that the case can be decided without going to trial or jury deliberation. As a matter of routine, defense attorneys often request a summary judgment once the prosecution has finished presenting its case. The judge usually declines to make that judgment.

TORT ▶ From the French for "wrong." Damage, injury or a wrongful act that a plaintiff claims was the result of willful or negligent action by the defendant. Torts most often refer to cases such as medical malpractice or product liability. Tort law results in more litigation than any other category of civil law.

VOIR DIRE ▶ The screening of potential jurors by the judge and attorneys representing both sides in a case. The action is taken to eliminate potentially biased jurors.

WARRANT ▶ A court order (also known as a writ) directing police to take a person into custody and bring him or her before the judge. Judges issue *bench warrants* for a person convicted of a crime who fails to appear for sentencing or is in contempt of court. A search warrant allows police to search a site or person for certain types of evidence. These warrants require detailed requests by police and prosecutors.

CHAPTER 8 ▶ Government

The shape and size of government vary among states and municipalities. Terms and definitions vary as well. The glossary below should provide a good start in understanding the language you'll hear on the job. You can also consult the online dictionaries referenced in the chapter. And because of the dizzying variation in the rules of capitalization, keep an *Associated Press Stylebook* for quick reference.

ALDERMAN, COUNCILOR, SUPERVISOR OR SELECTMAN ▶ Different titles for the same job the legislative position in city or town government. *Aldermen* and *city councilors* meet regularly to discuss budget issues and to vote on new rules, regulations and laws for the cities they represent. *Town councilors* do the same for their towns.

AT LARGE ▶ An elective office, usually for the city or town council, that is voted on by all voters rather than voters in specific voting districts called wards or precincts. These contests are at-large elections.

BALLOT INITIATIVE ▶ A proposed law placed on the ballot by citizens, usually in the form of a petition that is then voted on by the public. Ballot initiatives allow the public to sidestep state and local legislative bodies to pass a law. Different states have different standards for ballot initiatives. Federal law has no initiative provisions.

BILL ▶ A proposed law submitted to a legislative body. Bills can be proposed by legislators or citizens. A bill becomes a law when it is approved by both legislative chambers and signed by the chief executive — the president or governor.

BIPARTISAN ▶ An action or issue supported by both groups and political parties.

BUREAUCRATS ▶ Government employees, usually at the managerial level.

CHECKS AND BALANCES ▶ A basic design of our government that gives the three branches — the legislative, executive and judicial — the ability to limit powers possessed by other branches. The goal of this system is to keep the power of governance from being taken over by one section of government.

CHIEF OF STAFF ▶ The person who oversees the operation of an elected official's office. Presidents, governors, top legislators and some mayors have a chief of staff.

CIVIL LIBERTIES ▶ The freedoms and rights of the citizenry that cannot be altered or removed by government.

CIVIL SERVICE ▶ A merit-based system for the hiring and promotion of government employees. The system was established to prevent politicians from rewarding supporters, friends and relatives with government jobs. Civil service employees take competitive tests that determine who is best qualified for specific jobs. They cannot be fired when government changes hands. The federal civil service was established under the 1883 Pendleton Act.

CONCURRENT POWERS ▶ Powers of governance that may be exercised by both the federal government and the state governments. Some concurrent powers include the ability to set taxes, borrow money and spend funds for the public benefit.

CONSTITUENTS ▶ Citizens in a district who are represented by elected officials.

COUNTY ▶ Geographic areas into which states are divided. Counties can contain both municipalities and unincorporated areas. They may be governed by an elected board of commissioners or supervisors and can offer unified services, such as fire, police and schools, instead of requiring each municipality to run its own departments. The size and authority of county government vary from state to state.

DELEGATED POWERS ▶ A list based on federal or state constitution of what a government is allowed to do.

ELECTION COMMISSIONS ▶ Regulatory boards that oversee the election activities of political candidates. It is the duty of the *Federal Election Commission* and comparable state election commissions to enforce laws regulating the way candidates may gather and spend campaign funds.

EMINENT DOMAIN ▶ The power of government to take private property for public use and the "common good." The Constitution requires that government provide fair compensation to the property owner.

ENTITLEMENTS ▶ Government benefits provided to individuals or families meeting certain requirements. Social Security, Medicare and Medicaid are entitlement programs.

EXCISE TAXES ▶ Taxes on the manufacture, sale, or consumption of a product. Excise taxes can be levied by federal, state and local governments.

EXECUTIVE BRANCH ▶ The branch of government that oversees day-to-day operations. The chief executive is the president at the federal level, governors at the state level and mayors at the municipal level. Chief executives appoint — and fire — the next level of the executive branch, including heads of governmental agencies and departments.

EXECUTIVE SESSION ▸ An exception to open meeting laws that allows a government committee or board to meet away from the public to discuss sensitive personnel issues related to background information, pay or disciplinary inquiries. Each state has its own rules for when such closed meetings can take place.

FEDERAL SUPREMACY CLAUSE ▸ A section of the U.S. Constitution that establishes the precedence of federal law over state and local laws. Article VI of the Constitution says that constitutional guidelines and federal laws and treaties "shall be" the "supreme Law of the Land."

FISCAL YEAR ▸ A 365-day accounting period that differs from the calendar year of January 1st to December 31st. The federal government's fiscal year begins October 1st and ends September 30th — the beginning and end of the federal budget cycle. States have different fiscal years; many start July 1st and end June 30th.

FLAK ▸ Slang for a public relations person. The word derives from the World War II German acronym for exploding anti-artillery shells: *F*lieger *A*bwehr *K*anone (translation: "airplane defense cannon"). The word became a metaphor for criticism: *The president will catch flak for his position on health care.* Public relations people became known as "flak catchers" for their role in handling that criticism. That term was shortened to "flak."

FRANCHISE ▸ The right to vote.

FREEDOM OF INFORMATION ACT ▸ A federal law that compels U.S. government officials to release, at a citizen's request, copies of documents they might not readily disclose. Most states have similar laws. The acronym has become a verb (pronounced foy-yah) for a journalist's research into government documents: *He FOIAed the attorney general's office for details about the investigation.*

GERRYMANDERING ▸ A political tactic that manipulates the *reapportionment* of legislative districts to ensure the election of a party's candidate. In gerrymandering, district lines are redrawn to include voters most sympathetic to the party's philosophies within the boundaries of the district. The tactic is named after Massachusetts Gov. Elbridge Gerry, who redrew district boundaries in 1812 to benefit his party. The odd shape of one of those districts was said to resemble a salamander.

GRANTS ▸ Money distributed by government to pay for programs and policies. A *block grant* allows the recipient more flexibility in using the money. *Categorical grants* and *project grants* are given to fund specific programs.

HATCH ACT ▸ A 1939 law that prohibits federal workers from engaging in political activity, such as campaigning, polling, or telephoning voters. Most states have similar laws.

IMPEACHMENT ▸ The process taken by a legislative body to remove an official from office. The first step in that process is for the legislative body (Congress or state legislatures) to determine if there is evidence that the official has committed an impeachable offense. If the legislative body agrees, members vote to impeach the official. A trial is then held to determine guilt or innocence. President Bill Clinton was impeached by Congress but found not guilty of the charges.

INCUMBENT ▸ An official in an elected office.

LAME DUCK ▸ An elected official who will not return to office after the end of his or her term. The president and many governors can serve only two terms. They are considered "lame ducks" toward the end of their final terms because they have limited political clout and less concern about winning voter approval.

LEGISLATIVE BRANCH ▶ The branch of government with the authority to make and change laws and establish the government's budget. Federal, state and local governments have legislative branches whose members are elected by the citizenry.

LINE-ITEM VETO ▶ The power given to some chief executives, including governors and mayors, to eliminate specific spending provisions from a larger spending bill passed by the legislative branch. The U.S. president does not have such power.

LOBBYIST ▶ A paid professional employed by companies, industries, trade associations and special interest groups to influence legislation. The name is derived from lobbyists' original practice of meeting with legislators in the lobby outside their chambers. The activities of lobbyists are guaranteed under the Constitution's free speech provisions; however, their use of money, gifts and free travel to influence legislators is regulated by federal and state government.

MAJORITY RULE ▶ The requirement for some legislative votes that a simple majority — or one more than half the lawmakers — approve a bill or an action. Other votes such as a requirement to close debate on an issue require a two-thirds vote.

MANDATE ▶ A law that requires action or adherence by other agencies or governmental units. Federal mandates usually apply to states; state mandates apply to municipalities. *Unfunded mandates* require action by units of government but don't provide money to support the activity.

MEDICAID ▶ A program providing medical benefits to the poor. Medicaid is partly funded by the federal government; state governments also provide money to support the program. The growing cost of Medicaid has become an issue in Washington and in state capitals around the country.

MEDICARE ▶ A federal program providing medical benefits to the elderly. As with Medicaid, its costs have become a large and growing portion of the federal budget.

MUNICIPALITY ▶ A general term for the local form of government that includes *cities* and *towns*. Cities are typically governed by a mayor and a legislative body of councilors or aldermen; cities may be administered by a city manager. Towns are governed by a council without a large, full-time executive administration. Smaller municipal units include *villages* and *townships*.

OPEN MEETINGS/SUNSHINE LAWS ▶ Provisions in most states that require legislative bodies and governmental agencies to hold deliberations in public and provide a wide range of documents to public view. Rules to the extent of this openness vary from state to state. (See Freedom of Information Act.)

PATRONAGE ▶ Government jobs provided to people who have connections with politicians. Although this is prohibited for civil service jobs, administrative and appointed jobs can still be given to political allies.

PRIMARY ELECTION ▶ A vote within a political party to chose candidates for the general election. A *closed primary* restricts the vote to those registered with the political party. An *open primary* allows independent voters or voters registered with the other party to switch affiliation and vote in a specific party's primary.

PROPERTY TAXES ▶ A tax, usually determined by municipal officials, on residential and commercial properties within a city, town or county. Property taxes are a major source of income for municipalities. Taxes are based on the estimated value of the land, house and — in some cases — personal possessions of the property owner. In most cases the tax is a percentage of worth, such as a levy of 20 cents on each thousand dollars of a home's market value.

QUORUM ▶ The minimum number of members of a legislative body, such as a state legislature or city council, necessary to conduct the business of that group. A quorum requirement prevents a very few from passing laws or regulations that may not reflect the interest of a municipality's voters.

REAPPORTIONMENT ▶ The redrawing of legislative district boundaries for the U.S. House of Representatives and state legislatures. Reapportionment follows the federal census that provides information on the changes in the numbers of people living in the specific districts every 10 years. Politicians often try to establish districts that would benefit their party. (See Gerrymandering.)

REGULATIONS ▶ Rules based on laws passed by the legislative branch. The laws are translated into regulations by the executive branch, which then enforces the new rules.

RIDER ▶ An unrelated provision added to a bill during the legislative process. Riders often provide funding for a politician's pet project or place a regulation or law on the books that would be hard to pass on its own.

ROBERT'S RULES OF ORDER ▶ The bible for parliamentary procedure. Most government meetings are conducted under Robert's. At this writing the book is in its 10th edition.

STATEHOUSE ▶ A general term for state government. The statehouse, or state capital building, contains offices for the legislators and governor along with the chambers for the house and senate. The word is a synonym for the seat of state government.

TERM LIMITS ▶ Laws that restrict elected officials to a specific number of terms. The U.S. presidency has a two-term limit.

TOWN MEETING ▶ A form of direct democracy for local government, dating back to the 17th century, in which members of a community meet to determine policy and budgets. Town meetings still take place in New York, Michigan, Minnesota and the New England states.

VETO ▶ Latin for "I forbid," The president and governors have constitutional power to reject laws passed by Congress or the legislatures. If vetoed, a bill can still become law if two-thirds of both legislative chambers vote to override the veto. If the president or governor takes no action on a bill — neither signing nor issuing a veto — the bill will become invalid unless the legislature votes to override. Known as a *pocket veto*, this gives the president or governors the option of remaining mute on the issue.

ZONING ▶ Rules set by municipalities and counties that control what kind of building can be done in specific geographic zones. These rules determine areas where businesses and industry can be located. They can also set restrictions on the size and types of construction. Zoning regulations often are the result of a larger overview established by *planning commissions*. Zoning boards hold hearings to grant exceptions to the rules. These can be very contentious events.

CHAPTER 9 ▶ Education

As the child of several bureaucracies (local, state, federal, academic), education has a language all its own, populated with special terms and an alphabet soup of acronyms that the people you cover will use. You can find online glossaries and dictionaries more complete than the list that follows. School Wise Press (www.schoolwisepress.com/smart/dict/dict.html) offers a comprehensive selection, as does iseekeducation (www.iseek.org/education/terms.html). Keep a link in your Web browser to the sites you find most helpful, in case you need to check a definition on the fly.

ACCOMMODATION ▶ Actions taken by teachers and school administrators to address the requirements of special needs students. Accommodations can include individual lesson plans, special equipment and materials, accessible classrooms and different arrangements for testing, such as quiet rooms or additional time.

ADEQUATE YEARLY PROGRESS (AYP) ▶ A criteria established under the No Child Left Behind Act to determine how every public school and school district in the country is progressing academically. Standardized tests are used to determine if schools and school districts are improving from year to year.

ASSESSMENT ▶ The measurement and evaluation of how students are succeeding. Assessment can take different forms, including grades, tests and class work. In portfolio or performance assessment, students, teachers and sometimes parents select pieces from a student's work over a fixed period to demonstrate the student's level of improvement over time.

AT RISK ▶ Students considered in jeopardy of failing or dropping out or who are engaged in destructive behaviors. School counselors look for risk markers such as single-parent homes, family incomes at or below the poverty line, residence in higher-crime neighborhoods, emotional or physical abuse and trouble with the police.

BENCHMARK ▶ A point of reference against which something may be measured. The term is often used to refer to an early set of standardized tests that can be compared with future tests to see if a student is improving.

BROWN V. BOARD OF EDUCATION ▶ A landmark 1954 U.S. Supreme Court decision that found state laws establishing separate public schools for black and white students were unconstitutional. The decision overturned the Plessy v. Ferguson decision of 1896, which allowed state-sponsored segregation. The unanimous decision, which found that "separate educational facilities are inherently unequal," set the stage for school integration across the United States.

CHARTER SCHOOLS ▶ Elementary and high schools that receive both public money and private donations but are not subject to some of the rules and regulations at other public schools. In exchange for these freedoms, the charter school must meet established goals. Charter schools are attended by choice, but they are part of the public school system and do not charge tuition. Some charter schools provide specialized curriculum in areas such as arts or technology. Others attempt to provide a better and more efficient general education than nearby public schools.

COLLECTIVE BARGAINING ▶ The process of negotiations between employers and a union or other groups representing employees seeking an agreement over wages, benefits and working conditions. Teachers' contracts usually cover pay scales, rewards for service and continuing studies, pension arrangements and health care coverage. Although a majority of the states have permitted public employees to engage in collective bargaining, tight state budgets in recent years have caused some states to revoke the bargaining rights.

DISTANCE LEARNING ▶ A way of teaching that uses the Internet to conduct classes that can be accessed by students across town or across the country. Distance education courses that require a physical presence for special reasons (including taking examinations) are sometimes called *hybrid* or *blended learning*.

DROPOUT (DROPOUT RATE) ▶ Students who leave school before graduating. An estimated 1.2 million American students drop out of high school each year. The dropout rate is a major indicator of a school system's success or failure. Many school districts are debating raising or lowering the age through which students are required to stay in school.

GIFTED AND TALENTED EDUCATION (GATE) ▶ A broad term for special educational practices, procedures and theories used for children identified as possessing great potential in their studies or creative arts.

HIGHLY QUALIFIED TEACHER ▶ A No Child Left Behind term that requires teachers to meet certain standards to prove their competence in a particular subject area.

IDEA (INDIVIDUALS WITH DISABILITIES EDUCATION ACT) ▶ The latest revision of federal law that goes back to 1975, governing how states and public agencies provide early intervention, special education and related services to students with disabilities. The law outlines the educational needs of children with 13 specific categories of disabilities from birth to age 18. The legislation resulted from court rulings that found it illegal to keep disabled students from receiving a public school education.

INCLUSION ▶ The practice of placing students with disabilities in regular classrooms. Also known as *mainstreaming*, inclusion can create controversies over a disabled student's impact on classmates and the costs to the school district to accommodate the disabled student.

INTERNATIONAL BACCALAUREATE ▶ A rigorous college preparation course of study that allows motivated high school students to earn college credit from many universities if their exam scores reach a certain high mark.

MAGNET SCHOOL ▶ Public school with specialized courses and curricula. Magnet schools are so called because they draw students from across school zone boundaries. Some are established by school districts that draw students from their jurisdiction; others are set up by state governments and may draw from multiple districts.

MASTERY ▶ An alternative method of teaching that requires a student to reach a predetermined level of understanding before being allowed to progress to the next level. The process allows individual students to move forward at different time intervals from their fellow students.

PEDAGOGY ▶ The study of being a teacher or the act of teaching. The term generally refers to strategies or styles of instruction. Although educators use the term with regularity, substitute it with the simple word *teaching*.

PROFESSIONAL DEVELOPMENT ▶ Continued studies by teachers that may be mandated by the state or school system. These studies, which can include refresher courses in teaching methods or classes on new technologies, are often rewarded with pay increases negotiated by the teachers' union or professional organization.

PTO/PTA ▶ Known variously as parent-teacher associations, parent-teacher organizations or parent-teacher-student associations, these groups are established to encourage parent participation in their children's schools. Most public and private elementary schools have a PTA or equivalent organization; some high schools also support such groups.

RUBRIC ▶ A scoring tool to assess student performance on papers, essays and projects. The rubric sets criteria to keep evaluations consistent and understandable for students while describing steps to be taken for future learning and teaching.

SCAFFOLDING ▶ The use of instructional tools to help students grasp new concepts and skills. These tools, such as graphics or reviews, are intended to help students associate established learning models with new subject matter.

STANDARDS (OUTCOME-) BASED EDUCATION REFORM ▶ A national trend in public education that establishes clear, measurable standards for all students. A standards-based system measures each student against an established criteria rather than comparing a student's work with that of his or her peers. Curriculum, assessments and professional development are based on the standards. For the past three decades these standards have increasingly centered on statewide standardized testing in math, language and other core subjects.

TENURE ▶ A status granted to teachers based on their experience, education and other achievements that protects them against dismissal except in cases of extreme malfeasance known as *just cause*. Tenured teachers may not be fired or demoted at will. In recent years opposition has increased against the granting of tenure. Detractors say it allows poor teachers to hold on to their jobs. Proponents say tenure is a necessary tool to promote academic freedom.

TITLE IX ▶ A subsection of the federal Education Amendments of 1972 that makes it illegal to use gender as a reason to exclude anyone from an education program or activity that receives federal financial assistance. The law opened many doors to women — especially in college sports. Schools receiving federal funds must provide female students the same opportunities as males.

TRACKING ▶ Also known as STREAMING – A method of placing students according to their ability level. Students of different abilities (low, middle and high) are assigned to different educational "tracks" that can include vocational, general, college-bound, honors, and Advanced Placement. Tracking has come under debate. Some teachers believe it makes teaching more focused and manageable; others believe that it can wrongly trap a student in a lower track no matter his or her level of improvement.

UNDERPERFORMNG SCHOOLS ▶ Schools determined to be failing to educate students to an accepted level of competence. The standards can include student performance on standardized tests, grade averages, dropout rates and graduation rates. Schools found to be underperforming face disciplinary measures, including funding cuts or a takeover by state education authorities.

VIRTUAL SCHOOLS ▶ Also known as a CYBER SCHOOL. Term used for learning institutions that teach primarily online. Online high schools have proliferated in the United States in recent years, with some facing questions about their accreditation.

WHOLE LANGUAGE ▶ A teaching method that has students focus on word meaning and context rather than pronunciation and spelling — a strategy known as *phonics-based learning*. Whole language practitioners teach students to look at language as a complete system where words relate to each other in meaning and usage.

INDEX